SUCCESSFUL CHRISTIAN LIVING

Successful
Christian Living

Sermons on Christianity Today

by

HARRY EMERSON FOSDICK

PUBLISHERS

HARPER & BROTHERS

NEW YORK AND LONDON 1937

Contents

[v]

2134

Contents

SUCCESSFUL CHRISTIAN LIVING

Successful Christian Living

FOR a long generation a revolt has been in progress against old, familiar techniques of Christian living, such as private prayer, public worship, directed meditation, and family devotions. We are not thinking now of loss of faith in the profound verities of Christianity but of the lapse of those methods of Christian nurture which our forefathers used to call the "means of grace." How common that lapse has been is obvious.

Indeed, through this congregation now there may be running a mood of protest, as though to say, In a world so tragic, where immense social problems clamor for our thought and action, can it be that the preacher will spend a Sunday morning, even though the Lenten season is at hand, on the techniques of private, personal devotion? We liberal Christians in particular have grown accustomed thus to minimize "formalities." How many here habitually pray? In how many homes where little children are growing up are there family devotions? How many customarily direct periods of solitary reading and thought to religious ends? How many have any kind, mark this now, any kind of method whatsoever, cherished and faithfully practised, for the nurture and discipline of their inner lives?

Commonly, when we consider the breakdown of Christian living, we think of prevalent denials of faith. The immense upheavals of man's intellectual life that have shaken the creeds to pieces and plunged many into disbelief are in our thought. But millions of us in the churches are not disbelievers. We are neither atheists nor doubters of Christ's essential principles. Yet, for all that, we are living very shoddy, low-grade Christian lives. As we thus see how many of us are men of faith in theory but not men of successful Christian life in practise, how can we keep our eyes off this realm we are thinking of today? Something is the matter with what the engineers would call our techniques. We are not implementing what we believe. We have faith but we have thrown away the methods by which faith grows real. It may be there is something after all in that half-forgotten phrase of our fathers, "the means of grace."

When we turn from the spiritual life to consider any other realm, we have to stop condescending to method and technique. Method and technique are primary. In building a bridge across the Hudson River three factors are indispensable: first, a great body of mathematical principles; second, an ideal, a picture in men's imaginations of a bridge that should be there because it is vitally needed; third, methods, patiently worked out and practised methods, by which the principles are implemented until they are given body and substance in the realized ideal. It requires no long argument to show that here we are dealing with something universal. Always between the principles the mind assents to and the ideal the life desires lies this other realm where failure means failure altogether—the realm of methods by which the possible becomes the actual. It may be, then, that we have hold here of something more important than at first seemed probable. Millions of us in the Christian churches are failures, yet not for lack of Christian principles, which we never have denied, nor for lack of Christian ideals—how deeply we sometimes desire that inner power by which trouble is surmounted, sin conquered, and life made adequate! We are failures because, often unconsciously, we have dropped out of our experience the methods by which spiritual life is nurtured.

As we try to take the measure of this matter, consider the testimony of some of the most characteristic religious movements of our time. Here are three of them, for example,

Christian Science, the renaissance of ritualism as in the Anglo-Catholic movement, and the Oxford Groups. How diverse they are! The very naming of them sends the mind off in all directions. But one thing they have in common, one thing for which multitudes are hungry. They all present their devotees with methods. They all offer techniques for the nurture and guidance of the spiritual life. They do not, like much Protestant preaching, leave a man up in the air, with some fine ideas in his head but no practical, day-by-day things to do to weave the truth into the substance and texture of his daily life.

To be sure, the methods are diverse. An Oxford Grouper who always has believed in Christian principles now discovers that to take a quiet hour in the early morning and listen for the voice of the Divine gives him a sense of Providential guidance in his life which makes his faith in God a new and thrilling experience. And a friend of mine, one of America's leading novelists, whose books you all have read, each day goes to her Anglo-Catholic church to pray, before she undertakes her work, and once a week specially prepares her mind and receives the sacrament. "You may argue about the theory of it all you will," she says to me, "I know what it does to my life."

Surely, here is something to which we Protestants should give heed. For many years we have been throwing religious observance out the door and see, now, in what forms it comes back through the window!

Lest there should be misunderstanding, let me say frankly that many of these techniques are strange to me. I am not a Christian Scientist, an Anglo-Catholic, or an Oxford Grouper. By tradition and temperament I belong elsewhere altogether. My first and natural reaction to the whole question of religious observance is to attack it, to show how hollow and superficial it can be, to point out what peril of hypocrisy lies within it, to reëcho the cry of the ancient prophets against it as a dangerous substitute for righteousness. Did not Isaiah say, "What unto me is the multitude of your sacrifices? saith the Lord"? Did not Jesus denounce those "that devour widows' houses, and for a pretence make long prayers"? Have not the real saints and prophets always had as their chief antagonists the hypocrites who substituted outward form and pious observance for genuine goodness of life? No element in religious history is more futile than outward forms from which the life has fled, like dry irrigation ditches with no water in them; no factor is more shameful than the superstition by which men have thought they could content God with anything but living justly, loving mercy, and walking humbly with their God.

That would be my first and natural reaction to the whole matter of religious observance. But then I think of my own life and of yours. How many lives here are littered up with pious observance? Show me one person in this congregation who habitually fills his days with religious routine, thinking that thereby he placates God! That is the last thing we are even tempted to do. We Protestants, rather, have gone to the opposite extreme. We have sloughed off one observance after another. The more liberal we have grown the more we have emptied our lives of all methods of spiritual nurture, till I venture that many here would have to think hard to remember the last time they deliberately prayed.

What is the use, then, of hurling at our lives denunciations against religious formalism? That is not our typical trouble. We need to be told something else. We deeply need to be reminded that every realm of spiritual excellence requires practical methods of nurture and discipline. Did not Paderewski say that if he stopped practising on the piano one day he noticed the difference, if he stopped two days his family noticed the difference, if he stopped three days his friends noticed the difference, and if he stopped for a week the public noticed the difference? That represents a universal law of life.

We recognize the common sense of this in every area except our inner lives. From building bridges to surgery in our hospitals, from teaching in our schools to great music in our symphonies, we never expect beautiful consequence without disciplined method and technique. Yet who in this congregation does not have to accuse himself of haphazard, hit-or-miss dealing with his inner life, as though this thing, the most important in the world for our happiness, our influence, and our destiny, were not worth thoughtful, careful, yes, methodical, nurture?

Let us come at this matter now from another angle and see that here lies the explanation of some of our personal acquaintances whom in theory we cannot understand. Consider a Roman Catholic friend. Most of us cannot believe what Roman Catholicism teaches, but here, nevertheless, is a Roman Catholic friend, who is a lovely person. In the deepest sense of the word he is making a success of his spiritual life. The more we are acquainted with him, the more evident it is that not because of his theory does this fine consequence arrive but that the secret lies rather in his practical, day-by-day techniques. When he takes the sacrament, it is a great matter to him; into his life he welcomes the life divine, to which he must be true, and the world invisible grows real to him. When he goes to confession, he honestly searches his conscience and corrects his life. When he prays to the saints, it is not idolatry to him; he uses them to enliven and enrich his imagination of what the divine life is like. He steadily employs a whole series of spiritual techniques. Say with me, if you will, that you cannot use them, but there is no denying what they do for him.

Now, go to the other extreme, and think of an agnostic friend, who, while he has no religious theory, is a lovely person. He is wise in counsel and steady in a storm, sweet when others grow bitter and kindly when others are callous, and many turn to him in trouble who never turn to us. The better one knows him the more obvious it is that his secret too lies not in his theory or lack of it but in his day-by-day methods of living. You will see them if you look—his use of solitude, his choice of reading, his exposure of his soul to nature's beauty, his high employment of friendship, his inward ways of talking with himself. He has techniques by which his inner life grows fresh and wise and strong.

Are we really grasping the profound significance of this fact we are trying to state? That Roman Catholic friend and that agnostic are very different. Yet, considering their kindred quality, one sees that if we had to choose, as happily we do not have to choose, between theory and technique, it would be better to have a great technique for spiritual life, no matter what theory we had, than merely to have a great theory about life, however high and Christian, with no methods to make it work.

At any rate, I venture to put into three brief statements what seems to me to be the accumulated experience of the ages concerning the preconditions of great spiritual life. If some one thinks he has private and peculiar exemption from this testimony of the centuries, very well, but I doubt it. For here is the witness.

First, great spiritual life is never possible without solitude. We cannot live in the unrelieved din and confusion of the world and still grow a soul. There must be solitude, highly used, in the background of one's life, or there is no peace, no poise, no power. There must be some place familiar to our steps where, in Jesus' phrase, we can go and shut the door. That is the universal witness—no great thing ever dreamed or done except by men who knew the use of solitude "in deep mid-silence, open-doored to God."

Second, great spiritual life is never possible without fellowship. We are not individuals merely. Just as a single stick, if lighted, will go out, so a single soul, no matter how brightly kindled, in a world like this will be extinguished by itself alone. We must be thrown together if we are to keep our fire. Living a crowded life, where we meet teeming multitudes upon our lower levels, we need deliberately to seek the fellowship of kindred souls upon our higher levels. "Where two or three are gathered together in my name," said Jesus, "there am I."

Third, great spiritual life is never possible without disciplined habitual thinking. Habitual thinking is the inner loom on which is woven the texture of our real life. For a man, therefore, merely to have faiths about life, however high and Christian, is like having skeins of yarn lying idle on the shelf. Only by schooled and disciplined thinking are they woven into the texture and fabric of his common days. If any one supposes he can do that weaving by haphazard, casual carelessness, he does not understand himself. That deep and inward matter requires thought, time, care, directed meditation.

We are not saying that these three are the only preconditions of strong spiritual life, but they are central, and we are claiming that many here, by their wise use, could be thoroughly transformed and lifted to new levels of spiritual potency and achievement. In this modern world, of all places, why should that seem strange? For what made the modern world? Science. But what made science? The inductive method. That is the origin and fountainhead of all our scientific achievement. A new method made a new world. If a world can be so transformed by a new method, why should transformations of character seem strange to us, when folk in earnest accept the testimony of the ages concerning the high use of private prayer and spiritual fellowship and disciplined thinking?

Let us come at our subject from another angle and consider that in a day like this, when man's social life is so disturbed and disturbing, there is special need of strongly nurtured and well-disciplined inner lives. Some may feel, instead, that the world is so tragic, so hard bestead, so haunted by the fear of penury and war, that nothing except the social question matters and that it is trivial and selfish to talk thus about our private spiritual disciplines. That attitude, not uncommon among youth, springs from such generous motives that one admires its spirit, but the more one thinks about it the more one sees that it is mistaken.

A few weeks ago a young man attended service here and afterward wrote me a letter. He was impatient with our concern about the quality of our spiritual lives. He was thinking about the slums, he said, about poverty and industrial injustice, and he had worked out a philosophy, he wrote, which he put before me in bold capitals: "Take care of the body and the soul will take care of itself." So! *That* was his solution. But throughout this company are people whose bodies are well taken care of but whose souls are not taking care of themselves. And America, more than any other country in history, has been full of people whose bodies were well taken care of but whose souls did not take care of themselves. And that young man's letter, very long and self-revealing, showed that his body was being comfortably taken care of but that his soul was not taking care of itself.

Granted, I should say to him, that no Christian is genuine who does not deeply and sacrificially care about these appalling social conditions which fall with terrific incidence upon the souls of men and which deny everything that Jesus taught. But no Christian is wise who supposes that any change of outward circumstance can guarantee that the soul will take care of itself. At any rate, so far as our present problem is concerned, the more distraught and difficult our social situation the more we need strongly nurtured, well-disciplined inner lives.

To be sure, I am hoping that this thing we are saying is

[8]

being welcomed by the right people. There may well be some to whom we ought to say instead, Stop fussing about yourself; stop taking your own spiritual temperature; get away from yourself; find some public cause you care about, and serve it until you forget yourself; you never will be healthy-minded or spiritually well so long as you are obsessed with feeling your own pulse. Some people habitually need to be told that. But there are more here, I suspect, especially among the young, to whom one would like to say: When a flood devastates a great river valley, two duties concern the inhabitants—first, public service, doing the best they can for the common good, but, second, keeping themselves from going under. If they are submerged they will not help anybody else. How many need to be told that today! It is worth emphasizing: the more difficult the social situation, the greater the need of strongly nurtured inner lives.

See what this world does to us when we try to let our souls take care of themselves! See what we have to look at and read and hear, what obscenity faces us, what tragedy in the world at large confronts us, what selfishness invades us! I am not saying that we should run away from this. A hermit's escape is cheap. Live in the midst of the world, open-eyed to its folly and its sin. Let nothing that is human be alien to you. Live in the world but be not of it. If, however, a man is thus to be in the world but not of it, he cannot in any hit-or-miss fashion let his soul take care of itself. He needs methods.

If the Master were here, I do not think he would mind much just what methods we use. I think he would try to understand a sincere Quaker with his silence and a sincere Anglo-Catholic with his ritual. I think he would understand the high use of books and nature and art. He would know how we differ in temperament. He would not try to run us into one mold. But, friends, we need some means by which in time the Eternal grows real, the invisible shines through the seen, God becomes a speaking Presence, conscience is quickened, resources are deepened, and hope is renewed, until one hears the trumpets of the soul again and is adequate for life!

Our forefathers used to observe Lent with prayers and fasting. I am not appealing for any special method during our Lenten season. But I am haunted by the fact that hundreds here could be lifted to new levels of spiritual quality and power if they took in earnest what we have been saying. This thing particularly I lay upon your consciences: there is no more subtle and certain way of denying a great matter than by denying the means to it. Few people deny the principles of education or the desirability of an educated life, but by listlessness and laziness thousands refuse to master the techniques of study by which alone the educated life can come. They intend to refuse the road, not the goal, but, lo! he who refuses the road has refused the goal.

Alas for the bride and groom who, building a home with the highest ideas of marriage in their minds and the loftiest ideals of it in their hearts, yet as the years pass, while never denying the great principles on which they started, carelessly drop out the techniques of family life, the lovely, gracious methods and observances by which intimacy is made beautiful and romance is deepened into abiding friendship until, as with an old violin, the passing years add sweetness and mellowness to the tone! One often sees homes where the observances that make home life beautiful have been neglected until the ill consequence has gone so far that it is too late to mend. Nobody has committed adultery. Nobody has denied the principles of a great home. Only, dropping the means of grace, they have awakened to find that grace itself has gone.

Millions are so losing God. I know one student of music who hopes sometime to be a concert pianist and who in recent weeks has been practising five hours a day with his right thumb alone. That is the test of his sincerity, his teacher says to him. Does he want what he says he wants enough to master the techniques? Yet how many of us spend five minutes a day on the thoughtful nurture of our inner lives? "Be not deceived; God is not mocked: for whatsoever a man soweth, that shall he also reap."

Six Ways in Which Modern Man Can Pray

IF ONE could approach a subject like prayer freshly, could outflank the preconceived ideas of it and surprise people into the discovery of prayer's reality before they even guessed that one was talking about prayer, that would be ideal. For words like "prayer" have a long history. They come to us encrusted with old ideas which no intelligent mind can accept and with old practises in which no intelligent man can indulge. Today I am asking you not to blockade the road of this sermon with preconceived opinions. At least give us a fair chance to talk together about some of the real experiences of prayer.

To many people, for example, prayer suggests begging the cosmic God to run errands for us, and that seems to them absurd. Of course it is absurd. But why shut ourselves off from the rich and rewarding experiences of real prayer by preconceptions picked up in childhood, it may be, or heard of, heaven knows where?

Indeed, let us start with a word of Jesus which in the first instance had nothing to do with praying. In the parable of the Sower Jesus said of the seeds falling on thin soil among rocky places that "they had not much earth: and straightway they sprang up, because they had no deepness of earth: and when the sun was risen, they were scorched; and because they had no root, they withered away." So! Because they had no root—there is a text on prayer.

Consider, then, six ways of praying that bring to life deepness of earth and strong rootage—all of them possible to an intelligent modern man who believes in God at all, and in this difficult time especially and desperately needed.

First, *the prayer of interior relaxation and serenity.* It is a prayer which does not beg God for anything but in which the soul rests back on God. To be sure, if a man is to rest back successfully, he must have something deep to rest back upon, as did the Psalmist who said, "The eternal God is thy refuge, and underneath are the everlasting arms." Even in its simplest form prayer involves great matters. Tyndall, the nineteenth century scientist, although an outspoken agnostic, said this: "Often unreasonable, if not contemptible, in its purer forms prayer hints at disciplines which few of us can neglect without moral loss." Thus even an agnostic may have interior disciplines akin to prayer. But happy the man who, when he faces the inevitable necessity of resting back, has something strong to rest back upon!

Now, the God of the New Testament peculiarly meets this need. For where is the God of the New Testament? Granted that, as in the Old Testament, he still is the Eternal, holding Orion and the Pleiades in his leash, from everlasting to everlasting the Creator—yet where *especially* is God's dwelling as the New Testament pictures it, the place where we meet him, where our experience of him is consummated and fulfilled? "Know ye not that ye are a temple of God, and that the Spirit of God dwelleth in you?" "Behold, I stand at the door and knock: if any man hear my voice and open the door, I will come in to him, and will sup with him, and he with me." "God is love; and he that abideth in love abideth in God, and God abideth in him." Praying to such a God is not vainly reaching outside oneself to a distant deity, not exploding oneself, as it were, toward high heaven in a wild endeavor to catch the cosmic ear. Prayer to God, in its simplest form, is resting back upon a divine presence personally possessed and intimately known.

> Thou Life within my life, than self more near,
> Thou veiled Presence infinitely clear,
> From all illusive shows of sense I flee,
> To find my center and my rest in thee.

How do men live without that experience?

There are two aspects to every strong life—fruitage and rootage, activity and receptivity, tension and relaxation, working hard and resting back. When first we named this kind of prayer, some young, ardent spirit here may have felt scornful of it, saying, Such prayer is letting go, lying down, taking it easy, resting back, going to sleep. To that I answer: Do you really feel scornful about rest and sleep? Have you ever had insomnia, when you could not sleep, been so tense that you could not relax, so harried you could not let go? He who cannot rest cannot work; he who cannot let go cannot hang on; he who loses serenity within loses everything without. My consultation hours fill up with men and women who have mastered the techniques of activity and aggressiveness but whose lives are going to pieces because they have mastered no other techniques at all.

Listen, then, to this prayer from the great tradition of the church: "Let my soul take refuge from the crowding turmoil of worldly thoughts beneath the shadow of Thy wings; let my heart, this sea of restless waves, find peace in Thee, O God." Who said that? Saint Augustine. A weak man? One of the tremendous characters in history, from his early struggles with himself until at last, Bishop of Hippo in North Africa, he fell on sleep while the invading barbarians were hammering at the city gates and the Roman Empire was falling around his ears. He never could have stood up as he did throughout such a tumultuous life without that kind of prayer. That man had roots.

In the second place, *the prayer of affirmation*. This prayer also does not beg God for anything but goes up before the face of God and there remembers and affirms the great convictions which blow trumpets in the soul and rouse its powers to action. "The Lord is my shepherd; I shall not want"—that is prayer. "Our Father who art in heaven, Hallowed be thy name"—that is prayer. "I thank my God upon all my remembrance of you"—that is prayer. "Therefore will not we

[14]

fear, though the earth be removed, and though the mountains be carried into the midst of the sea; though the waters thereof roar and be troubled, though the mountains shake with the swelling thereof. . . . The Lord of hosts is with us; the God of Jacob is our refuge"—that is prayer. It is not begging; it is affirming, putting at the center of one's mind those great convictions of faith which enlarge and elevate, empower and dignify the soul.

One of the most moving sermons of our generation was preached some time ago in Aberdeen by Dr. Gossip, a powerful Scotch minister. His wife had died without warning and one of the loveliest of homes had been broken up with terrific suddenness. Taking for the subject of his next sermon, "But When Life Tumbles In, What Then?" he made an affirmation of faith which shook Aberdeen and which even in cold print cannot be read now and soon forgotten. Of course that man prayed, but evidently it was the kind of praying that held at the center of his thought not so much his trouble as his faith, that threw around and over and underneath his trouble great convictions, as though, like the Psalmist, he too were saying to God, "Though I walk through the valley of the shadow of death, I *will* fear no evil: for thou *art* with me; thy rod and thy staff they *comfort* me." And so powerful is such affirmatory prayer that he could end his sermon to his people by quoting Hopeful from *The Pilgrim's Progress*, halfway through the last dark river, calling back to his friend, " 'Be of good cheer, my brother, for I feel the bottom, and it is sound.' "

Indeed, so influential is this affirmatory process that it makes praying dangerous. I mean that some people pray about trouble in such a way that, putting trouble in the center of attention, they come out more troubled than they were before. Some people pray about sexual temptation in such wise that, putting that in the center of their thought and keeping it there, though they are talking to God about it, they end worse than they began. Some people pray about discouragement so that they emerge more discouraged than they started, because their prayer has only served to concenter their attention the more on their disheartenment. You will find no praying like that in Scripture. Paul was in trouble, in prison, facing death. Listen to his description of his own prayer: "I bow my knees unto the Father, from whom every family in heaven and on earth is named, that he would grant you, according to the riches of his glory, that ye may be strengthened with power through his Spirit in the inward man; that Christ may dwell in your hearts through faith; to the end that ye, being rooted and grounded in love, may be strong to apprehend with all the saints what is the breadth and length and height and depth, and to know the love of Christ which passeth knowledge, that ye may be filled unto all the fulness of God." That is affirmatory prayer. How do people live without it?

An old legend says that after the angels had rebelled in heaven and had been cast out of paradise they were asked what they missed most and they answered, "The sound of the trumpets in the morning." Aye, that is prayer.

In the third place, *the prayer of spiritual companionship.* This prayer also does not beg God for anything but habitually enters into inward fellowship with him. It is the prayer that says with Jesus, "I am not alone, because the Father is with me." Who can properly estimate the control over our lives conferred on us by the fact that we can choose our interior spiritual companionships? Many things in the outer world we cannot choose; there necessity often decides not only the circumstances that shall befall us but even the company that we must keep. But within ourselves we can choose our company. There no hand can shut the door against a visitor whom we would entertain. There we are masters of our hospitality. There we can maintain an habitual spiritual fellowship.

Some one here may be saying, This is a modernist's idea

of prayer and not at all the old conception on which the historic church has been nourished. I answer, Who was it taught that if a man uses words, that is not prayer; that if a man uses ordered thoughts, that is not prayer; that only when one goes deeper than words and ordered thoughts can go and is wrapped in the sense of a spiritual companionship is he praying? Who taught that? Savonarola. Who was it thought of prayer as establishing "ourselves in a sense of God's presence by continually conversing with Him"? Brother Lawrence, a seventeenth century Catholic mystic. Who was it to whom prayer meant making "frequent colloquies or short discoursings between God and his own soul"? Jeremy Taylor, an old Protestant leader. Friends, to the great souls of the church prayer has meant the maintenance of an habitual spiritual fellowship.

Here the limelight falls upon one of the most important things that can be said about prayer: its worst perversions, superstitions, and caricatures are associated with the idea of it as an emergency measure. Men get into a tight place and then try to pray themselves out of it. As the Psalmist says, "They . . . are at their wit's end. Then they cry unto the Lord in their trouble." That is a third-rate way of praying—trying to use God, as the old Greek dramatists used Zeus, a *deus ex machina* swung over the stage to unravel the plot when it was so tangled that human wit could not unravel it. Who so thinks of prayer has made magic of it and at the last will discover that the great God is too august to be a suddenly called errand boy running to answer our frantically pushed buttons. The worst perversions of prayer come from treating it thus as an emergency measure. That is not the way we treat friendship. The glory of a friend is his dependable fellowship. The glory of the Unseen Friend is his habitual companionship. Then when an emergency comes ones goes, like Jesus to the garden, traveling an accustomed path to a familiar Presence for a brief colloquy, to emerge

[17]

again to face the wrath of devils and the scorn of men. Souls who pray this way have roots.

In the fourth place, *the prayer of moral conflict*. The most decisive battles of the world are fought not on external battle-fields but in the consciences of men. The destiny of Israel's nation was in the wilderness with Moses alone beside the burning bush. The destiny of mankind was with Jesus in the desert alone with his temptation. The hope of the church was on the Damascus Road with Paul "not disobedient unto the heavenly vision." One stands in awe before these inner battlefields. What thus is true in the large, in the small is true of each of us—our major conflicts are within.

Praying means carrying these conflicts up before the face of God and fighting them out in the light of the Highest be-fore we have to fight them out in the world. *No man can ex-temporize character*. Our great decisions have to be made tri-umphantly within before they can be made triumphantly without. Alas for a man who does not know that inner place of prayer where the great decisions can be made!

Consider this autobiographical reminiscence from Robert Louis Stevenson. "Go," he says, "the first grey, east-windy day into the Caledonian Station, if it looks at all as it did of yore: I met Satan there." One wonders what it was he met there. All unsuspectingly young Stevenson passed into the Caledonian Station, but years afterwards he was still re-membering the terrific impact of that shock—he met Satan there. So in every realm life does ambush us. We must be ready beforehand. It is too late to get ready after the ambush has been sprung. No man can extemporize character. We need an inner place where the decisions are made first.

As you see, I am talking today not so much about the theory as about the experience of prayer. All through life run vital functions whose theories keep changing but whose experience persists. Agriculture, for example. How changing and varied have been the theories of agriculture this last quarter of a century! But agriculture persists; we must go on growing things to eat, no matter how the theories shift. So prayer's explanations alter but its experiences persist. We, like our fathers, must have a high and inward place where we fight out our major conflicts in the presence of God before we have to fight them out in the world.

No one, I think, ever described this function of prayer so vividly as did Chinese Gordon. He had temptations so terrific one wonders that he ever withstood them. He whimsically named one of them Agag after the Amalekite king in the Old Testament. Listen to him then in a letter to his sister: "My constant prayer is against Agag, who, of course, is here, and as insinuating as ever," and, again, "One feels inclined to withdraw from the combat altogether, and go into seclusion; but even there I expect Agag would pursue in some form." Says one biographer, "He wrestled with 'Agag,'" and George Adam Smith reports that more than once he said, "I had a hard half hour this morning hewing Agag in pieces before the Lord." I commend to you this indispensable experience—"hewing Agag in pieces before the Lord."

In the fifth place, *the prayer of strong desire*. As some of you have been correctly thinking, prayer is more than resting back, or affirming faith before the face of God, or seeking an interior companionship, or carrying our conflicts up into the light of the Highest. Prayer is strong desire. It comes out of our deep needs and it cries for the things we want.

Were I to ask you about the condition of your "prayer life," that might sound to you like a pious question and, half-sheepishly, you might try to tell me that you have very little of it. But if I should ask you about your life of desire, you could not tell me that you have very little of that. That is the heart of you—your strong and clamorous desire. Well, let us not fool ourselves with the conventionality of language. Desire *is* prayer. Beneath all the things we commonly call praying, what we do verily want of life is our genuine prayer.

We never know any one, then, until we know his desire. We know Admiral Peary when we hear him say, "The determination to reach the Pole had become so much a part of my being that, strange as it may seem, I long ago ceased to think of myself save as an instrument for the attainment of that end." We know John Knox when we hear him pray, "Give me Scotland, or I die!"

Have you ever read the Beatitudes of Jesus and been astonished that prayer is not mentioned? Strange, isn't it? that this master of prayer, to whom it meant so much, should speak these great beatitudes of the spiritual life and leave prayer out! But we are mistaken. Prayer is there, not in word but, deeper, in reality. "Blessed are they that hunger and thirst after righteousness: for they shall be filled." That is prayer, life's hunger and thirst.

So prayer is a tremendous force. Controlling desire can roll down through the center of a man's life like the Mississippi, which, flowing through the center of the continent, calls in tributary streams from every side until, a flood, it pours out into the Gulf of Mexico.

Because desire is one's real prayer, praying is dangerous. We commonly hear folk complain because their prayers are not answered, but alas, look around you and see the people on every side ruined because their real prayers have been answered! Underneath the formal supplications which we offer when we put on court clothes and come up to the sanctuary piously to ask what it seems meet to ask—beneath such formal praying, our veritable demands on life, the cravings around which our lives are organized, inevitably tend to be answered. Indeed, we use a slang phrase when some bitter rebuff or unkindly consequence falls upon a man. He asked for that, we say. Just so! Of how much of our trouble is that true— we asked for it!

Go through this congregation now and is it not true that our major problems concern our desires—their conflicts, their perversity, their waywardness, their power, so hard to handle? My soul, carry up your life of desire before the face of the Most High, there to be unified, organized, elevated, purified, directed to great ends, and say as Jesus did in the garden, "Not my will, but thine, be done." How can a man live well without some such process in his soul?

In the sixth place, *the prayer of released power*. One never ceases to be astonished at the number of people who think that prayer means getting God to do what they want done. But the very saying of that ought to prove its fallacy. God, at my beck and call to do what I want done because I want it—the perspective is all wrong in that, as though the mountain must come to Mahomet and not Mahomet to the mountain. No! Prayer is not a way of getting God to do what *we* want but a way of putting ourselves in such relationship with God that he can do in and for and through us what *he* wants. Prayer is not a magic means by which we control God but a humble means by which God can control us, find gangway through us, release his power and purpose in us.

Did you ever try to teach music to a child who did not want to learn music? That is a baffling task. Here is the whole world of music, and you, more than willing to give a creative share in it to the child, are baffled, frustrated, and estopped for this so simple reason: there is no prayer for music in the child. So at last, like a great reservoir waiting in vain for an outlet, the world of music finds in that child no release and through him no revelation. So, without prayer there are some things God cannot say to us, for prayer is the listening ear. Without prayer there are some things God cannot give to us, for prayer is the hospitable heart. Without prayer there are some things God cannot do through us, for prayer is the cooperative will.

When, therefore, this sermon is done, I beg of you not to go out saying that I presented prayer merely as a subjective experience without objective consequence. The most tremendous objective consequences on earth come from released power. Even in the physical world we do not by our sciences create power; we release it, with world-transforming consequence. So, when David Livingstone prayed about Africa, "May God in mercy permit me to do something for the cause of Christ in these dark places of the earth!" he did not change God's intention but he did change God's action. He did not alter God's purpose but he did release it. There was a fresh invasion of the world by God through Livingstone. Who can set limits to the possibilities of that?

Six kinds of prayer that give us deepness of earth and strong rootage in it! Not one of them, I think, is shut out from any intelligent man if he believes in God at all. Friends, we miss such praying, not because of the keenness of our intellects, but because of the shallowness of our lives.

Discovering What We Can Do with Ourselves

ONE of the profoundest mysteries in the universe lies in the fact that inside each of us there are two of us— I and Me. That is why a man can talk with himself. Observing an abstracted look in a friend's eye, we know what is happening—he is talking with himself. So inside each of us dwell two of us.

Psychologists may describe this phenomenon as the subjective and objective aspects of personality, but a technical name by itself never solved a practical problem and still the mysterious fact remains that I am not simply I but I and Me, locked in an enforced companionship, talking together, planning together, quarreling together, trying somehow to manage life together. Moreover, I cannot get away from Me. Sometimes from other people one can escape, but not from oneself. Lo! here we dwell, I and Me together in an indissoluble marriage, from which there is no divorce. This is, I should suppose, the innermost, basic fact of human life.

Sometime since, a cartoon pictured a woman on shipboard, saying to a traveling companion, "I took this trip just to get away from myself." It takes more than a sea trip to do that; it takes death itself, and, if we who believe in immortality are correct, even death will not succeed. When we consider the hectic feverishness with which people live, when we ask why they drink so much, drive themselves so furiously, preoccupy themselves with such trivialities, the reason is plain— I is endeavoring to escape from Me; with hectic excitement and stimulation I is trying to blanket the protests, anesthetize the pains, and evade the pursuit of Me. Always the endeavor fails. For the fleeing I at last slackens pace, the pursuing Me catches up, and the old problem emerges again, the deepest,

[23]

most secret problem in human experience—how can I manage to go on living with Me? Even Dwight L. Moody said that he had had more trouble with himself than with any other person he had ever met.

Some one may say, I do not wish to think about this today; I am interested not so much in what I can do with Me as in what we all together can do with the world; that is the great problem. I answer that I too am concerned about the world and that, if we follow far enough this trail we have started on, it will land us in the thick of the world. But, certainly, it is far easier to discuss the problems of the world in general than to face this interior challenge: The world being what it is, what can I get out of Me that is likely to do the world any good? That is not evading or forgetting the world's problem but bringing it close to one's doorsill.

In all human history has anything of importance ever happened except as somebody discovered what he could do with himself? At the Last Supper, as the Fourth Gospel pictures it, Jesus summed up the secret of his world-transforming ministry in three words—"I sanctify myself." So! I and Myself, and what went on between them! To be sure, he said, *"For their sakes* I sanctify myself," or, as we should say, For their sakes I dedicate myself, consecrate myself—in Burne-Jones' phrase, make the most of my best for the sake of others. Jesus' interior transaction with himself had the world in view, but let no one miss the profound significance of that collocation, I and Myself. Whether in art or music, in morals or science, in social reform or religion, nothing has ever happened of importance apart from this most intimate, searching experience of humankind—discovering what one can do with oneself.

In the first place, consider the inevitableness of this problem. We have to do something with ourselves. We have ourselves on our hands. Other problems a man may shunt off, find proxies for, discover substitutes and surrogates to care about, but not this. Here is one of life's inevitables—I have Me on my hands.

Moreover, multiplied as it is as many times as individuals are born on earth, this problem soon becomes a public matter. In New York State, for example, one person out of every twenty-two in the population, at some time in his or her experience, has to be confined in an asylum for the mentally unfit—one out of every twenty-two. This means that, if we are average people, over one hundred persons in this congregation either have been or will be incarcerated in asylums. When one deducts the congenital reasons for that calamity and the environmental reasons easily imagined as removable, the residue is very large—cases where the real trouble lies inside, I living wretchedly with Me. On what unhappy terms I and Me commonly dwell together! What interior wrangling, quarreling, backbiting, flights from reality, mutual hatreds, are in that deep and silent center of our lives where I and Me are trying to live together! Said a modern novelist about one of his characters, "He was not so much a human being as a civil war." So I and Me too often dwell together. Sometimes we go insane because of it and commonly we make a sorry mess of living.

Such is the characteristic externalism of our time, such the dominance of things, that many people never come to grips with this most intimate problem until it is too late. We habitually talk about adjusting ourselves to our environment and our environment to ourselves. Important as that doubtless is, there is no adjustment we can make between ourselves and our environment that matters much if we cannot adjust ourselves to ourselves. The I-and-Me relationship is central. That is the main implement I have to work with at any other task. That is the only standing-ground I have for spiritual leverage upon the world.

So in "The Green Pastures" Noah said to the Lord, "I ain' very much, but I'se all I got." So! "I'se all I got." With that much I was fitted out to start with, to see what I could do with it, and I cannot do much at anything else if I fail in that primary commission—I entrusted with Me.

In this regard our fathers were right when they said that the soul of the world's salvation is the salvation of the soul. Whatever Wordsworth did for the world in his own realm went back to an interior conference where I decided about Me that Me must be, as Wordsworth put it, "else sinning greatly, a dedicated Spirit." Whatever Florence Nightingale achieved for the world in her life went back to an interior transaction whose anniversary she always kept, February 7, 1837, when her two selves agreed that she had been called of God to a special type of service to mankind. All that Jesus did for the world stems out from an inward transaction on what quiet days, upon what silent hills in Galilee, when first he began saying, "I dedicate myself." And anything we ever do for the world will, one way or another, go back to the manner in which we handle this I-and-Me relationship. As Ralph Waldo Emerson put it, "Souls are not saved in bundles. The Spirit saith to the man, 'How is it with thee? thee personally? is it well? is it ill?'" If some are so modern-minded that they do not wish to take that from a now old-fashioned man like Ralph Waldo Emerson, hear it in other language from one of the greatest of our psychiatrists: "Our problem is not primarily to fit a man to face his environment, but . . . to fit him to face himself. A man is impotent to face the onslaughts of the objective world until he has restored harmony within the borders of his soul; only when he has resolved these conflicts in his soul is he fitted to face his environment. With peace in his soul he is capable of facing the most terrible experience, as has been proved by the war; without it he cannot face the responsibility of writing a letter."

In the second place, what even the least of us does with himself makes a difference to the world. Some here doubtless have been saying, All that the preacher claims is true but true only of the creative geniuses; the major achievements of mankind do go back to turning points where stand great individuals whose influence was determinative. If on that first sea trip Columbus had not dealt courageously with himself, America would have had to wait to be discovered. If, in many a difficult place in his experimentation, Edison had not dealt resolutely with Edison, the story of electricity's development would have been different. But in such a day as this, when economic and nationalistic forces rage across the planet like Caribbean hurricanes, how disproportionate, how empty of large consequence, seems what happens deep in my life where I am dealing with Me! To that natural and modest statement, with truth in it, I venture two answers.

For one thing, it makes a difference to you, at any rate, how you live with yourself. That much of the world has everything at stake. Even war and unemployment do not matter more to you. For, difficult as hard times are, a man can live through them pretty well if he knows how to handle himself, but he can be as rich as Dives and as unhappy as perdition if he does not.

One of our leading university presidents tells us that one springtime he was in the north of Canada when the frost was breaking up and the roads were well-nigh impassable. He says that at one crossroad he saw this sign: "Take care which rut you choose; you will be in it for the next twenty-five miles." One would like to say that to many a youth! Living ignobly with oneself is an easy thing to start, and more than one youth here must have started it—I doing things that Me is ashamed of; Me furtively hiding conduct he does not want I to refer to; not much serenity within to come home to at night; no spiritual allegiance that draws life together and gives direction, meaning, and integrity! It makes a difference to you how you live with yourself.

"Take care which rut you choose; you will be in it for the next twenty-five miles."

Moreover, it makes a difference to the world how you live with yourself—at any rate to some people in the world. "For their sakes," said Jesus, "I dedicate myself." Could even he have guessed how many people at last would be taken into that enlarging company? As he first spoke the words, he appears to have been thinking primarily about the few at the table. Numbers do not decide everything. There are at least some people for whom the most important thing in the world is the way you handle yourself. You know who they may be—father, mother, lover, fiancée, wife or husband, children—somebody. What you do with yourself carries in its hands more destiny for them than anything else in the world. For their sakes then, and, because they touch others, for *their* sakes, and, because they touch still others, for *their* sakes, what is I doing with Me?

In the third place, consider that through this truth lies one of the most fascinating approaches to practical living. We may not be pioneering cosmologists or even explorers of the stratosphere, but we can explore the possibilities of ourselves and see what, by God's grace, we may succeed in doing with ourselves. That is within our reach.

In a class for young children the teacher was endeavoring to make vivid to imagination the newness of inventions such as airplanes and radios, which a few years ago did not exist. "What is in the world," she said, "that was not here fifty years ago?" and quick as a flash an eager voice cried, "Me!" There is a young philosopher for you. He knows what is the most important of new things that ever comes to earth—Me. *There* is something to look deeply into and explore, finding what in it can be brought out into the light—Me!

Such eager expectancy could get even into us if we would have it so. What a rallying-cry it is for flagging spirits on difficult days—Come, now, let us see what we can do with ourselves!

We face suffering, let us say. That is difficult. One wants to collapse into plaintiveness and fear. In the face of pain I can have a dreadful time with Me. Yet, after all, suffering is part of life, one of life's inevitables. Do we ask for a golf course without bunkers that we ask for life without pain? Let us see, then, what we can do with ourselves, joining the honorable company of those who by well-sustained endurance have incomparably lifted the estimate of man's moral possibilities and from the land of suffering have brought back insights never to be found on easier ground.

Or we face handicap. At the start we thought we were a thousand-acre farm. Now we know the truth. A one-acre lot—that is what we are, and the soil is none too good. We are handicapped by our limitations within and by circumstance without. I can have a disastrous time with Me about that. Yet while creative geniuses have nobly served the world on a great scale and so have served us within it, when one thinks of the most secret, inward, redemptive, spiritual help one ever has received, how much of it has come from handicapped people! Remind us of Copernicus or Sir Isaac Newton, and we respond with admiration. But remind us of Helen Keller, and we feel something else and something deeper. How often in the interior silence of her life she must have said to herself, Things being as they are, still I will see what I can do with Me!

Or it may be we face moral defeat, which all our trying has been unable to prevent. We are tired of trying. Again and again we have stepped on the gas of our volition only to have it peter out. Effort of will is getting us nowhere—in beating off temptation, or in facing daily strain, or in quelling our unruly feelings. Let us see, then, what we can do with ourselves by resources of the Spirit from beyond ourselves! Edison did not light the world by individual effort

[29]

only but by harnessing a universal power. So in every realm science works its miracles, not so much by vigorous volition as by released power. We never out-of-hand create power. All our power is appropriated, assimilated, released. Great is the hour, then, when a man, in whom I stands dismayed at the powerful unruliness of Me, reaches out for superhuman help and finds it. Amazing have been the transformations so begun. Out of such experience rises a host of witnesses to testify: You do not need to stay the way you are; you can be changed as a desert is changed when it is irrigated, not by effort expended but by the power released.

I deeply wish that this experience might be opened now to some here who need it. It makes small difference what you call it. If you are accustomed to the traditional language of Christianity, you will call it being born anew. So it is. But being born anew is no unique specialty of religion. In no realm do we amount to anything without being born anew. When, as a young boy, I first heard a great symphony, it meant nothing to me. I thought the violins were dreadful, and an internationally famed artist who played a solo on the 'cello seemed endlessly tiresome. If to me now such music is, as it were, the breath of life, my volition did not work the change. Rather, as once again I sat in the presence of great music, it found in me an open door. It came in and took possession. More than my will wrought the saving transformation. I was invaded by a realm from beyond my volition and was born anew into a fresh relation with a reality greater than myself. So said Paul—"If any man is in Christ, he is a new creature."

We have run here upon one of the profoundest truths about our subject: in the I-and-Me relationship religion has its central residence. While by vigorous effort, without conscious religious faith we can handle fairly well this or that item in our external environment, when I confronts Me, and with any intellectual and spiritual competence takes the measure of that situation, two needs rise up that only religion can meet—the need of faith, which will put abiding spiritual meaning at the heart of life, and the need of power greater than our own, to live it with. That is why modern psychology, at first materialistic, mechanistic, behavioristic, now that it emerges into practical application and tries to help I handle Me, confronts religion. One of the greatest of psychologists, Jung, calls his last book *Modern Man in Search of a Soul,* and among other things interesting to men of religion he says this: "Among all my patients in the second half of life—that is to say, over thirty-five—there has not been one whose problem in the last resort was not that of finding a religious outlook on life. It is safe to say that every one of them fell ill because he had lost that which the living religions of every age have given to their followers, and none of them has been really healed who did not regain his religious outlook." Twenty years ago one would not have expected such testimony from such a source.

Finally, however, some here may not be facing the things we have been speaking of. You are not confronting suffering or handicap or moral defeat. You are young, strong, gifted, ardent for life. Ah, then, see what you can do with *yourself!* Make the most of your best for the sake of others! Say to yourself that one thing in the world not here fifty years ago is Me. See to it that you explore that. I bring you no negative counsel of self-repression. I bring you positive counsel of self-expression. Get out of yourself, for the world's sake, all the best in yourself—as old Jacob Boehme, the mystic, put it, all your fiery energies harnessed to the service of the light.

If some one is troubled because this I-and-Me relationship is inward and psychological while the problems of the world are external and sociological, I beg of you to see the two not apart but together. I never can make the best of Me by thinking only about Me. We must change the social structure, change it deeply, for, as it is, it impinges on individuals with such cruel inequity that I has no fair chance to make the most of Me. You are right about that. When on the hills of Galilee Jesus first began saying, "I dedicate myself," he was not thinking primarily of himself but of the world. That world desperately needs thinking about still. Nothing more stimulating comes to any one, especially a youth, than a call for help. Let the call for help from the social need of the world reach you, draw out from you all the intellectual ability and moral courage you have anywhere concealed about your person. Find your social cause and serve it or you never can make the most of yourself. But remember, Alexander the Great was not the only one who found it easier to conquer the world than to rule himself. Robespierre was not the only flaming servant of a social cause, called by those who knew him best "the incorruptible," who went to pieces at the last because he could not handle himself. No public service can make up for that inward lack. Many a promising career of public service has gone to pieces because of it.

> . . . To thine own self be true,
> And it must follow, as the night the day,
> Thou canst not then be false to any man.

On Finding It Hard to Believe in God

SOME atheism, dogmatic and intolerant, deserves the Psalmist's indignation—"The fool hath said in his heart, There is no God." Familiar today, however, is another kind of atheist altogether, puzzled, wistfully wishing there might be a God but finding it desperately difficult to think there really is. One cannot be indignant about *that*. Such difficulty in believing in God is a human problem so inclusive that even the most confident man of faith would feel himself in a glass house if he tried to throw stones at it, remembering how often he, too, has found it hard to believe in God. For such souls the text is not the Psalmist's "The fool hath said . . . There is no God," but rather the kindly, understanding attitude of the Master toward the man who cried, "Lord, I believe; help thou mine unbelief."

Our sermon, then, is not an attack on atheism or even an argument for theism, as though in a few moments one could marshal reasons like squadrons and make them march to a victorious proof of God. Our aim is more modest—the sympathetic endeavor to suggest to some who are finding it hard to believe in God considerations which may make their problem simpler and its effect upon their lives less perilous.

In the first place, we might say to them that no one believes in all of God. No one can. All of God is too vast to be comprehended in anybody's faith. We cannot even believe in all the physical universe. How can we? It is too great. As was said of Mrs. Einstein, she did not understand Mr. Einstein's ideas of relativity, but—what was more important to her—she understood Mr. Einstein. We all are thrown back on some such attitude. We cannot take in all the cosmos, but some of

[33]

it we can. Often what is most important to us we can take in and believe.

If this is true about the physical universe, how much more true about God! Many people, I am sure, lose faith in God because they are not willing to take him, shall I say? in instalments and believe in as much of him as they can. Starting, rather, with an all-or-none attitude and finding all of God too great for the comprehension of their faith, they feel thrown back on disbelief. But when one is dealing with the idea of God which represents the most august and profound reality one can think about, an all-or-none attitude is preposterous. No! Believe in as much of God as you can—that surely is the first good counsel to one who is finding it difficult to believe in him at all.

The prevalence of the all-or-none attitude is evidenced in people who come asking the minister for his definition of God. As though God could be defined! A little girl, asked how she drew her pictures, answered, "First I think, and then I draw a line round my think." It would be difficult to improve on that as a description of artistry, but no ultimate reality can so be dealt with. If any one tries to have a "think" about God and then put a line around it, one knows that the God whose judgments are unsearchable, as the New Testament says, "and his ways past tracing out," has been missed. Far more modestly than that, a man must believe in as much of God as he can.

Some one probably is feeling that what we are saying is typical of vague, evasive modernism and that it lacks the clear, definitely outlined idea of God our fathers used to have. This shows how little we know about the religious ideas of our fathers at their best. Who was it said, "At present we only see the baffling reflections in a mirror"? That was Saint Paul. Who was it said, "All that can be said about God is *not* God, but only certain smallest fragments which fall from His table"? That was Saint Catherine of Genoa, born in 1447.

Who was it said, "His essence, indeed, is incomprehensible, utterly transcending all human thought"? That was John Calvin. Who was it said, "Our safest eloquence concerning him is our silence, when we confess without confession that his glory is inexplicable, his greatness above our capacity and reach. He is above, and we upon earth; therefore it behoveth our words to be wary and few"? That is Hooker in his book, *Of the Laws of Ecclesiastical Polity,* one of the great Christian works of the sixteenth century. Our forefathers at their best did not have that neatly outlined God whom we have sometimes heard presented in Protestant pulpits. They had a God so great that they stood before him in humble awe and, knowing that they could not comprehend him altogether, believed in as much of him as they could.

This comforts me on days when I find it hard to believe in God. I am not called on to believe in all of God. I cannot. He is too great. But as for disbelieving all that the word "God" stands for, I cannot do that either—not even on dark days. Here and now we verily live in two worlds, one visible, tangible, physical, the other invisible, intangible, spiritual. The rocks we touch and the stars we see are not more real to us than the love of goodness, beauty, truth. The visitations of divinity are not strange to us. There are hours when we are conscious that the realest forces in this world are spiritual. "God," says the New Testament, "is love." So there is always some of God we can get at and believe in. Do at least that much. Do not say, I disbelieve, putting the weight of your affirmation upon the negative side. Say, I will believe in as much of the Divine as I can. For then you will join a great company of souls upon whom the Master has looked with understanding, as they said, "Lord, I believe; help thou mine unbelief."

In the second place, to those who have difficulty in their faith about God we might say that, while philosophically we may deny God, psychologically we always are constrained to have a god. One of the most mysterious facts about human nature is that we never can content ourselves with things beneath or things around, but must always have something above, to which we give ourselves and concerning which we feel we belong to it. Reverence, according to Goethe, is the "one thing" on which "all depends for making man in every point a man." Each member of this congregation is instinctively a worshiper. We must give ourselves to something, make a god of it and serve it, or there is no meaning or direction in our lives, so that even when we get rid of God philosophically we have not gotten rid of God psychologically. A man, wrote George Herbert Palmer, requires a transcendent object of loyal devotion.

This in large measure explains the fact that in recent years, when so many people have given up God philosophically, there has been so luxuriant a crop of psychological substitutes for him. People say, for example, that God is like Uncle Sam or Alma Mater, a picturesque representation of our social devotion and enthusiasm, so that, when at Commencement time we go back to our college and sing our ardent devotion to Alma Mater, that is most like being religious. God and Alma Mater, they say, are not philosophically real but they are useful as psychological pictures to point up our devotion. Do you see what all this signifies? It signifies multitudes of people feeling psychologically the need of God in a world where philosophically they have denied God. That is a pathetic situation—to have your psychological needs pulling one way and your philosophical conclusions pulling another, to feel a deep want of a transcendent object of loyal devotion in a universe where you think there is nothing worth being transcendently loyal to.

H. G. Wells is far from being an orthodox believer but he is talking about his profoundest spiritual experience when he says: "At times in the lonely silence of the night and in rare lonely moments I come upon a sort of communion of myself with something great that is not myself. It is perhaps poverty of mind and language which obliges me to say that this universal scheme takes on the effect of a sympathetic person—and my communion a quality of fearless worship. These moments happen and they are the supreme fact of my religious life to me, they are the crown of my religious experiences." There are many modern people unable to affirm God, who yet psychologically find their deepest experiences thus involving God. On the one side they hold inward communion with what seems like God and on the other side they live in a universe where they are tempted to think there is no God.

In the face of this dilemma, which today is literally tearing multitudes of lives apart, it seems clear that there is something the matter with a philosophy which leaves out what is deepest in man's life. Whatever else philosophy takes in and gives a just account of, it should be *that*. If some one is here not believing in God or finding it difficult, while still, like all the rest of us, having experiences which suggest God, I say to you, Trust what is deepest in yourself. If you cannot trust what is deepest in your own life, what can you trust in this strange universe? And since what is deepest in your life lifts up its hands for God, have as great a God as you can. Do not thin him down and water him out and make him Uncle Sam or Alma Mater. These people who, having philosophically denied God, now go about trying to keep themselves clothed in the shreds and patches of their psychological substitutes, are pathetic figures. That is not the last word about a great subject like God.

Dr. Rufus Jones says that a kindly gentleman, summering on the Maine coast and discovering on an island off-shore a group of children who were receiving no religious training, went out on Sunday mornings to instruct them. On the first day, wishing to start with something close at hand and familiar, he asked all of them who had seen the Atlantic

Ocean to raise their hands. Not a hand went up. He thought
they were shy, so he pressed the question. But they were
quite in earnest—they had never seen the Atlantic Ocean.
All their lives they had lived in it. Their boats had been
sailed upon it. Its waters had sung their lullaby at night
when they were babes, and the rhythmic beat of its waves
upon the shore had waked them in the morning. But they
did not know it was the Atlantic. How like to them many
of us are about God! All that is deepest in our spiritual life
is the near end of him. All the best in us is God in us. We
cannot run away from him. As soon as we deny him we
start calling him by other names and making substitutes for
him. Since, then, we must have a God, let us have a great
one. Do not say, I disbelieve. Say, Lord, I believe; help thou
mine unbelief.

In the third place, if you are finding it difficult to believe
in God, remember that there are also towering difficulties in
the way of disbelief in God. Of course it is difficult to believe
in God. Great faith has always carried a heavy burden of
doubt. The Psalmist in a confident mood said, "The Lord
is my shepherd; I shall not want," and every one remembers
that. But most people forget that the Psalmist also said, "Why
hidest thou thy face from me?" Who can look at the vast
stellar spaces, unmeasured and immeasurable, and easily
saturate them with kindly purpose? Who can regard the
strange history of this planet, with its volcanic furies, its
huge and useless beasts, its cruel parasitic life, its strange
evolving miseries, and not find it difficult to fit God in? Who
can look out today upon this chaotic world or bear, it may be,
in his own life the shocks of an unkindly fate and find it
easy to say, Our Father? A man who thinks it easy to believe in God does not know what believing in God is.

So it may be difficult for you to believe in God. If it is,
far from being discouraged about you religiously, I should
say that, if you handle it aright, you may yet join the suc-

cession of the great believers. For the great believers are those who, finding it hard to believe in God, have found it harder still to disbelieve.

In the grand days, alas, now gone, when Toscanini reigned like a king in Carnegie Hall, I have come from listening to symphonies there absolutely certain that the materialistic explanation of the universe would never do. Such beauty— the minds that created it and the souls that loved it—could not be the accidental consequence of colliding atoms. When an atheist like Krutch says, as in all good logic he must say, that life is "merely a physiological process with only a physiological meaning," that is nonsense, and as Professor Montague puts it, the chance of that's being true would have to be represented by a fraction with 1 for the numerator and with a denominator that would reach from here to one of the fixed stars. For in all our great moments the realest forces in the world are spiritual—goodness, beauty, love, and truth— and in the face of them it is desperately difficult to disbelieve in God.

If some one says, But look at the trouble in the world, I say, Yes, but the bitterest trouble we face is an argument not against God but for him. The existence of God does not mean that all life must be pleasant. That is a popular fallacy. Friends, the first implication of the existence of God is that we live in a moral order where men and nations can no more break the laws with impunity than they can break physical laws and get away with it. Who was it said, "If you eat salt herrings, even the grace of God won't keep you from being thirsty"? I should say so! If, now, the origin of the universe were merely material, why should there be a moral order which so inevitably searches out and punishes our spiritual mistakes? We complain about life's trouble but much of the bitterest trouble we face today is what the Lord Chancellor in Gilbert and Sullivan's opera, "Iolanthe," called "an affidavit from a thunderstorm." The aftermath of human sin is just that. That is what war's consequences are, what our economic depression is, what many of our personal troubles are—an affidavit that we are living in a moral order, where no man can disobey law with impunity and no nation can obtain blessing without fulfilling the conditions. And the existence of such a moral order is an argument not against God but for him.

As for life's beauty and loveliness, there is so much of it that as the years pass I find it ever more difficult to disbelieve in God. Even the stellar universe is not simply huge, as we so commonly think. It is unified—not a multiverse but a universe coherent and integrated. It is orderly—not whimsical and capricious—with never a slip anywhere between cause and consequence. It is simple—not complex and multifarious, but simple—with less than a hundred elements in it, whose formulas, when we grasp them, bind everything together into uniformity from here to the farthest star. And it is intelligible, as though, mind having made it, mind could enter into and understand it. Well, read the great scientists and see. It is desperately difficult to ascribe all this to chance and disbelieve in God.

Or when one comes closer home to the life of mankind upon this planet, there does seem to be something afoot here with meaning in it. A small boy was asked in fun how many lives a cat has and, as so often happens, the questioner got the surprise of his life in the boy's answer. "Cats," said he, "have nine lives, but they do not need them all in these days because of Christianity." There is something to be said for that. Even in the few millennia that mankind has been upon this planet, finer principles of action have arrived, nobler possibilities have emerged, than the first humans could have dreamed. With all our difficulties, man never faced the future with more power in his hands and more possibilities before his feet. Now, over this planetary process atheism has to hang a sign, "Nothing ultimately doing." That is difficult to think. In view of what has been and may be, I cannot believe it.

And when one comes still closer home to think of souls near and dear through whom the divine life has shined upon us, the homes from which we came, the mothers whom we recollect with deathless gratitude, the fathers who cared for us, the children who have come to us, the friends who have nurtured us, to say that such spirits are but accidents without any root in eternal fact, that they bear no news of what is ultimate, that we never have seen the light of the knowledge of the glory of God in a face like Christ's—that is difficult to do.

They say that a Russian girl took a government examination under the Soviet *régime* and, after the examination was over, feared she might have failed. In particular she worried about one question—"What is the inscription on the Sarmian wall?" She had written down what she thought it was—"Religion is the opiate of the people"—but after she was through with the examination she walked seven miles from Leningrad to the Sarmian wall to be sure. There it was just as she had written, "Religion is the opiate of the people." Then falling upon her knees she crossed herself and said, "Thank God!" Hard to believe in God? Of course it is; he is so great and the problem is so vast and so deep. But it is harder yet to disbelieve in him. Lord, I believe; help thou mine unbelief.

Finally, if you find it difficult to believe in God, ask yourself whether you would not like to have this a world where your children would find it easier to believe in God than you have found it. For faith is not simply a theoretical but a practical matter. Most people in the United States who disbelieve in God do it, I think, because they are discouraged about life. We Christians are constantly told that our faith in God is a defense mechanism, a fantasy to which we run away for comfort from life's stern realities, a kind of wishful thinking. Now, to be sure, there is an aspect of faith in God that lends itself to such description. It *is* a comfort; it is backing, sustenance, and security in times like these to believe in God and feel that, even if the horse does seem to be running away, there are stronger hands than ours upon the reins. So Bishop Quayle, we are told, put it with characteristic picturesqueness. He was lying awake at night worrying—worrying himself to distraction about problems that he could not solve—until he heard God speak to him. "Quayle," God said to him, "you go to bed, I'll sit up the rest of the night." If you are an atheist you will call such an experience a fantasy but you must confess that it is keeping multitudes of people out of the insane asylum. And what if it is true, what if stronger hands than ours *are* upon the reins, what if there is an *"enduring power, not ourselves, which makes for righteousness"?*

At any rate, if you insist that our faith in God is the rationalizing of our wishes, hopes, and ideals, I know one answer. Your denial of God is mostly the rationalizing of your discouragements and your disillusionments. Yes, it is. I venture that nine-tenths of the atheism in the United States is the rationalization of discouragement. Take frustration and bafflement, anxiety and fear, futility and grief, and pile them so high that a man cannot see over them or around them, and not far off is the cry, There is no God! *If much of our faith in God is wishful thinking, much of our denial of God is discouraged thinking.* Plenty of people come to see me to talk about God, with whom I do not bother to talk about God. Help the man—that is the first thing to be done; throw a little friendliness around him, lift if you can an intolerable burden off him, let a little light shine upon his darkness. Faith in God will often take care of itself if you give it a chance. That will happen in Russia. Let them continue to improve the conditions of their people and open ever wider the doors of hope and opportunity, and multitudes will be on their knees, saying, Thank God! The wisest observers of Russia say it cannot stay atheistic.

If, then, you are having difficulty believing in God, say at least this to yourself: I can make my life an argument for God; I can help make this world the kind of place where our children will find it easier to believe in God than it has been for me. God is not simply an idea to have faith in; he is a living Presence, a Toiler, lifting an ensign for the people and calling us to follow him for justice, brotherhood, and peace. You must not deny *that* God. For your soul's sake you must not say, No, to that God! Lord, I believe; help thou mine unbelief.

When God Lets Us Down

GREAT hymns, such as we just have sung,* sound as though in our experience and in the experience of our fathers God had been found to be altogether satisfactory. Commonly in our services of worship, in our hymns and anthems, in the Scriptures read, prayers offered, and sermons preached, God is unanimously praised, and our experience with him, barring our own sins, is presented in terms of complete contentment. Realistically, however, the truth is that God often seems to let us down.

This painful collapse of trust in God comes most intimately in individual tragedies, ruinous to things beautiful for which God ought to care. Marriages that seemed made in heaven are ended by what insurance men call an "act of God"; promising children whom the world desperately needed are untimely carried off; men rendering to the cause of God inestimable service are stricken down at the height of their strength, so that God at times seems to be arrayed against himself and to be fighting his own interests. Beyond such individual tragedies, moreover, men who have high hopes about the world at large—praying earnestly, working laboriously, sacrificing greatly for peace and justice—see the total drift of their generation set in against them, until, far from being backed by the Eternal, their best efforts sometimes appear like whistling in the teeth of a hurricane. It is this that often breaks down the faith of men. In the worship of the church they hear experience with God presented in terms of complete satisfactoriness, but in private they often feel that any God they know is letting them down. The Bible

* "Our God, our help in ages past,
   Our hope for years to come."

[44]

does not leave this problem out. The Bible is an inclusive compendium of all the experiences the human soul has had with God, and from beginning to end this problem runs.* Jeremiah, for example, a believer in God if ever there was one, talks to God with forthright candor. He has been sacrificing terribly for the cause of God's righteousness among his people and, seeing everything going wrong, with himself, with his family, with his nation and the world, he says to God, "Wilt thou indeed be unto me as a deceitful brook, as waters that fail?" Any one who has been in Palestine understands what a devastating picture of the Eternal those words present. In the rainy season there are brooks aplenty, transient rivulets running through the watercourses and in a few days gone. Unhappy the man who banks on them! They are no reliable resource for hopeful agriculture. Says Jeremiah to God, Are you like that? I trusted you deeply; will you turn out to be a deceitful brook, waters that fail? When one thinks of the grand metaphors by which we commonly describe God, our king and father, our rock, fortress, and high tower, our shepherd and our savior, with what shocked surprise and yet with what admiration for candor does one run on this picture from one of his most devout servants—a deceitful brook, waters that fail!

What are we to do when God looks to us like that? Where does the trouble lie?

To start with, if we are to take our cue from Jeremiah, we will not hastily try to solve our problem by giving up God. Many do that. Beginning in childhood with beautiful pictures of God, mediated to their imaginations by the loveliest symbols human experience provides, such as shepherd, friend, and father, they grow up to face life's tragic realities, and, seeing the incongruity between the sweet fatherliness of God that they have believed in and the cruel calamities

* E.g., Exodus 5:22-23; Job 10:1-3; Psalm 22:1-2; Jeremiah 20:14-15, 7-8; Habakkuk 1:2-3; Matthew 27:45-46.

they endure, they give up God. Then, coming to the church on Sunday and hearing us present our experience of God in terms of unalloyed security and peace, they cry, These Christians do not see the facts. Of course we see the facts! How can a man help it? To feel that God is not living up to his good reputation is one of the most poignant, unescapable experiences his saints ever face. Who was it cried on a cross, "My God, my God, why hast thou forsaken me?"—which is to say, My God, why hast thou let me down?

Nevertheless, if some one advises giving up God, we say, That is too swift and easy a response. Even on *a priori* grounds the probabilities are that so impulsive a solution is superficial. Consider an analogy. In the early days of modern science, men looked upon the diverse, chaotic processes of this huge cosmos with an idea in their minds that nature might be law-abiding. It was a tremendous idea, which nature commonly seemed to contradict. Law-abidingness gave nature a reputation for order, unity, cohesiveness, and regularity, but nature in one area after another refused in appearance to live up to it and kept letting down those who sought to hold the faith. There were multitudes of facts not to be subsumed under any law and many such exist even yet. Suppose, then, that the first, swift reaction of light minds had been general and that the idea of nature's law-abidingness had been given up—what a sorry loss, ending in what colossal fallacy, would have ensued! No, this universe is profound and any solution that matches it must be profound too. A man must have a kind of stubbornness in holding to great ideas about the universe even when they do seem to let him down. That is as indispensable in science as it is in religion.

This morning we cannot state the full grounds for holding hard by the great idea of God but this seems to me to be the gist of it: we human beings have spiritual experiences that a materialistic explanation never really explains. That is the gist of it. I too once tried to give up God. How can a minister help the people if he never has gone down into the valley of doubt, where all the saints have gone before him and where God sometimes seems like a deceitful brook, like waters that fail? But always there has remained this deep, indubitable fact—spiritual experiences that no materialistic explanation really explains. The love of beauty, of goodness, of truth, conscience within, personal relationships that make love seem the most powerful force in the world, and great hours when the Eternal seems real indeed and the world invisible shines through the seen—a whole series of spiritual facts which constitute man's life at its highest, and which, when the materialists have talked themselves hoarse, they have not begun to explain.

Sometimes on a mountain's crest, hugely wrought in the rock, one can see the outlines of a human face. It is, we know, the result of casual, accidental, cosmic weathering. But there are other faces—those of our friends, our poets and musicians, our saints and prophets, our Christ—and we are told in effect by the materialists that these too are the result of casual, cosmic weathering. It will not do. Friend, you are asking us to believe in magic if you ask us to believe in that. Everything, even the least, must have adequate causation, and casual, cosmic weathering is no adequate causation for the towering and significant facts of man's spiritual life. When, therefore, God seems to let us down, the first response is not to give him up.

In the second place, if we are not to give up God, let us see what we can do with our problem by changing some of our own attitudes, ridding ourselves especially, so far as we can, of self-centeredness. There lies the nub of our difficulty. When our egos push themselves up into the center of attention and we think it the chief business of God to keep us from trouble, we begin to feel let down. The self-centeredness of much popular Christianity is appalling. I have watched a great convocation of Christians singing at the top of their voices,

> O that will be glory for me,
> Glory for me, glory for me,

until sick at heart I thought it about the most irreligious and unchristian spectacle I ever had looked upon. Consider even the fascists and communists. They are calling on multitudes to give themselves to something larger than themselves, a cause concerning which they say, Not my will, thine! and so to get themselves out of the center of the picture. We never will match them with the kind of self-centered religion that has been encouraged in many of our churches.

George Eliot, in *Middlemarch*, reminds us of old mirrors which, after generations of polishing, are covered with innumerable, infinitesimal scratches, and she says that when, in the dark, a lighted candle is brought close to one of them, the markings arrange themselves in concentric circles around the image of the candle flame. So our lives become egocentric. We think of our friends, our family, our nation, our world, chiefly in terms of what we can get out of them. If, then, a man is religious, he brings God in, and his religious faith and reliance are added to the concentric circles. God's meaning for him lies in God's ability and willingness to save him from trouble. It is that picture of the Eternal which lets us down. God never yet guaranteed to keep any man out of trouble, not even his Christ.

Indeed, consider the paragraph of Jeremiah's confessions from which our text arises. Jeremiah was one of the most devout and sacrificial servants God ever had, but, like the rest of us, he had hours when his ego marched up into the center of the universe and stood there clamorous. Listen, then, to the paragraph from which our text comes: "O Lord. . . . remember *me*, and visit *me*, and avenge *me* of *my* persecutors; take *me* not away in thy longsuffering: know that for thy sake *I* have suffered reproach. . . . Why is *my* pain perpetual, and *my* wound incurable, which refuseth to be healed? wilt thou indeed be unto *me* as a deceitful brook, as waters that fail?" So his clamorous self walked up into the center of the universe. And when any man gets the universe so disfocused, he is bound to be let down. That picture of the cosmos, with the ego at the center, does not correspond with reality.

About the hardest thing in the religious life is to get oneself out of the center of the picture and genuinely to practise self-renunciation. An earnest Sunday School teacher, having done his best to present to his class of boys the parable of the Good Samaritan, asked them what lesson they had gained from it for themselves. Immediately one boy answered, "What I get out of it is that when I am in trouble my neighbors ought to help me out." That incorrigible slant, even in human relationships, is bad enough, but when it takes God in, when it regards God, shall I say? as a cosmic nursemaid to keep us comfortable, then we are foredoomed to be let down.

In this last generation many Christians have been disturbed by the new astronomy, which opens to one's eyes and imagination such vast expanses that the soul seems dwarfed in contrast. In reality, however, the stars should be among the most valued ministers to the spiritual life. We need them. They help us get ourselves out of the center of the picture. They say to us, This universe isn't centered in you. You have not the slightest reason to expect any exemption from trouble or tragedy. This universe is centered in God, in whose eyes a thousand years are but as yesterday when it is past, and as a watch in the night. Play your small part like a man. Stand what you have to stand like a man. God is not letting you down because you suffer. See how far beyond your beholding sweeps his eternal purpose. Get *that* for the center of the universe.

At any rate, such self-renunciation is indispensable to great religion, and it certainly belonged to the essential quality of the religion of Jesus. He never expected God to take care of him in the sense that God should save him from suffering. From his early ministry he knew that God would lead him into suffering. What, then, was he doing that tremendous hour in the garden before he went out to be crucified? Trying to get himself out of the center of the picture! "Not my will, but thine, be done." Three times he went to his knees with that cry—*not me, thee*—trying to get himself out of the center of the cosmos and to focus the universe rightly, with the eternal purpose there. Ah, Christ, that is our problem too.

In the third place, if we are to handle well the heavy hours when God seems to us like a deceitful brook, we shall have to recognize that God is greater, sterner, and more austere than our sentimental popular Christianity commonly suggests. For our difficulty with this problem is not simply self-centeredness but sentimentality. If a man starts with a picture of the universe as run by a sweet, indulgent deity, he is doomed to be let down. In saying this, one need not deny the gentle aspects of Christian experience. There are hours when the unseen Friend within makes real everything that Jesus said about the Father's individual care. It is true of him that,

> . . . warm, sweet, tender, even yet
> A present help is he.

While, however, that is true, it is not the whole truth, and whenever partial truth is taken for whole truth dangerous fallacy ensues. The loveliest forget-me-nots I have ever seen are in the high Alps. They are beautiful, running their blue glories up to the very edges of the snow. But, lovely as they are, they are not the whole of the high Alps. The high Alps are towering altitudes with austere aspects that forget-me-nots do not exhaust. So is the great God.

The most obvious exhibition of this fact is to be seen first in the law-abiding nature of the universe, not only physically but spiritually. "Be not deceived; God is not mocked: for whatsoever a man soweth, that shall he also reap"—on that point God is inexorable. He plays no favorites. He has no softness. Age after age the law-abiding conditions in this universe wait, offering the curse or the blessing, and the curse falls remorselessly or the blessing arrives as the conditions are fulfilled. Jesus likened God once to an austere man. My word! that is putting it mildly.

Suppose I should preach a sermon here about the wrath of God; what would you make of it? Our fathers used to hear powerful discourses about that; in this pulpit you have never even heard the phrase. Well, I do not like the phrase. "Wrath" applied to God is an archaic Hebraism, a symbol suggesting to us ill temper and vindictiveness. Behind that phrase, however, is a prodigious fact at the heart of this universe. The penalties of God's broken laws fall with inexorable austerity on men and nations.

At no point has our too sentimental religious liberalism done more harm to the truth than here. Mark Twain once reported the saying of Darwin's father that Unitarianism was a feather bed to catch falling Christians. Unitarians need not feel specially hit by that. The same thing is true in general of the whole modern, liberal movement in religion. We rose in holy indignation—mark it, rightly so!—against the old theology with its cruel and barbarous presentation of divine wrath and hell, and, throwing the whole incredible and horrid business out, substance and symbol, we left ourselves with the gentle, sweet, lovely, comfortable aspects of Christianity. We lost the high Alps in the fog and kept the forget-me-nots. Our religion often became much like a feather bed. Many preachers became religious crooners. The drums and trumpets died out in our orchestra and sometimes only the flutes were heard. God seemed very sweet.

Then the inevitable aftermath followed. Men, picturing to themselves this indulgent God, went out into the real world, where in very truth, as Paul's ancient phrase put it, "The wrath of God is revealed from heaven against all ungodliness and unrighteousness of men," and, struck by the incongruity between their, shall I say? heavenly sweetheart on one side and these tremendous facts on the other, they said, God is only a deceitful brook. Surely, the cure for that is not to give up God but to get a fresh grasp on the reality of the real and great God.

At this point, in spite of the horror of much of their old theology, our fathers had the advantage of us in realism. We discover God almost exclusively in the lovely, desirable, beautiful aspects of life. Our fathers discovered him there too, but not exclusively. They found God also in the stern, severe, sometimes terrific facts of life. They saw the penalties of eternal laws falling terribly on sinners, and they saw God himself behind the laws, not trying to make life easy for man but trying to make man great enough for life, holding him up to high standards, drawing him by opportunity, pushing him by punishment, letting the curse fall when he refused. Friends, that austere view of God is greater and truer than much of our popular sentimental Christianity.

At any rate, long ago Jeremiah recovered himself from his low hour by a fresh grasp on the greatness of the austere God. If one could meet him now one might say to him, Jeremiah of Anathoth, prophet of the living God, even you feared once that your Lord was a deceitful brook. Moreover, the facts that made you feel so were real. Disasters did fall terribly upon your people. They went into exile in Babylon, and you died, an unwilling refugee, in Egypt. But that exile was like a refiner's fire—the finest elements of the Old Testament came out of it. And back from it came a remnant and from the remnant Christ, and the world now claims you in the great succession—Hosea, Jeremiah, Isaiah of Babylon, and Jesus. I can imagine Jeremiah's saying, So that was the way it came out! I could not foresee all that, although I rose to a strong faith that God was in the fire I hated as much as in the favors I desired; he was a great God after all, and in the end he did not let me down.

This, then, is the conclusion of the matter, that, if we are to handle well the hours when God seems like waters that fail, we had better interpret our relationship with him not so much in terms of comfortableness as in terms of power. That distinction is not absolute. The noblest kind of comfort is power—not nursing but inward power adequate to stand up against life and carry off a victory in the face of it. Nevertheless, no distinction between religious people, I suspect, goes deeper than this: some in their religion are chiefly concerned to make life easier, some are chiefly concerned to make life stronger.

Those whose chief concern with religion is to gain ease inevitably tend toward a religion of escape, an otherworldly, lotus land of fantasy to which they run away. And, because that otherworldly land is none too realistically associated with the facts, they can dress it up in all the loveliness they may desire. This is a dangerous kind of religion, comparable with taking drugs; it makes religion an opiate of the people. A leading official in the Chamber of Commerce of one of our New York towns indignantly reports that he heard a man of means, who had contributed to Christian service among the underprivileged, say about it, "Keep 'em religious in order to keep 'em quiet." Such religion is dangerous socially and pernicious personally. God does not let us down; it is otherworldly religion, running away from the facts, which inevitably turns out to be a deceitful brook.

A deeper kind of faith and experience than that is found in those whose chief concern is not an easier but a stronger life. There lies the great tradition, from Moses, associating himself with his oppressed people in Egypt, to Kagawa in the slums of Tokyo, and many an unnamed and obscure soul in difficulty, living with courage and triumph. What tragic facts have such spirits run away from? What stern tragedies have they not looked in the face? What suffering have they not borne? Their relationship with God was interpreted in terms not of comfortableness but of power. They were strengthened with might by God's spirit in the inward man so that they could stand up to life, socially overcome evil, personally transmute hardship into good. Such religion does not let a man down. Out of such religion come souls like Jeremiah, human enough at times to think of God as a deceitful brook but habitually saying that God is a "fountain of living waters." Out of such religion came Christ, human enough in an hour of bleak despair to cry, "My God, why hast thou forsaken me?" but not ending there—ending with faith and confidence and power: "Father, into thy hands I commend my spirit."

The Contemporary Prevalence of Polytheism

ONE of the commonest elements in popular religious thinking is the idea that either a man believes in God or he doesn't. If a man believes in God, he is a monotheist; if he disbelieves, he is an atheist or an agnostic—so runs the popular classification. And behind this classification is the idea that there is only one God and that our religious life or lack of it depends on our attitude toward him. There is truth enough in this popular way of thinking to keep it alive but it presents an inadequate picture of the situation. It presupposes that polytheism is dead, whereas polytheism, I suspect, is far and away the most prevalent religious attitude in the world.

This ought not to be difficult to see. What is really a man's god? Not what is his theory about God, picked up on the surface of his mind because he happens to have been born in the twentieth century, when all intelligent people speak of God in the singular number, but what is verily his god? Surely, a man's veritable god is that factor in his life, whatever or whoever it may be, that he does truly worship and serve, belong to and care most about, the unifying loyalty which draws his life together and gives it centrality and singleness of aim. That is a man's real god.

As soon as the matter is so stated, it becomes clear that millions of us are not monotheists. We have no *one* such God who so commands our lives. We are polytheists. We worship a pantheon of deities—multiform and various objects of devotion, now one and now another, often as conflicting as the diverse altars of the olden time when polytheism was in flower. That is the realistic fact.

Until we see this clearly we fool ourselves about ourselves

and about our real religion. We take it for granted that polytheism is obsolete, but polytheism is obsolete only in its outward forms so that we no longer use the old vocabulary or practise the old cults. Polytheism, however, always has meant something deeper than *that*. It stands for the varied claims life makes upon our loyalty, not at one point but at many, calling out our clamorous desires, now here, now there, and our passionate devotions, now to this and now to that. Go through this congregation. How many of us really have one God? If we doubt the application of this question to our individual lives, how can we doubt its application to the world at large? Is Mars dead? Is Bacchus dead? Is Venus dead? Is Mercury, the god of slick and crafty contrivance in diplomacy and commerce, dead? Are they not all alive, along with many more? Is not polytheism our prevalent religion?

When thus we turn from the smooth surface of our theoretical monotheism to the actual situation inside our lives, some texts in the Bible that once seemed outgrown come alive again. Here is one from even so early a book as Joshua: "Choose you this day whom ye will serve; whether the gods which your fathers served . . . or the gods of the Amorites, in whose land ye dwell: but as for me and my house, we will serve the Lord." How ancient that sounds at first! Yet in our actual experience the problem of conflicting gods is far from obsolete.

In the first place, consider that in the light of these realistic facts there is no such person as an atheist. If we start with one God, Creator and Father of all, then, of course, there are disbelievers in him and, so, atheists. But if we start with our actual lives and agree to call that a man's god which he does verily worship and serve, to which he belongs and for which he most cares, then there is no such person as an atheist. We all have gods.

Often when one thus turns from theology to psychology,

from the theories we have inherited to the actual processes of our living, one runs on disconcerting revelations. I doubt not that in theory most of us here are monotheists. But ask where that monotheism came from and obviously most of it came from our tradition. Long since, monotheism conquered polytheism, and we have so inherited the consequence that we have never been even tempted in theory to believe in many gods. Moreover, to this inherited faith in one God we have added our own thinking, that this is a universe and not a multiverse, and that its ultimate explanation must lie in one Power, one Mind, one God. So in tradition and in theory we are monotheists.

Look inside our lives, however, and how far different from this tradition and theory of monotheism is the situation there! Daily within our lives many altars smoke with sacrifice to many gods. We adore our homes; we would give our lives for them. We do not talk about the Penates, the ancient Roman deities of hearth and household, but psychologically we worship them. We are devoted to our vocations, in letters, in art, in science. We do not talk about the Muses, goddesses of science and the fine arts, but psychologically we serve them. We are devoted to social betterment and for it many a fine life is spent in unstinted zeal. We do not make our vows to some demigod, Prometheus, who at the cost of unutterable sacrifice dared steal the sacred fire from heaven to warm the hearths of men, but psychologically we serve Prometheus. And many serve Bacchus or Mars or Venus or Apollo, the god of physical beauty, or Minerva, the goddess of wisdom. Indeed, how many try to serve a mixed medley of these gods, the Penates and Venus, Apollo and Bacchus, Prometheus and Mars! What a polytheistic mess of incoherent gods the typical living of millions of us reveals, although this is the twentieth century! As one looks at it, one sees clearly that there is not an atheist among us, not one; we all have gods.

Far from being discouraging to religious people, this fact we are dealing with is one of the guarantees of religion's indestructibility. For here we run upon one of the deepest, strangest, most revealing facts in human life: we must give ourselves to something, we must belong to something, we must have gods. Life is dull, stale, flat, and unprofitable save as we find something to love and adore. Let it be the smallest imaginable sort of god, yet that god, something that matters most to us, for which we care, is our very life. What god we serve is the central question. On the one side are the things that serve us, the ingenious conveniences and gadgets that minister to us, and on the other side are the values we serve, the loyalties we love, the gods we worship. And not all the things that serve us can make life worth living unless the gods whom we adore are worth adoring. Moreover, because in this sense there are no atheists, the problem of our gods presents us with a forced decision. Because we must have gods we must choose which gods. So across the centuries that ancient challenge comes, which by no psychological possibility can any man avoid, "Choose you this day whom ye will serve."

In the second place, note the light thrown by this upon the fact that commonly so little consequence follows believing in the God of the creeds and of the churches. In a nation-wide poll made some time since, ninety-one per cent of the answers revealed belief in God. But look at the character and conduct of this large percentage of our population that believes in God, and see how little difference such faith makes. So the enemies of religion have ample occasion to blaspheme.

Of course, a merely theological faith in one God may have no more effect on character than believing in the rings of Saturn. If, however, we approach this question by agreeing to call *that* a man's god which he does verily serve, then the issue is plain. Show us the god who really gathers up a man's devotion and we will show you the real man. Jesus

[58]

habitually approached the matter so. He was as stout a monotheist as ever lived, but, thinking in terms of the living loyalties of men, the actual deities between whom they make their choices, his message was, "Ye cannot serve God and mammon." In that statement Jesus personified riches. He fell back, as it were, on polytheistic language, as we are doing, to get the truth expressed. He saw the conflicting loyalties that demand our service, and bade us choose, saying, "Ye cannot serve God and mammon."

That kind of choice is still the central fact in every life. At the long last, life is compelled by its gods. They are the determinative factor there. So in Norris' novel, *The Pit,* Jadwin cries, "The wheat cornered me, not I the wheat." Mammon has so treated more than one of his devotees— cornered him. Or here is another man, who chose Bacchus for his god, not intending him to be his only god but, as a true polytheist, to have him among other gods. Yet now he is saying that if a glass of whiskey were put close to his hand and he knew that to drink it would plunge him into hell in ten seconds, he would drink it without an instant's hesitation —he could not help himself. So our gods get us. Venus, Bacchus, Mammon, Mars—our gods get us. There sets in an ever increasing central current, on which float the back-eddies of our lesser loyalties. Life is compelled by its gods.

If some one says, I cannot distinguish in my life those devotions or deities outside myself to which this polytheistic vocabulary would apply, I answer: Still you cannot escape inevitable psychological processes, and, if you have no such gods outside yourself to worship, then you become your own god. The Greeks had a word for that too, "Narcissus," the fair son of a river god, who fell in love with his own reflection in a fountain. So can a man become his own chief concern, himself his god, unable to get himself off his hands, until Whittier's lines come true:

> Oh, doom beyond the saddest guess,
>   As the long years of God unroll,
> To make thy dreary selfishness
>   The prison of a soul!

I call you to witness—we are polytheists. From Mammon to Narcissus, we worship many gods, and so, alas! the one God, high over all, blessed forever, is often not our god at all. He becomes to us a marginal reference, what another called a spare tire, but the deities we really serve are not he. Ah! you ancient polytheists, whose outward altars perished long ago—still you triumph; still we serve your gods.

In the third place, consider the light thrown by this on one of the most confusing problems of our lives, the conflict between our gods. The old stories of the quarrels of the deities on Mount Olympus have seemed to us primitive, incredible, disgraceful. But here, again, polytheism tells the truth about something going on in every life in this congregation—the conflict between our gods.

Look out upon the world at large today and see, for example, two strangely unlike gods that all mankind is serving, Mars and the Penates, war and the home. Man everywhere is devoting himself to both. Men and women adore their homes and their children. It is a sustaining and lovely blessing in a man's life to have a hearth of his own and some one there who deeply cares whether he comes home, and growing children in whom he lives more than in himself! Were there no other altar on the earth, I would worship at the altar of the home. And mankind as a whole feels thus but still strives to serve war too, and the Hitlers and the Mussolinis and all their kind are crying out today for boys, more boys, more babies to be born, that there may be more soldiers for more wars. And man, this foolish, polytheistic creature, is trying to worship war and the family.

Some of the saddest news that comes from Europe is not so much political as domestic. A teacher of boys in France

said, some time since, that he found the boys of France in
their early years eager, ardent, wholesome, but that when
they turned the corner, at about fourteen or fifteen years of
age, and woke up to see the kind of world they were living
in, they became dull and stolid and cynical. "I find it impossible," he writes, "to awaken their ambition after they get
to be fourteen or fifteen years of age. 'What's the use,' they
say, 'of working ourselves to death in preparation for a
career which we shall not live to carry out? Our elder
brothers are dead or crippled by the last war, and so we will
be before we are twenty-one.'"

We think of the horrors of war in terms of the bloody
slaughter while it is in process. That is not half the story.
We think of the horrors of war in terms of the long-drawn-
out and lamentable aftermath when it is past. That is not
half the story. The horror of war begins before its coming, in
a world visibly preparing to plunge into war, where boys
and girls, foredoomed to death or mutilation or war-widow-
hood or worse, grow up saying, What's the use?

There are scenes in the Old Testament that once seemed
obsolete, which today wake up again. Would God another
Elijah might arise to summon the peoples of the earth to
meet him on the crest of some Mount Carmel, confronting
them there with the choice between their baals and the
true God! For still that ancient word might well ring across
this modern world: "How long go ye limping between the
two sides? if the Lord be God, follow him; but if Baal, then
follow him." So man does stand today between his wars and
his homes. Choose which ye will serve.

Forgetfulness of this profound and realistic conflict between the deities we serve is in no small wise responsible for
the sentimentality of much of our religion. For much of our
religion is soft and sentimental. It lacks the stimulating challenge which our fathers' faith met when the cry went up
that there were many conflicting gods on earth and that true

religion meant a true choice between them. At the heart of all great religion is this consciousness of conflict in the cosmos. The Hindus called it reality against unreality; the Zoroastrians called it light against darkness; the Greeks called it spirit against matter; the early Christians called it God against Satan—all of which are symbols of something everlastingly true, to neglect which is to denature and enfeeble religion. For the gods are struggling for the possession of this earth and of our lives upon it, and to see that realistically and to choose courageously the true God makes religion heroic. I should be content to preach this sermon if one soul only, some youth, God grant with his life still in his hands, should see the heroism of choosing the true God instead of the false and should say, "As for me and my house, we will serve the Lord."

Finally, consider the light which this throws upon the profound meaning of having one unifying God. For polytheism, as we have interpreted it, means a scattered life, dispersed, incoherent, uncoördinated, like a broom ending in a multitude of small straws. Such a life is a sorry sight to the observer and to the possessor a fretful misery.

This is no preachment from the pulpit only but the major message and chief concern of our modern psychology. What is the great word of the psychiatrists today, which in their parlance sums up all good and, as it were, takes the place of the old religious word, "salvation"? The great word of the psychiatrists is "integration," getting life together, giving it coherence, centrality, unity. But when the psychiatrists have done their best, integration still remains, as the best of them know well, a question of one's god. What gods have you that so split up and tear your lives apart, that shred them out into scattered and unwoven filaments? Or have you happily one God, a supreme devotion that draws life together, that makes a federal union of your else divided and belligerent states, and gives centrality and meaning to your existence? Only when thus we translate monotheism versus polytheism into the terms of our inward life does their profound significance appear.

Doubtless some one has been saying, But is it not right to have many devotions—friends, home, romance, science, art, music, the social good? We do have many loyalties whose diversity enriches life—is this not wise and right? To which I answer, Of course it is wise and right if—*if* first we face the supreme test of the difference between the true God and the false ones. Here it is: the true God unifies life, the false gods split it up. Nationalism is a false god. You can tell—it splits life up. If we serve that god, then we are shut out from serving other gods we ought to serve. It plunges the world into unresolved discord. It disintegrates life. So Bacchus is a false god and Venus is a false goddess. If we serve drunken license and unbridled lust, we are shut out from serving other devotions we would love to serve. That is the mark of every false god—it disintegrates life.

But the true God is inclusive of every lovely loyalty. That is the mark and sign of him. He draws life together. I do adore my home but my home is a revelation of, and a pathway to, my God. I do worship at the gates of beauty, and music, letters, the magnificence and loveliness of nature are my resource, but all beauty is a highway to my God. I could, as it were, burn incense on the altar of science, it is so holy a thing, this disinterested love of truth, but all truth is a revelation of my God. I do give myself to my vocation and for some causes on the earth might even dare to die, but all good work and all fine loyalty are service to my God. The true God is inclusive of every lovely loyalty. Even what Venus spoils he elevates, and every noble attribute of man he gathers up. In the grand phrase of the Bible, "He is God of gods, and Lord of lords."

Christians have called Jesus God. In some meanings I cannot consent to that. I do not think that Jesus was omnipotence, omniscience, omnipresence, masquerading in a human body. That would make of him a monstrous, unreal being, impossible to imitate. But if, approaching him by the road which we today have traveled, we think of God in terms of our real loyalties, then I would, like Thomas, cast myself at his feet and cry, "My Lord and my God." I cannot imagine a higher object of devotion than Christ presents. I cannot think of any lovely loyalty that he excludes. He takes them all in. Alas for these false gods, which preëmpt the worship of our hearts! The ancient idols still infest the world, while the true God says to our unhappy race what Christ once said to the sick man, "Wilt thou be made whole?" Choose, then, this day whom you will serve!

On Being Civilized to Death

IN A western New York community stands a house, still occupied, the original portion of which was a log cabin. That log cabin my great grandfather built. Hardly three generations are represented in the years that have passed since then and yet how startling have the changes been! When my grandsire played as a lad about a log cabin, there was not anywhere in the world a railroad or a telephone or a telegraph. There were no matches to light fires with or gas or coal ranges to light them in. There were no elevators or refrigerators, no plumbing, no electric lights, no sewing machines, no furnaces. Letters were written with quill pens because steel pens had not been invented, and were dried with sand because blotting paper did not exist. And, of course, there were no Victrolas, radios, typewriters, bicycles, automobiles, or airplanes. With what absorbed preoccupation during three generations has mankind been engaged in inventing and producing the external paraphernalia of civilization!

Let us phrase the situation in the convenient terms used by sociologists. Man's life can be divided into two distinguishable though closely interrelated areas, civilization and culture. Civilization is the complex of devices, mechanisms, techniques, and instrumentalities by means of which we live. Culture is the realm of spiritual ends, expressed in art, literature, morals, and religion, for which at our best we live. Civilization is made up of things which we utilize to get something else. Culture is made up of values which we desire for their own sakes. Civilization is what we use. Culture is what we are.

For three lifetimes we have been busily engaged in building a civilization, a vast complex of implements by means of which to live, but we have not with any similar intelligence and care been engaged in creating a culture of spiritual ends, personal and social, for which to live. In the mordant phrase of G. Lowes Dickinson, we have been "contemptuous of ideas but amorous of devices," till now mankind stands, its hands filled with devices, but as bewildered and unhappy as mankind has been in centuries. Listen to Jesus, then, though he did live nearly two thousand years ago, speaking as if to us: "A man's life consisteth not in the abundance of the things which he possesseth"; "What shall it profit a man, if he shall gain the whole world, and lose his own soul."

The meaning of such words, applied to individuals, is clear but today they constitute a searching diagnosis of our social ills. Though mankind amass things without end, achieving even the marvelous apparatus of modern civilization, that alone is pathetically not enough. Ingenious devices to live by without worth-while ends to live for, a material civilization without a soul to guide it, as though a magnificently furnished ship had no idea what port it was headed for—that situation underlies every lesser problem of mankind today.

In endeavoring to see the significance of this, consider first that here lies the explanation of the optimism which characterized our early American forefathers but which among us has commonly collapsed into disillusionment. We whose memories go well back into the nineteenth century recall that, whatever else we Americans were then, we were optimistic. We were sure that we were continuously growing bigger and better. Progress was our real religion, in which if a man did not believe we thought him damned indeed. We lived in the time of the first telephones, the first express trains, the first uses of electricity, the first internal-combustion engines, the first of so many astonishing devices that life became an eager standing on tiptoe, wondering what new marvel would arrive tomorrow. So, when philosophers like Herbert

Spencer told us that man's progress toward perfection was an inevitable necessity, we believed them. This illusion of progress so possessed us, from day laborers to philosophers, because all alike we had our eyes primarily upon one thing, civilization—the invention, production, utilization of the marvelous new apparatus of living. We were on our way then from the log-cabin stage to cities like New York. And because this multiplication of the means by which to live was our serious aim, we thought we were successfully headed toward a great end, and our life was pitched in an optimistic key.

Now, however, we have plunged headlong against a stubborn fact—all this boasted civilization we have gloried in is nothing but means, only implements to be utilized, and the more powerful the implements become the more insistently the question rises, on the answer to which man's destiny hangs: To what end will mankind use them? To that question civilization does not possess the answer. The answer to that question is found not in a nation's civilization but in its spiritual culture. For civilization is merely what we use; culture is what we are.

Some in those old days foresaw the *dénouement* we were headed for. Henry D. Thoreau, retreating to Walden Pond, watched from a distance the process we have just described and visited upon it a devastating comment. With all America busily engaged in producing the paraphernalia of living, he said, "improved means to an unimproved end." Thoreau was referring especially to the new and marvelous Atlantic cable, concerning which he said, "The first news that will leak through into the broad, flapping American ear will be that the Princess Adelaide has the whooping cough." How many improved means to unimproved ends we have today! The phrase suggests not simply the way we can create the cinema and degrade morals with it, create the radio and give nonsense a wider hearing with it, create the automobile and implement gangsters with it, and the countless ways in which the old vulgarian and the old barbarian reach out controlling hands for the new devices. The phrase suggests also that society as a whole can so utilize the most amazing industrial equipment mankind ever had as to plunge millions into unemployment and penury, or, furnished with world-wide intercommunications, can make of them world wars, armed, moreover, with techniques that would cause the very devils in Milton's hell to blush with shame—"improved means," there is no doubt of that, but to an "unimproved end."

For three lifetimes we have been thus engaged in building civilization, as though man's life could consist in the abundance of the apparatus which he uses. But this other realm, where man's real life lies, his spiritual culture—the profound faiths that alone give life intrinsic meaning, the great goals that give life direction—has often been popularly treated as a decoration, an afterthought, an addendum. And now the God of judgment speaks—The end of this road you are traveling is irretrievable perdition; if you love your lives and your children, recenter your attention; one thing supremely matters to mankind today, the quality of spiritual life which will use these amazing implements. What shall it profit a man or a nation or the race, to gain the whole world and lose the soul?

In the second place, consider that while, at first hearing, this diagnosis and prescription may seem rather general, the more closely one regards it the more intimately personal it becomes. One clear difference exists between civilization and culture. Civilization is easily handed down. Contrivances invented in one generation are taken for granted as a matter of course in the next; they are improved, expanded, and they go marching on. The apparatus of civilization is easily transmissible. But a profound spiritual culture is not so. It must be reëxperienced by every soul, its insights and devotions individually reproduced, its values inwardly possessed and

[68]

assimilated. No one in my stead can love great music or as my surrogate and substitute possess Christ's spirit. There are no proxies for the soul. It happens, therefore, that while the apparatus of civilization piles up and moves on, there is an appalling lag in spiritual culture until mankind stands, as it stands today, with vast new implements to use and the old barbarian using them.

In our homes, for example, it is not difficult for parents to hand down to children the civilization developed in our time. The young take to Victrolas, radios, automobiles, and all the gadgets and devices of civilized society, as ducks to water. But not so simple is it to hand on to them profound spiritual culture. From the love of great music to the love of Christ and all he stands for, parents cannot give *that* to children as they give telephones and automobiles. The onward march of civilization and the appalling lag of spiritual culture are not simply a general problem; they constitute *the* problem in how many families here! The houses in which we live come from civilization but the homes for which we ought to live are the fruit of spiritual culture, and as one sees some houses and some homes within them the description holds good, "improved means to an unimproved end."

Far from being merely general, therefore, this truth knocks intimately on every door. From childhood we have heard of the dangers of wealth. That a rich man can hardly enter the kingdom of heaven we have been told as long as we can recall. But this truth rolls from us without appeal. We are not rich, we say; we must watch our step financially to get along at all; the least of our moral dangers is the peril of wealth. If, however, a man will cease thinking of his individual pocketbook and will think of his inevitable share in modern civilization's amazing opulence in things—marvelous, rapidly accumulating things, whose ingenuity outdoes the magic of Arabian Nights—he must feel the pertinence to himself of wealth's peril. See how millions of us live! The focus of our lives is in civilization; we are absorbed and centered in its material opulence; while spiritual culture, which alone gives life intrinsic dignity, worth, and meaning, is crowded out.

It is one thing to have an automobile—that is a part of civilization. It is another to be carried by it on a summer's day into the loveliness of the countryside and so to use the experience that one returns saying,

> He maketh me to lie down in green pastures;
> He leadeth me beside still waters.
> He restoreth my soul.

That is not a means to an end, but an end in itself. It is one thing to own a printed book—a marvelous civilized device. It is another thing so to use it that one knows the seer's meaning when he said that the greatest day in a man's life comes when he runs into a new idea. *That* is not a means to an end but an end in itself. It is one thing to share the great heritage of scientific inventions; it is another to share the greater heritage of the world's seers and prophets. The first is something we use; the second is something we are. And such is the hypnotic power of civilization's wealth in things that many a man, of lowly financial rating himself, may well face the warning, "How hardly shall they that have riches enter into the kingdom of God!" Indeed, some of us could talk sensibly to ourselves like this: Beware of too much civilization, too many gadgets and devices that surround life, impinge on it, steal its time, invade its privacy. Especially beware of the false impression which this accumulation of apparatus makes on men, as though, because they can run cars, press buttons with almost magical results, tune in on the radio, and ride in airplanes, they must therefore be superior persons themselves.

Did some one here instinctively pity my grandfather because he lived in a log cabin? You may spare your pity.

Before he was through he was Superintendent of Education of the City of Buffalo. Though he did live in a meager civilization, he was himself a superior person, whereas the truth about multitudes of us amply apparatused moderns is, as the old Latins put it, *Propter vitam vivendi perdere causas*—in the process of life they lose the reason for living.

I wish I could bring the figure of Jesus up over the horizon of some soul here. His words have an applicability to us that he himself could never have foreseen. It is not simply the individual possession of money that misleads us, it is our common social possession of this apparatus of civilized society, as though in that alone there were any hope, as though that by itself alone did not present to man his most stupendous problem and peril. For even when we define "things" in terms of all this paraphernalia, man's life consisteth not in the abundance that he possesses.

In the third place, let us face the imminent impact of this truth on our present world. Not only vertically, from parents to children, is civilization easily transmissible; it is as well swiftly transmissible horizontally, from nation to nation and from race to race. Start a contrivance anywhere and in the long run it will be everywhere. Nothing is much more easy to copy than civilization. An illustrious example of this is Japan, which within hardly a generation has absorbed, mastered, and made her very own the characteristic techniques of Western society. It is inevitable, then—a most stupendous fact—that in the end we shall have one identical, world-wide civilization. But spiritual culture, the profound faiths that give life meaning, the moral ends to which this vast agglomeration of mighty implements will be devoted, has no such swiftness of transference. A man of realistic mind, therefore, who would not live in a fool's paradise, must confront the fact that a vast, single, world-wide civilization run by barbarian cultures means suicide. If ever mankind needed to cry, What must we do to be saved? it is today.

Do not, I beg of you, misinterpret this as discouragement. Upon the contrary, the positive assets in our present situation are very great. Professor Whitehead of Harvard truly says, "On the whole, the great ages have been unstable ages." Out of the wracked agony of disturbed generations man's greatest gains have come. Moreover, our modern problem is not handling weakness, as has often been the case in history, but handling power; and handling power, while dangerous, is promising. "The greater the civilization," says Professor Mac-Iver, "the more numerous are the alternatives which are opened up to human endeavor." That is encouraging. In the log-cabin civilization, narrow limitations surrounded man's immediate possibilities, but in our new civilization doors of promise are open before man the like of which he never dreamed before. Nevertheless, we may not rest back comfortably upon these encouraging factors as though they were self-operative. They are not. There is nothing automatic about them. "Power," said Alfred the Great, "is never a good, unless he be good that has it." *Unless he be good that has it—* that shifts the problem to the profound and central place where the destinies of mankind will be decided this next generation.

In 1876 Thomas Huxley visited America especially to speak at the new Johns Hopkins University, and this was his message: "I cannot say that I am in the slightest degree impressed by your bigness or your material resources, as such. Size is not grandeur, territory does not make a nation. The great issue, about which hangs a true sublimity, and the terror of overhanging fate, is, What are you going to do with all these things?" So today the wise man addresses himself to civilization as a whole. Not for a moment would one belittle the intelligence, skill, and devotion which have been invested in creating the apparatus of civilized society. But the predominant problem is no longer there. The apparatus of civilization will inevitably accumulate, pile up, march triumphantly on. If, however, we use all this agglomerated might for war we are irretrievably undone—that is the inevitable problem. If we let it be utilized by selfish acquisitiveness in a dog-eat-dog economy, bloody revolution waits like Judgment Day—there the real problem confronts us. Man never had such a civilization to use; therefore man never so desperately needed a spiritual life to use it.

Finally, then, consider the responsibility which rests upon all agencies of the spiritual life, and especially upon us in the Christian churches. I know this sermon has been preached in so serious a mood that some souls, coming here for cheer and comfort, must have felt it dour. Yet all the time we have been pleading for man's happiness. We inventive moderns thought we knew better than Jesus did how to get that. We will give men happiness, we said. Bestow on them devices, gadgets, appliances, give them not only things but things made magical by harnessed power, and they will be happy. So we have furnished ourselves with civilization and in consequence multitudes of us are accurately portrayed by the cartoon in Punch where an irate parent on a public holiday at some English replica of Coney Island holds his tired and whimpering offspring by the ear and angrily demands, "Now then, are you going to enjoy yourself or shall I make you?" So foolish have we also been to suppose that happiness ever can consist in the abundance of the apparatus we employ.

A strange paradox is man's search for happiness. Francis of Assisi was the gay and wealthy son of a prosperous merchant, with ample means to live by, and he was not happy. Then he stripped his gay robes from him, espoused "The Lady Poverty," washed the sores of lepers, and made himself one with the famished poor. And lo! *that* Francis of Assisi preached joyously to his brothers the birds, sang the "Canticle of the Sun," and, incidentally, shook Christendom to its foundations. He found happiness at its residence, not in the means by which but in the ends for which he lived. I am not recommending literal copying of Saint Francis. To each generation its own way! But this is clear: not only bad times in the social order but wretched times in the individual life lie ahead of us if we have merely a vast civilization and lack a profound spiritual culture.

We need not lack it. For hardly more than three lifetimes have we been so busily engaged building the apparatus of civilized life. That is not long. Nor is it to be expected that mankind will be so permanently insane as to absorb itself in providing improved means to unimproved ends. Already millions of ordinary folk look at the world with vision clarified by our imminent peril. The road we have been walking on leads to perdition. We have tried to civilize our apparatus of living till we are well-nigh civilized to death. The problem of our salvation lies elsewhere—in our spiritual culture. Ah, Church of Christ, what a clarion call you might sound in such a time as this! For while Jesus could help us very little in devising a civilization, who could help us half so much in creating a spiritual life to use it? And still he waits. What shall it profit—like the tolling of some great bell those ancient words sound on—What shall it profit if a man or a nation or the race gain this whole world and lose the soul?

On Being Christians Unashamed

AT LEAST one kindred element joins Paul's generation with our own; there were plenty of things in Paul's time, too, of which to be ashamed. Paul was ashamed of himself, first of all, and of many of his friends. He was ashamed of the Christian churches of his period, with their divisions and quarrels, mortified by the way in which his own people and nation were behaving, and of Gentile civilization he said as blistering things as ever have been said of public morals anywhere. One suspects that out of this experience of general disgust with a disgraceful generation Paul's resounding affirmation arose concerning one thing which called for no shame. "I am not ashamed," he wrote to the Romans, "of the gospel of Christ."

Granted sensitiveness of conscience, how can any one of us read the morning paper without being morally humiliated? Of what sordid details is the minor news compounded! And as for the major news, with nations plunging headlong into war, with societies surrendering priceless human freedoms, with the return of barbaric extremes of racial prejudice, with bloody civil war abroad, the meanness of partisan politics at home, and needless poverty everywhere, does not mankind present a disgraceful spectacle? It is true, is it not? that when we are not doing anything else we spend a good deal of time being ashamed.

This capacity to feel moral shame, while it is one of the distinguishing faculties of human nature and ennobling in many of its uses, can easily overplay its hand and well-nigh ruin us. Moreover, it is ruining many people today. Sensitive of conscience and caring deeply about the world, they are so ashamed of the human spectacle that they are disheartened, humiliated, and dismayed. Read Santayana's *The Last Puritan* and see. When a man is fine, as Santayana is, all the more he may be shamed by the world until chronic disgust becomes his habitual mood.

Some of us who are older can remember times when disgust was not our chronic mood at all. We thought of mankind in elevated terms and supposed that everything was getting bigger and better. Far from shame, enthusiasm was our mood. We joined in Browning's singing,

> How good is man's life, the mere living! how fit to employ
> All the heart and the soul and the senses forever in joy!

Well, times change. Most of the Browning circles have broken up. Read our modern poetry, novels, drama, and see the prevalent mood of disgust and disillusionment.

When I cannot stand it any longer, when I have been disgusted with things that a man ought to be disgusted with until I have reached the saturation point, I find myself seeking recovery of spirit by recalling some things that do not cause shame. The Ninth Symphony, so conducted by Toscanini that we came down from hearing it as from a Transfiguration mountain, trailing glory into the common street—that was something, at any rate, which man had done, of which we need not be ashamed. Or the tennis champion in the Middle West who lost his right arm in an accident and then relearned tennis with his left arm and became a champion again—there is a brave conquest of calamity, of a kind one sometimes sees, of which one need never be ashamed. So in these days, we find ourselves almost of necessity seeking some things we can glory in.

But these, you see, are items; they are details picked up here and there. What if there is within our reach something more than that—a whole philosophy of life, a majestic movement of the human spirit inspired by the Divine, which we can claim for our own and glory in? *That* was Paul's affirmation. He had found something which put elated significance into the whole of life. "I am not ashamed of the gospel of Christ: for it is the power of God unto salvation to every one that believeth."

Let us see what that means and, like Paul, let us make it our personal confession!

For one thing, I am not ashamed of the gospel of Christ as a message of monotheism. It is that to start with. It is, I think, the most distinguished announcement in human history of one God, Father of the whole human family. One ought not to be ashamed of that. If ever this embittered world needed to recover the meaning of monotheism, it is today.

One of the most thrilling adventures of the human mind has been the endeavor to see this cosmos as one system, one integrated and coherent universe. To the wondering eyes of primitive man the stars were first like swarms of flies and then like marshaled armies marching. But now go to the Planetarium and see! Apparent chaos has been conquered by man's mind and order reigns. Whatever else this amazing cosmos is, it is one system, unified, integrated, coherent—from top to bottom, from center to circumference—one vast whole.

We never succeed, however, in getting the whole cosmos really together on a materialistic basis only. For the most amazing thing in this universe is not matter but mind. The visible stars are marvelous enough but they are not so marvelous as the invisible mind that comprehends them. And this mind, which has conquered chaos, must not be left out of the explanation of the very universe which it has, as it were, created. That is the assertion of monotheism. It is the high refusal of the human intellect to leave out of the explanation of the universe the most momentous factors here—mind, spirit, creative purpose. Until these have been brought into the very center of the explanation we have not got our universe together. I am not ashamed of monotheism. It is the most adequate statement of the truth we have. From all detours philosophy keeps coming back to it, teased by the fact, as Jeans the physicist says, that this universe is more like a great thought than like a great machine. Indeed it is—one Power, one Mind, one God. That insight alone gives us a real universe.

Even more does one glory in monotheism when one thinks of its moral implications. Has some one here been thinking that, after all, monotheism is an ancient achievement of thought? Rather, monotheism is so new that it has barely gotten started, and the people on earth today who really believe it are so few that mankind is sick for the lack of them. For monotheism is the doctrine that all men and women, of all nations and all races, have one Father and are one family. How many really believe that? "I bow my knees unto the Father, from whom every family in heaven and on earth is named"—how many do that? "I saw, and behold, a great multitude, which no man could number, out of every nation and of all tribes and peoples and tongues, standing before the throne"—how many see that?

Even in popular Christian thinking the common supposition prevails that the primary enemy of monotheism is intellectual doubt. No, the major antagonists of monotheism today are not intellectual but moral and social. Nationalism and racialism are the great denials of monotheism. And they do deny it terribly. With fearful explicitness of prejudice and slaughter, they say to all the world, There is not really one God and one human family. And amid the consequent storms, which all but beat our common life to pieces, like a beacon shines the gospel, to believe and practise which is the hope of the world—one God, one Father of all, one family. A man ought not to be ashamed of that. Whatever hopeful future there is on earth belongs to that. One wishes that gospel could be shouted from the housetops.

For another thing, I am not ashamed of the gospel of

Christ in its insistence on the tragic sinfulness of man and his desperate need of interior salvation. I can remember days when that deep and tragic message about man could easily be side-stepped and forgotten. We did not think ill of mankind. Leaders of thought like Herbert Spencer told us that progress was a beneficent and inevitable necessity, and poets like Tennyson assured us that "the thoughts of men are widen'd with the process of the suns." In those days we felt as though on the broad bosom of an ample river we floated to some heavenly ocean, the predetermined goal of human perfection. Of course, if we pulled hard on the oars we might get there sooner; still, whether we pulled on the oars or not, we were bound to arrive anyway, because we were afloat on a strong current of inevitable progress.

That was a fool's paradise, you say. Indeed, it was! Inventive science had given us some new and startling contrivances, like railroads, which predisposed our minds to temporary optimism. Now, however, it is plain that no contrivances can save us. Our need is far too deep. Like Roman candles and skyrockets, our mistaken dreams of salvation by ingenuity have gone off, and some of us begin to see again the abiding stars.

The gospel of Christ always has been right about the deeper matter. There is no such thing as inevitable progress. This is a tragic world where what man sows he reaps. The eternal laws of cause and consequence turn not aside for any man or nation, and history is the record of the rise and inexorable fall of societies and empires that tried to build on the foundations of unrighteousness. It cannot be done.

We thought that science might save us, but see how we ruin ourselves with the very implements that science gives! We thought that education might save us, but see to what more accomplished and destructive deviltry the trained mind turns its evil instincts! We thought that patriotism might save us, but see the murderous consequence which now we face! No! Something greater than science, deeper than education, more inclusive than patriotism, must save us. I am not ashamed of the gospel of Christ.

Indeed, in these difficult days one seems to discover its deep meaning all over again. In the gospel stands the most sober, realistic statement of the tragic need of man that the race has ever faced. Why should we balk at the great word "salvation" in view of our desperate want of it? Does not scientific medicine set itself to save us from disease? Do not schools exist because we need salvation from ignorance? Do we not institute philanthropies and pioneer more equitable economic orders because we need to be saved from poverty? Salvation is the chief preoccupation of all intelligent and earnest minds. But behind disease, ignorance, poverty, and running through the causes which produce and perpetuate them, is this deeper thing, the tragic selfishness of the unredeemed human soul. That is the sober, realistic fact. So the gospel of Christ has always taught. We may well be ashamed of much that is associated with the history of organized Christianity and with much that goes on in the churches today, but the gospel of Christ—*that* presents the soberest statement of realistic human need the world has ever faced.

For another thing, I am not ashamed of the gospel of Christ in its insistence on the prodigious lifting power of vicarious sacrifice. Vicarious sacrifice is the most impressive fact in the moral world. What one of us has not been saved from something because another, who did not need to do it, voluntarily took on himself our calamity or sin and by self-sacrifice redeemed us? And wherever that spirit of the cross appears and the ancient words come alive again, "He saved others; himself he cannot save," there is the most subduing, humbling, impressive fact we see. How can a man be ashamed of that?

This last week we buried Mrs. Anne Macy, Helen Keller's lifelong friend and teacher. Nearly fifty years ago, a little girl barely seven years of age—imprisoned behind doors so firmly locked it seemed they could not be unclosed and walls so high it seemed they could not be overpassed—was given to the care of this sacrificial teacher. For Mrs. Macy too had met blindness and, having partially surmounted it, vicariously gave herself to the blind. How subtly she passed through those fast closed doors! How marvelously she overpassed those high, strong walls and became to that imprisoned child the great emancipator! Years went by and Helen Keller passed her entrance examinations to college. Years went by and Helen Keller graduated from college *cum laude*. More years passed and Helen Keller was a world figure, known by every one. Still in the background was this magician, this self-effacing teacher, putting her life into another's and liberating it. It is one of the most amazing stories in the human record. And so powerful is such sacrifice that, because of this example of what can be done, new hopes have come, new methods, new open doors for blind and deaf folk everywhere, and the story has no end. Once more vicarious sacrifice works its miracle. How can one be ashamed of that?

To be sure, our world is disgraceful with the opposite of it, man's callous selfishness. Has some one here supposed that Paul, a man of piety and faith, must have been, therefore, a sentimentalist and looked at life through rosy spectacles? You should read the whole of this first chapter of the letter to the Romans, where our text appears. It is one of the most vehement eruptions of disgust with human life ever written. Listen to Paul in his denunciatory summary of humankind, "filled with all unrighteousness, wickedness, covetousness, maliciousness; full of envy, murder, strife, deceit, malignity; whisperers, backbiters, hateful to God, insolent, haughty, boastful, inventors of evil things." So he goes on, paragraph after paragraph, and at times is so specific about human perversity that I could not quote him here. He is no sentimentalist. He wears no rosy spectacles. But ever and again, in this same letter, he takes, as it were, the shoes from off his feet, for the place whereon he stands is holy ground. He comes within sight of the cross. He sees that most moving exhibition of self-sacrifice in history. He feels the lift of that power, which could save the world if we would let it. And before the marvel and mystery of that he bows in awe.

Like the law of gravitation running through the physical world, the law of vicarious sacrifice runs through the spiritual. No scientific medicine, no high education, no great music, no social progress, no lovely home, has ever come save as some one has voluntarily taken on himself a creative task. That is true of the cross on Calvary. That is true of Noguchi, going to South Africa to find the secret of a human plague and dying in consequence. That is the law of the spiritual world. If some one here is almost letting go and sliding to the dogs but still is held back from the last surrender, what is holding you is some one's vicarious love and sacrifice on your behalf. That is the most powerful force in the spiritual world. One should not be ashamed of it.

Once more, I am not ashamed of the gospel in its emphasis on what it calls the eternal purpose which God purposed in Christ. That is to say, before the gospel urges us to do something it tries to get us to see something, to see something everlastingly so about this universe: namely, that our world is not a feckless wanderer, coming from nowhere and going nowhither, but that an eternal purpose runs through it in which we can invest our lives, with which we can coöperate, and so be, as Paul said, "God's fellow-workers."

In this regard, the process of great religion is much like the process of great science. For great science also at the first stands aloof from practical problems, goes apart from the too clamorous demands of the world, and in isolation from the strife of tongues seeks to discover something everlastingly so about this universe. And, lo! when that has been discovered, the by-products begin to come, amazing by-products, from seeing something true, so that the face of the world is changed. So the gospel begins by asking us to *see* something, an eternal purpose through this universe with which we can coöperate.

Personally, I deeply need to see that. All the substitutes for it in our generation have blown up and gone to pieces. Only a few years past, non-theistic humanism was acclaimed as the great new religion. Never mind about God, it said; never mind about what this universe really is; let us blow on our hands anyway and save mankind. But in morals and in social hopes, as much as in science, what the universe really *is* is the basic matter. What if the universe is only chance and chaos? Suppose Schopenhauer is right, that all human history is nothing but a tragi-comedy played over and over again with some slight changes of scenery and costume? Then what is the use of blowing on our hands? Only one philosophy can undergird a long sustained and arduous investment of self-sacrifice—the idea that there is something at the heart of this universe greater than ourselves, a Power that makes for righteousness with which our little lives can ally themselves and coöperate.

One of the most surprising confirmations of this in our times has come from communism. That is the last place I expected such confirmation from. The communists started by saying they were atheists. We naturally supposed they meant that the universe in their eyes was without source, without purpose, without goal. But now the truth comes out as communist writings become available. The communist leaders say stoutly that they do not believe in mere mechanistic materialism. They go beyond it. They believe in dialectical materialism, which apparently teaches that, while there can be no such God as we believe in, history is so channeled, society by its own nature is forced to flow in such currents, that the kind of society they want is predicted and furthered by the nature of things. So they find cosmic backing from beyond themselves to make their enterprise reasonable. "Dialectics"—I quote a communist—"gives the proletariat the certainty of victory, it is to a certain extent *the guarantee of this victory.*" So the communists threw theistic religion out of the door only to find that part of it came back through the window. For all their talk about atheism, they cannot make sense of their arduous, sacrificial enterprise without having a cosmic backing.

That is an amazing confirmation of what Christianity has always said, that the only philosophy which makes long sustained and sacrificial labor reasonable is one recognizing something greater than ourselves in which we can invest ourselves and with which we can be fellow-workers. Well, then, if we are going to have *that,* why not have it at its best—the living God and his eternal purpose purposed in Christ? I am not ashamed of that.

We have picked four elements, out of many in the gospel, in which to glory, and, so doing, we have been attacking the timid, negative, apologetic attitude on the part of multitudes of Christians, as though they were half ashamed of being Christian. When one listens to the resounding cries of those who serve other causes—as though it were a glory to say, I am a Nazi, I am a fascist, I am a communist— one sees how outclassed we Christians are with our apologetic attitudes. I have dared to hope that some of us might go out from this service today with our heads higher, with more confidence and assurance saying, I am a Christian. Let that banner catch the winds once more! One God and one human family, the deep need of man for interior transformation and the Spirit that can meet it, the powerful lift of genuine self-sacrifice, the stimulating message of the eternal purpose which God purposed in Christ—what a gospel! When we see it burst into a life, when it is incarnate, from Christ to his humblest disciple, we cannot be ashamed of *that*.

The Most Durable Power in the World

NO SAYING in the New Testament is much more familiar than our text, and yet, when with cool, appraising eyes one regards it, how incredible it is —"Love never faileth"! Paul said that in the thirteenth chapter of First Corinthians but, beautiful and desirable though it sounds, how can it be true? Love does fail, obviously, egregiously, tragically.

Love sometimes fails because of lack on the part of those who exercise it. Even mother-love, becoming unwise, over-indulgent, possessive, can have appalling consequence, and as for the love that makes a home, who cannot understand the psychiatrist's remark that of all the emotionally upset people who seek his help half come because they are not married and the other half because they are? Indeed love can fail!

Moreover, love sometimes fails, not so much because of lack on the part of those who exercise it as because of callousness, obtuseness, imperviousness, on the part of those on whom it is bestowed. Only sentimental fiction can suppose that sacrificial love is so powerful that, sooner or later, it must overcome all obstacles and melt the most reluctant heart. Certainly, it did not work that way with Judas Iscariot. Can we imagine affection more unselfish and sacrificial than Christ's? He gave his love to Judas. Well, the scoundrel sold him out for thirty pieces of silver. Certainly love can fail.

Moreover, love fails as an adequate, cohesive power in society. Were we dependent for our basic social order and security only on the love which men voluntarily have, one for another, we should be in a bad way. Our social security rests back on coercive force, upon governments and laws, upon courts and prisons, upon armies and navies even. This is not commonly said in the pulpit but it had better be. We Christians, customarily proclaiming our reliance on the persuasiveness of sacrificial goodwill, need a factually true picture of our situation, depending, as we do, for our common security upon coercive force. Were that organized social coercion to disappear and nothing be left except voluntary friendliness to hold society together, society would fall apart, as though, as another put it, we had trusted the personal friendship of the engineer for the conductor to hold a railroad train together.

How comes it that we have even freedom from smallpox epidemics? Does some one answer that scientific medicine has provided us with vaccine which confers immunity? That is no adequate explanation. We are free from smallpox epidemics, not simply because of vaccine but because of compulsory vaccination. Had it not been for that coercive factor there would have been in the population a lunatic fringe ample enough to have refused vaccination and kept smallpox going. So we Christians, taking full measure of our constant and habitual dependence on coercion, may well ask what Paul could have meant when he said, "Love never faileth."

At this point, so it seems to me, Christianity stands or falls today. Only a few years ago our difficulties in being Christian lay in another realm. Could we as Christians accept the new science, and evolution in particular? How hotly we debated that and how comparatively obsolete the problem seems to us today! For now our bafflement about Christianity's truth lies in another realm. We are committed to a gospel of love. We proclaim God as love, exalt Christ's life of love, appeal to the noblest motives of mankind responsive to love, endeavor in practical service to express the principle of love. "By this shall all men know that ye are my disciples, if ye have love one to another"—that is the core of Christianity and without that there is no Christianity at all.

Once Henry George, the social reformer, and Cardinal Manning, prince of the Roman Church, were introduced, and one who was there has never forgotten the two strong profiles, as they faced each other in the gathering dusk, and the tone of emotion with which each professed his faith. Said Henry George, "I loved the people and that love brought me to Christ as their best friend and teacher." Said Cardinal Manning, "And I loved Christ, and so learned to love the people for whom he died." Well, have it either way; that is the core of Christianity. Some love the people and so are brought to Christ, and some love Christ and so learn to love the people, but, either way, this thing that Paul was trying to say in the thirteenth chapter of First Corinthians is the essence of Christianity: "Love never faileth." Yet look at the world depending on force, coercive tyranny, organized ill will, bloody violence! Do we really believe in the efficacy of love? The cross still stands above the altar, a symbol of our reliance on self-sacrifice to win the world. Do we honestly believe in that? In comparison with this, all other difficulties in being Christian today seem to me relatively simple.

Let us see, then, what true and realistic things we, as Christians, can say about this matter.

In the first place, love does not fail in so far as man always has to come back to it when he wants something constructive done. Granted the necessity of force. Granted that in the background of our lives coercion stands sometimes like a great dike holding back floods of disorder. Granted even that force may sometimes be necessary to give an obsolete social order a final push and send it sprawling. Say your best about force and its functions, but the limits to what it can do are set and inexorable. Napoleon

[88]

Bonaparte was probably, as he has been called, the greatest wielder of force in the modern world, but in his consular days he made this remark: "Do you know what amazes me more than all else? The impotence of force to organize anything. There are only two powers in the world: the spirit and the sword. In the long run, the sword will always be conquered by the spirit." So! He ought to know and we ought to know, too. We have lived through a generation swept by such massed violence as the earth has never suffered from before. What beautiful and constructive thing has all this violence built for humankind? The world's present situation does not argue the failure of love, as so many seem to think it does; it displays on a planetary scale the impotence of force.

Here in our own state and nation we are trying now to solve the problem of crime by force—by rigorous penalties, Baumes laws, G-men, and what not. Granted the necessity of marshaling effective force in our appalling situation. Yet our social workers have carefully mapped out in our large cities definite areas where, all the time that we are trying by force to solve the problem of crime, we are producing criminals faster than we can handle them with all our laws and prisons. Force cannot solve the problem of criminals constantly produced, as they are, in the slum areas of our cities. Only constructive goodwill can solve that problem—goodwill which cares about decent homes, decent recreation, decent neighborhoods, decent opportunities for boys and girls to live normal lives without being twisted out of shape in their early years. Realistically we are shut up to goodwill for the solution of the problem. Force has failed lamentably.

In 1919 Franklin D. Lane was Secretary of the Interior in the Cabinet of the United States. A high-minded, thoughtful man, he was watching from Washington the consequences of the World War—not a single constructive thing done by it that it had promised—and while, being himself, as he confessed, very uncertain about his own religion, he wrote this to a friend of his who was in Europe: "As for your religion, various of your friends think it odd. I think that you are a subject for real congratulation. A man who can believe anything is miles ahead of the rest of us. . . . John, if you have a religion that can get hold of people, grip them and lift them—for God's sake come over and help us." So, after every momentous exhibition of violence, the human heart cries out thus, as though to say: Physical force can repress, restrain, coerce, destroy, but it cannot create and organize anything permanent; only spiritual forces can do that. "Now abideth"—yes, after man has wielded all the massed violence he can get his hands upon—"Now abideth faith, hope, love, these three; and the greatest of these is love."

Sometimes from our mad world, where men so trust in force, I come into this church alone and look at the cross above the altar. It seems to say to me: I am a symbol of apparent failure; I represent the crucifixion of love by men of violence; but long ago they passed away, and the empires which by violence they founded passed away, and I still am here waiting; there is no way out of human misery but by love; whoever believes in violence trusts in a god who cannot create or organize anything permanent; in the long run it is only love that does not fail.

In the second place, love does not fail in so far as it creates a standard of judgment by which anything less than itself is shown up as inferior, and erects a goal of endeavor toward which, even despite ourselves, we are pulled from all lesser ways of handling life. Whenever anything beautiful comes into any realm it immediately sits in judgment on the ugliness there. The beautiful thing may seem very small —surrounded, impinged upon, and almost submerged, by the accepted ugliness—but, small though it seem to be, there it is, a standard of beauty, simply by being what it is judging the ugliness, showing it up, making it seem inferior and low, until at last the ugliness shrinks back from the silent but tremendous condemnation of the criterion which beauty has set up.

So love has come into the world and whenever we see it beautifully exhibited in persons, in families, among friends, in any degree in any social situation, we know that it is standard, that in so far as we fall short of it we fail, that in so far as we approximate it we succeed. When one takes a long look back across human history, the tremendous changes wrought by this silent influence of the criterion of love cannot be denied. Our forefathers of northern Europe used to think of Valhalla as a place where every day they would "put on their armor and go out into the court and fight, and fell each other." Who now, after only a few centuries, could dream of such a heaven or even desire such an earth? Another standard has come even among us ferocious folk of the northern races so that we know that any human relationship, if unfriendly, is so far wrong that, as Professor MacIver of Columbia University puts it, "When force is much in evidence it is a pathological symptom." Almost despite ourselves, we do judge human relationships by the criterion of goodwill, by our approximations of it and our lapses from it.

The first group of true friends in human history, whoever they were, certainly started something. They never could have guessed how much they started. Imagine them, the first group of true friends in a world where there never had been friendship quite like that before. How weak at first, in a world of violence, the principle of their relationship must have seemed, but how immediately it began sitting in judgment upon any other principle of human relationship, showing it up, making it appear foolish and fallible, until Plato came with his belief, as Professor Whitehead of Harvard phrases it, that even creation was the victory of persuasion over force, and Aristotle devoted two chapters of his great work on Ethics to the friendship that "holds mankind together in communities and cities," and Jesus came and set the criterion of love where it cannot be displaced. There it stands judging us, however we may twist and squirm and try to escape—still judging us, in our individual attitudes, our families and communities, even in our international relationships. Moving out, as we are, into an intermeshed, reticulated, interdependent world, the criterion of goodwill becomes for us not less but more imperious. By that criterion we sink or swim, survive or perish.

If, now, some one protests that, even so, it is not possible for us as nations and as individuals to live in the world as it is today on the pure and absolute standard of love, I agree. Alas, we have to modify our love with shrewdness, canniness, caginess, hard-headedness! It does nobody any good to let him use us for a doormat to wipe his feet upon. As Jesus said, we have to be as wise as serpents while we are as harmless as doves, and that is a difficult combination. What I fear for myself and you, however, is that, easily impressed by this aspect of the facts, we shall neglect the Christian venture—pushing love out in every relationship of life as far as we can make it go. Make that venture your own, I beg of you. Take risks for it, stake your life on it, stop being cynical about it, widen the margins of its application. Push constructive goodwill out as far as you can make it reach in every realm. The future of mankind depends on that. For, mark it, when Hitler and Mussolini are gone and their policy in retrospect looks as Napoleon Bonaparte's looks now to one historian, as an irrelevant episode, still the love standard will be here judging us, saying, Approximate this or perish—*In hoc signo vinces*.

In the third place, love does not fail in so far as it makes beautiful the personal lives of those who exercise it. Commonly we think of love in terms of those on whom it is bestowed, but I am sure Paul was thinking here as well of those who, possessing love in themselves, have lives in which the spirit of goodwill makes the whole house beautiful.

The old world in which Paul lived was as violent and vicious as ours, and yet see the quality of magnanimous life, lived within it and despite it, that this thirteenth chapter pictures! To dwell in a bitter world and not be a bitter person—if you know any one doing that, you need no preacher to explain that love is not a failure. *That* is one of the shining successes of mankind. Those who achieve it—the men and women of undiscourageable goodwill—are, in a world like this, to use George Eliot's figure, like "a fine quotation from the Bible . . . in a paragraph of today's newspaper." Certainly in private life this triumph of love is clear, for the most powerful influences that ever came into our experience flowed from persons, like fathers and mothers, in whom love was regnant and potent and persistent. Such love is not weak; it is the strongest force in the world in producing great character. As Shakespeare said, love is

> . . . an ever-fixed mark
> That looks on tempests and is never shaken;
> It is the star to every wandering bark.

Even in the rough, callous public life of the world, how men have been glorified by the spirit that could say, "With malice toward none, with charity for all!" Indeed, after all these centuries of human history, of what have we most right to be proud? Only one thing supremely, I suspect— the men and women who have loved the world, who, rising above life's bitterness, have cared for the people even when the people seemed little worth caring for, and who, so loving them, have given their best ability to the people's good. That and some of the consequences of that are the chief causes for just pride and hope we have from the long story of mankind. For, wherever else love may seem to have failed, it has not failed in producing the world's great souls.

Take not a conventional saint, much less a sentimental emotionalist for an example, but a scientist like Pasteur, creator of modern medicine, with his profound Christian faith and his single-minded devotion to the welfare of the people. "He was," says his biographer, "convinced that a man of pure science would complicate his life, the order of his thoughts, and risk paralysing his inventive faculties, if he were to make money by his discoveries." So Pasteur disciplined himself in single-minded devotion to his vocation and to the service of mankind. What that life has done for the world has long been an open book, but what that spirit did for the man who possessed it, who can estimate? No, love does not fail.

Yet many modern sophisticates who consider themselves shrewd and hard-headed talk of coerciveness, pugnacity, ill will, as being strong and of love as soft and weak. But ill will does not build strong character. See what it does to its possessor! It disintegrates his personality; it blurs his mental vision; it makes objective judgment impossible; it muddies up the waters of his soul. Ill will does no good to any one. It is an emotional debauch, whose worst ill consequence befalls the one who indulges in it. In comparison with that are the lovers of man soft? Pasteur soft? David Livingstone soft? Sir Wilfred Grenfell soft? Jesus soft? Despite our ill will and violence we still date our calendar from the birthday of one whose life was incarnate love. In building great character, love is the strongest force in the world.

Finally, love does not fail in so far as it keeps discovering possibilities, both personal and social, among the actualities, and brings them out. Ill will has chronic eye trouble —it cannot see far. It becomes angry about what is and so lacks insight to see what can be made of it. But love has eyes; it keeps discovering not simply what individuals and social situations are but what may be made of them if they are treated rightly and all their potentialities brought out.

Surely, many of us here are ourselves illustrations of that. Wherever should we have been if love had not discerned in us what only love could have guessed was there and then by patient faith and sacrificial care brought it out? Ah, family of mine, that years ago, when no one else would have taken pains to care, dared suspect that beneath the unlikely surface of a small boy's life was metal that might well be mined! If any one of us has ever discovered aught of value in himself, somewhere in his career love must have furnished the eyes.

Here is a neglected aspect of our truth. We habitually think of love as emotional. We have an unruly *penchant* for interpreting it in sentimental terms. But love is cognitive. By it alone can some truths be discerned. It only has eyes to see some realms of knowledge. For, while sheer intellect can discover the actualities in human life, only love can see the possibilities. There are truths about humanity that never would have been known unless love had discovered them. That we could run schools by goodwill, without corporal punishment, without any violence in the background, that we could make schools victories of persuasion over force—it took love to discover that. That we could have families without giving the father power of life and death over his children, as was once considered indispensable, and without the constant flourish of the rod and threat of violence—it took love to discover that. That we can have an economic life free from the terrific coercions which keep millions down, and can even run our nations without the insanity of war, is the kind of knowledge which always must exist first in the insights of goodwill before it can exist in the area of demonstrated truth. Love has eyes to see in souls and in societies what may be done with them, and if ever the eyes of love should close, the hope of the world would be forever dead.

Ah, Cross of Christ, grow real to us again. For the violence of this world often discourages our faith in thee and almost persuades us that love has failed. We need to see again that everything else, without love, has failed and that, lacking it, even our Western civilization will wretchedly collapse. We need a fresh vision not only of love's grace and beauty but of its abiding and dependable durability.

> In the cross of Christ I glory,
> Towering o'er the wrecks of time.

When Conscience Outruns Religion

ONE of the most disastrous evils that can befall religion is to have the best moral conscience of its generation get ahead of it. When the effective goodness of one's time moves on before while religion ethically lags behind, religion is obviously in a bad way. The assumption of conventional preachers is that men ought to become religious in order to become morally better. The realistic fact, however, is that often the most important and far-reaching ethical insights and endeavors of a generation are pioneering on ahead, while organized religion is behind, stuck in the mud or reluctantly dragging its feet.

We are familiar with the fact that the church has often let the intelligence of its generation get ahead of it. Organized Christianity, refusing to believe the insights of the scientific seers, from Copernicus to Darwin, faced the new science with ecclesiastical opposition—that is a familiar and often deplored fact. But, after all, that is not so strange, because science is not religion's specialty and in opposing new science at its first appearance religious leaders have done what the older scientists themselves have often done. So, when Harvey discovered the circulation of the blood, it is said that no scientist of that day over forty years of age credited his findings. It is not strange that religion should often have let the pioneering intelligence of its time get ahead of it. But morals, the principles and practises of the good life, are of the very stuff of religion. When they move ahead and religion lags behind, a situation arises to cause religious people deep, not to say desperate, concern.

When one thinks of any faith not his own, whether historic or contemporary, this phenomenon is obvious. In many an ancient faith, human sacrifice was a religious ritual to which religion clung with stubborn fidelity long after the best conscience of the people had overpassed it, and to this day in India the caste system, one of the cruelest of human institutions, against whose extremes men like Gandhi are making vigorous protest, has its support and will have its long lingering defense from orthodox Hinduism. When one thinks of religious faiths, historic or contemporary, other than one's own, one can plainly see the basis for the judgment of one of our foremost students of society, that "the religious manual of conduct almost always lags behind the current moral standards of a people." The question with us today is whether we have enough clarity of vision and objectivity of thought to see that same situation in our contemporary Christianity.

It is not difficult to understand why religion is thus continually tempted to let the best moral conscience of its time go ahead of it. For one thing, religion has the inveterate habit of making everything it touches sacred. It is easy to pass from bicycles to automobiles, or even to airplanes, because, religion having nothing to do with them, bicycles have never become sacred. But it is far more difficult to pass from one religious creed or ritual or ethical idea to another, because religion always adds the powerfully preservative feeling of sacredness. When, therefore, religion becomes entangled with a moral or social custom, like slavery, and especially when it can find in its ancient books slavery accepted or approved, a powerful bulwark is erected against attacks upon the system. So, as late as 1864, a lengthy and fervent defense of slavery was written in our own country by a bishop. Moreover, that bishop did not say that slavery was permissible; he said it was a sacred institution ordained of God, although already the best conscience of the nation, North and South, had gone beyond it.

For still another reason religion is in danger of letting the best moral conscience of its time outrun it. One of the major functions of religion is to bestow interior security and steadiness upon individual souls. Perhaps the most mysterious fact about our bodies is that in health they maintain a steady temperature of about 98.6°, no matter what the weather is outside, from Greenland to the Equator. But man's spirit has no such automatic guardianship against the heats and colds of this feverish and troubled world, and religion endeavors to supply the need. Now the need is deep and religion's service, in giving men what the saints have called "the peace of God, which passeth all understanding," is real and enduring. But if a religion absorb itself merely in endeavoring to keep a steady temperature in individual souls, it can easily become the friend of the established *status quo* and the enemy of all disturbing change. So while the real pioneers of goodness in a generation are forging on ahead, often with tormented hearts and lives linking themselves with the disinherited and fighting for a more decent social order, saying, it may be, as they go to prison for it, what Eugene V. Debs said, "While there is a lower class, I am in it; while there is a criminal element, I am of it; while there is a soul in prison, I am not free," the church may be lagging far behind the lines, absorbed in trying to keep the spiritual temperature of a few individuals at 98.6°.

When, then, a candid mind not only finds in other faiths the universal danger of conscience outrunning religion but sees as well the inherent and ever present reasons for that, it is hard for him to think that his own Christianity escapes the peril. So today I plead for a religion that will not let the best conscience of our time get ahead of it.

We may begin with a familiar and comparatively simple illustration. One of the most admirable factors in the goodness of today is the scientific conscience about truth. Science is not simply intellectual or inventive. It is a moral matter, a disinterested care about the truth, the whole truth, and nothing but the truth. There is in science at its best a certain rigorous honesty about facts and the statements one makes concerning them, which constitutes one of the noblest elements in the morals of today, whereas, in general, organized Christianity is far behind science in that regard. That hurts. One can understand and excuse the churches for sometimes failing to see the pioneering insights of highly specialized investigators, but to have the religion of one's time less honest than its best conscience is deplorable.

Can you imagine groups of scientists standing up to make formal confession of their faith in solemn words beginning, "I believe," when they do not believe? It is unthinkable. The scientific conscience would not tolerate that. Ponder these words of Thomas Huxley: "The longer I live, the more obvious it is to me that the most sacred act of a man's life is to say and to feel, 'I believe such and such to be true.'" That is from a scientist—"The most sacred act of a man's life is to say . . . 'I believe.'" Yet every week in many of our churches Christians repeat historic formulations of faith beginning solemnly with "I believe," when in multitudes of cases they do not believe. The ministers themselves, dragooned by ecclesiastical necessity, who lead the recitation, do not believe and say so. They solemnly affirm that they believe in the virgin birth, and they do not believe. They solemnly affirm that they believe in the resurrection of the body, and they do not believe. As one clergyman put it to me, "I get around that; I make the choir chant the creed." I know all the arguments in defense of such practises in the churches and I would not for a moment charge any devoted man with conscious, personal dishonesty, but still I say that the best conscience of our time about what honesty means has gotten a long way ahead of *that*.

Moreover, this kind of practise in the church does irreparable harm. Young men and women trained in our universities, catching something of the scrupulousness of science about facts and statements concerning them, see this loose, and to them apparently unscrupulous, affirmation in the church and have one more excuse for surrendering religion. They think that even in the matter of sheer honesty the best conscience of our time has outrun the church.

Let us turn now to a larger field for the illustration of our problem. The best conscience of our time is profoundly disturbed about the inequalities in our social order. The statistics concerning this, according to the Brookings reports, for example, are plain enough but one needs no statistics to make the matter clear.

Recently I spoke to you here about the enduring experiences that can begin in childhood and go through with one to the very grave—the love of nature, the companionship of books, the love of music, the profound interior satisfactions of an unashamed conscience, and an enriched spiritual life—and I said that they are the most democratic and accessible experiences we know, costing the least in money and most openly available to all the people. Then I went home and thought about it. I think that what I said is true, that such experiences as the love of nature, of books, of music, of an enriched spiritual life, are the most accessible we know and lend themselves least to the privilege and monopoly of the few. Yet imagine yourself living under the conditions that millions of people face in New York today, impoverished, trying to bring up children in old-law tenements that in all good conscience should have been torn down half a century ago, facing environments fairly represented in a play like "Dead End," and tell me frankly how much you would be interested in these abiding and most accessible experiences, how much margin of spiritual resilience and energy you would have to care for them, and what chance you think your children would have to be the kind of persons to whom such experiences would matter. So, with a disturbed conscience I saw that I had been talking about the most available experiences in human life to you who could understand and have them, while all around were multitudes of people who could barely understand them and would do little about them in any case. Surely, the best social conscience of our time must be disturbed, as it is disturbed, about the appalling inequalities of our social order.

Now, for the most part the churches are associated with the privileged. Where in this congregation are the slum dwellers who tonight will sleep in the 250,000 bedrooms in this city that no sunlight ever enters? They are not here. Would they not be welcome? Most welcome, but they are not here. Where are the day laborers, the toilers with their hands, the thousands of men, for example, who every morning in this city deliver milk at our doors? They are not here. Would they not be welcome? Most welcome, but they are not here. So across this country our churches for the most part are allied with, supported by, directed to the needs and attitudes of the comparatively-privileged, and the consequent temptation to ignore the problems of other classes besets us all, ministers and laymen alike.

For out there the disinherited, the underprivileged, the hard-hit, the restless, dreaming of a better day for their children, whom they love as much as we love ours, are trying to do something about the situation. To be sure, they often turn to crazy panaceas, yet they are planning, hoping, working for a better day, and in the best and most intelligent areas, mark it, they forge ahead—the best social conscience of our time set on such a reformation of the social order as will make impossible the continuance or recurrence of our present inequities. So, once more, organized religion is in danger of letting the best social conscience of its time get ahead of it.

Therefore let me address myself to you as I address myself to my own conscience. The privileged are not merely a few of the conspicuously well-to-do. We are all in this situation together, practically everybody in this church today. And if we are Christians in the serious sense that we want the spirit of Jesus operative in the world, when it comes to building a social order with open doors of decent opportunity before all people, we ought to be out in front. The worst disservice that we as individuals or churches can do to Christianity is to become the sponsors and supporters of the *status quo*. The Russian church did that, allied itself with the *status quo* while an unhappy people under the Czar were trying to feel their way forward to a better day. This is the tragedy of the Russian church, that in the day of its power it allied itself with privilege and let the best conscience of its time get ahead of it, and, lo! the nemesis of that fatality has been overwhelming and conclusive. How often has religion gone down, chained to a *status quo* it allied itself with! Could that not happen to our own privileged Protestantism?

In all this I am thinking not simply of Christianity but of democracy. I care about that too. And democracy came out of, depends on, and is indissolubly connected with, a certain comparative equality of condition. It was said of New Haven a century ago that "no man was too poor to own a carriage, and no man was rich enough to own two." Read Daniel Webster if you want some of the sturdiest statements ever made about the indissoluble connection between equality and democracy. "A great equality of condition," as Daniel Webster said, is "the true basis, most certainly, of a popular government." What we are saying now is not new radicalism but old Americanism. Today democracy faces one of the most critical eras of its history. On the one side are fascism and communism—although ultimately there is more hope in the latter than in the former—and on the other side democracy. For one, I am all for democracy, but the basis of democracy is not mainly political, it is economic. We cannot go on in this country with successful democracy in the face of the embittering inequality that exists today, so that, in spite of all the natural and inevitable differences of opinion about ways and means that must exist in such a congregation as this, there ought to be no difference of opinion about the necessity of profound social change. Let no man here who cares for Christianity or democracy, because of any private privilege or any reactionary fear become the sponsor and supporter of this *status quo*, while the best conscience of our time goes on ahead.

Having thus illustrated our problem in two diverse realms, let us turn the kaleidoscope and see our proposition in a new relationship. There is a kind of religion which, far from being left behind by morals, has been the pioneer of morals—prophetic religion. When, in the Scripture, Isaiah, the prophet of God, said to his people, "Wash you, make you clean; put away the evil of your doings from before mine eyes; cease to do evil; learn to do well; seek justice, relieve the oppressed, judge the fatherless, plead for the widow," there was religion, you see, far out ahead, calling to the morals of the people to come after it. So although ecclesiastical religion is commonly outrun by conscience, prophetic religion, represented in the Old Testament by men like Amos, Micah, Isaiah, and Jeremiah, and in the New Testament by Jesus himself, has been a trail-blazer for morals. Today, therefore, we are pleading for prophetic religion, and these, I think, are two of its typical attributes.

First, again and again in history, far ahead of the moral conscience of the people, prophetic religion has seized on a great and revolutionary truth, and with that truth, like a pillar of cloud by day and of fire by night, has gone ahead and morals have come stumbling after.

One such pioneering truth was the idea that all men are equal before God, who is no respecter of persons. That is a religious insight, the first entrance into human thinking of the idea of equality. In spite of all the rankings and discriminations that seem important on earth, when men and women stand before the face of eternal God they stand alike. When that idea of equality emerged in religion there was no equality elsewhere, no equality before the law, no equality of the sexes; slavery was taken for granted, tyranny was taken for granted. In only one place had that concept arisen: where men face eternal God the differences vanish and they are alike. As every student of the history of thought knows, that has turned out to be one of the most revolutionary ideas in man's record, because, if men verily believe that they stand alike before God, they cannot help seeing that something is wrong with slavery, with tyranny, with the subjection of women, with crushing poverty. So prophetic religion with a great truth went ahead, and morals are still trying to trail after.

Another such pioneering idea is the belief in the essential dignity and infinite value of every human soul. That is a religious insight. It rose high in Plato and in Jesus higher yet. When that idea arrived in religion, the human soul was not practically treated as of infinite value. That was a trail-blazing concept in religion and, as Professor Whitehead of Harvard has made clear, no one can understand the rising conscience of the Western world across the centuries against slavery, against tyranny, against illiteracy, against the mistreatment of children, women, the sick, the insane, against industrial despotism and crushing poverty, without taking into account the creative influence of this religious idea, which made men see that, if every soul is infinitely sacred, then something is intolerably wrong with our societies. So once more prophetic religion went ahead, and morals followed.

So we could go on showing that, while ecclesiastical religion is continually left behind, prophetic religion is consistently a trail-blazer for goodness. That is why we never catch up with Jesus. In physical presence he is back in history; in creative ideas he is out ahead of us, with his religious insight challenging our morals, condemning them, inspiring them, calling them to arise and follow him.

Put it this way. There are two kinds of causation in the world, one forcing us from behind, the other drawing us from before. When we eat food we are forced to it by hunger, but when we paint a picture or write a symphony or build a cathedral, we are drawn from ahead by something that we would like to translate out of the ideal world unseen into the world visible and tangible. Every man's life has these two forms of causation, one pushing him from behind, the other drawing him from before. The more a man is pushed from behind the less of a man he is; the more a man is drawn from before the more of a man he is. And of all influences that have gone ahead and drawn morals after them, nothing so much as prophetic religion has been the pathfinder that human goodness has stumbled after.

The second attribute of prophetic religion, briefly put, is a certain clairvoyant prevision of practical possibilities and an undiscourageable faith in their achievement. At the beginning of this sermon I know well that I was encouraging some doubters here in their distaste for religion and confirming one of their worst suspicions about it, that it lags behind while conscience goes ahead. Listen to this then: "They shall beat their swords into plowshares, and their spears into pruning-hooks; nation shall not lift up sword against nation, neither shall they learn war any more." Is that a resolution of a modern peace society? On the contrary, that is the prophecy of a man of God in the eighth century before Christ. Did the world then look as though peace were possible? On the contrary, despite all our discouragements, the practical chances of peace now are a thousand to one compared with those of Isaiah's time. Was ecclesiastical religion then in sympathy with such pacific aims? On the contrary, ecclesiastical religion, then as generally, was just as nationalistic and militaristic as the common run of morals. That was prophetic religion in the eighth century before Christ. As from the heights of Zion, looking eastward, one sees the first edges of the dawn come up from the desert far across the Jordan gorge, the prophet saw, afar off, premonitions of peace. That certainly is not religion lagging behind morals.

A generation ago some of us were deeply upset because the intelligence of our time was getting ahead of its Christianity. To see the best thinking of our day forging ahead into a new scientific world view, while religion lagged behind, was intolerable and we bestirred ourselves. Whatever else happened, we said, we would have a religion that kept up with the best thinking we knew. Today another problem challenges us. Our danger is that the best conscience of our time should get ahead of us.

Wherever else Christ is, he is out ahead. For peace against war, for a world community against our suicidal nationalism, for human brotherhood against the rising tide of racial prejudice, for freedom against fascism, for human equality against our prevalent inequities, for the motive of service against the motive of gain—there is no mistaking the general direction in which Christ moves. And we belong with him.

Christian Attitudes in Social Reconstruction

JESUS faced his disciples with a question which in these days of social unrest and reconstruction ought to disturb our consciences: "What do ye more than others?" The Master fairly taunted his followers with the similarity between their attitudes and the attitudes around them. "Do not even the publicans the same?" he said; "do not even the Gentiles the same?" "What do ye more than others?"

Today we face that question, especially with reference to our social attitudes, as we move out into one of the most disturbed eras in history. Obviously in this nation we have a trying time ahead—economic hardship for millions, irreconcilable conflicts of economic opinion and policy, bitter partisanship coming perilously near to class war, it may be even the threat of fascism, and all this only the American foreground of a planet everywhere disturbed by dangerous turmoil. With such a situation in view, what about our social attitudes? What do we Christians more than others?

To be sure, many of the qualities needed for a successful solution of our social problems are not specifically Christian. Intelligence, for example, is no prerogative of ours. If, however, Jesus is what we say he is, if as the captain of our salvation he moves on ahead and we are his disciples, there ought to be in us some qualitative superiority, some observable distinction to mark us off from the common run of men. Yet look at the social attitudes of our churches. Do not even the publicans the same? What do we more than others?

To start at the beginning, Christians, more than others, ought to be deeply and sensitively interested in social questions. Christianity is a two-way street. It tries to change men's souls in order to change their societies, and it tries to change their societies in order to give their souls a chance. Certain reactionary groups wish to persuade the church that Christianity is a one-way street, concerned only with individual souls in their relationships with God. It is, they seem to say, no particular affair of ours that slums damn souls, that some millions of young people in our country, out of school, have no work to do, that we have an economic organization where share-croppers, who raise the cotton, cannot possess enough cotton for their own underclothes, that dictatorships issue in wars and then wars issue in dictatorships, in hideous and ruinous succession.

I shall not insult your intelligence by lengthy argument against this one-way-street idea of Christianity. On the face of it, it is absurd. By logical necessity the individual gospel involves the social gospel. The more we care for the souls of men, one by one, the more we must care for the social conditions which so vitally affect them.

Even on grounds of self-preservation, Christians, more than others, had better be sensitive about social problems. Some of us have been indignant about the "no-God exhibits" in Russia. The Soviet Government took great cathedrals, where for centuries the praises of the Lord had sounded, and there set up "no-God exhibits" deriding all religious faith. We have been indignant about that. We might well spare a little of our indignation. We have plenty of "no-God exhibits" here. If war and slums and lynching and penury in the midst of possible plenty are not "no-God exhibits," then there never has been one. We Christians have been tremendously concerned about theoretical denials of God in philosophy but we never have been enough concerned about real denials of God in society.

There are some sixty million Christian church members in this country. Suppose they could see our cruelest social wrongs for what they are, "no-God exhibits," downright denials of the God of righteousness and brotherhood, more explicit and more dangerous to Christianity than any theoretical denial can ever be. They could be no longer deceived by the idea that Christianity has no concern with social questions.

In the second place, Christians, more than others, should have a clear criterion and standard of judgment in dealing with social problems. The Christian philosophy of life stems out from a profound sense of the value of personality. Personality is the most mysterious and marvelous factor in the universe. A being, mark you, with consciousness of his own life and power over it, possessing capacities of intellect, purposefulness, and goodwill, with possibilities of development inherent in him nowhere else existent within our ken—such is personality. Says Professor MacIver of Columbia University, "Personality is the only intrinsic value we know." That idea was Jesus' specialty and every situation he faced he judged by what the situation did to persons. One can briefly sum up the Christian ethical attitude by saying that whatever elevates, enlarges, and liberates personality is right, and whatever crushes, smirches, and degrades personality is wrong.

Here, then, is the specific Christian approach to social problems. If, speaking as though I were an expert in economics, I should say, I will now solve the economic problem and tell you in outline what the new order ought to be, you might well move to adjourn. That would be outside my competence. I might retort that it seems also to be outside the competence of everybody else, especially the economists and politicians. That, however, would be no real answer. You are under no obligation to listen to me as though I were an expert builder of economic systems. But if I should say, In the name of Christ I appeal for the rights of persons; there are situations which open doors to personality and there are situations which damn personality, imprison it, buy and sell it as a thing instead of a spiritual treasure; in the name of that test, and of the Christ whose test it is, I appeal against the bitter wrongs which crush the people's souls within them—then I would not be off my beat and you would know it.

This special Christian test of social situations is not vague and general; it brings one to particular conclusions. As a Christian I am against the totalitarian and dictatorial state, whether in its fascist or its communist form, because the dictatorial state makes itself into a wheel in which personalities are merely spokes, and that will never do.

As a Christian I must be against sex discrimination, because sex discrimination thinks of woman first, last, and all the time as though she were only woman, whereas the far deeper fact is that she is a personality and must be so regarded.

As a Christian I must be against race prejudice, for race prejudice thinks first in terms of blood and color, but blood and color are superficial in comparison with the deeper fact that every man of every race is a personality and must be so treated.

As a Christian I must carry on my conscience heavy burdens—the burden of the slums; the burden of millions of youths to whom the world is saying, We have no need of you; the burden of poverty in the midst of luxury—and I must judge the economic organization which issues in such results as intolerable.

As for war, in view of what it does to persons, I must adjudge myself a fool that twenty years ago I thought there might be a Christian defense of that. An American woman working in the devastated areas of France during the war, saw the troops come back from the trenches after the Armistice. "I had expected," she says, "to see them gay, hilarious, effervescing. But among all those thousands I saw only one gay soldier." She tells of a boy lately released from a German prison camp and coming back to France. "In three hours," he said to her, "I'll be home. I'll see my father and my mother—even Toto, my dog." Then she asked him where home was and he answered, "La Faux." Alas! She had been in La Faux and all that was left there was a sign, reading, "HERE USED TO BE THE TOWN OF LA FAUX." So, in three hours he would be home!

If I were a citizen only or a politician or an economist, I might have this or that attitude toward war, but as a Christian I must have a special attitude. See what it does to persons! See what it inevitably, needlessly, deliberately does to persons! So judging it, I know as a Christian that it is irremediably wrong.

This special Christian test, then, is no mere generality, and one particular consequence seems clear. No genuine Christian can ever be a reactionary, a mere defender of the *status quo*. Always, at the heart of the Christian attitude, there is a judgment seat to which the organizations and institutions of mankind, however venerable they may be, are brought and this question put to them: What are you doing to personality? Are we then Christian? Do not the publicans the same? What do we more than others?

In the third place, Christians, more than others, ought to inject into this social situation an indispensable quality, humility. Nothing more bedevils our social problems and holds up their adequate solution than group pride. As individuals we may be modest but, when we get together into political parties, economic classes, and patriotic nations, we at once fall victim to pooled pride. It becomes a positive virtue— loyalty, we call it—to believe that our group is mostly right and other groups mostly wrong. I plead today for a quality which should lift Christians above the shibboleths and prejudices of class and party, *humility,* the consciousness that all of us together—democrats, republicans, and socialists; rich and poor; employers and employees; Europe and America— share a common guilt and need a common penitence. If we

could get our parties and classes to stop saying, as did the
Pharisee in Jesus' parable, "God, I thank thee, that I am not
as the rest of men," and could get them to praying like the
publican, "God, be thou merciful to me a sinner," we might
at least produce a climate in which a better social order would
have a chance to grow.

To many humility will seem a weak thing to recommend
in so vehement a world, but the fact is that the lack of it viti-
ates everything we do. Allow me to apply it for a moment
to the class most represented here today—to us, that is, who
more than others have had access to the world's good things,
especially its economic and educational opportunities. O privileged class in America, I should say, you had best be humble. I fear for a church like this where, from the pulpit to
the pew, we come from privileged backgrounds, when I remember how often in history the underdog has been right.

A century ago in England, in 1834 to be exact, six men
formed a branch of the Grand National, an early labor union.
They were, according to the record, God-fearing men, two
of them Methodist lay preachers, but they "conspired"—so
runs the charge at their trial—"to preserve," as they put it,
"ourselves, our wives and children from degradation and
starvation." Well, the privileged class, represented in the
Government, promptly crushed the conspiracy and those six
men were exiled to penal servitude in Australia. Now, however, a century afterward, an impressive memorial has been
erected in their honor, to say, what so often has had to be
said in history, that privilege was wrong and the underdog
was right.

Fellow members of the privileged class in America, we had
best achieve humility. When we talk about social evils we
generally think of their disastrous effect on the underprivileged. But listen to one of the most thoughtful men among
our fellow citizens. "It is an evil thing," he says, "to starve
in the midst of plenty. It is an even more evil thing to enjoy

[113]

plenty in the midst of starvation." So would Christ say. Well, are we Christians? What do we more than others?

In the fourth place, Christian faith ought to throw eternal horizons around these temporal conflicts. I do not mean that it should be a chloroform mask, as another put it, into which men can thrust their faces and so forget the temporal conflicts. That is a caricature of religion, which makes it "the opiate of the people," substituting, as the radicals say, "pie in the sky" for righteousness on earth. I mean that faith in the living God revealed in Christ ought here and now to bring to us new dimensions, new height, depth, breadth, and length, and so, contributing vision, wisdom, and power, lift our social attitudes above the common run.

In a few paragraphs let me sum up the influences which such faith should bring to bear upon our thinking:

A Christian ought not to be so easily discouraged as are other men. One does not mean that Christians should be easy-going optimists like a barometer stuck on "Fair," and refusing to change no matter what the weather is. Such lush expectancy that all will be well is no true result of a deep and serious religion. Let all Christians remember that the New Testament begins with a massacre of little children, is centered in a crucifixion, and ends while the souls of the saints under the altar cry, "How long, O Master?" In no book is there more exaltation of spirit than in the New Testament, and in no book is there more trouble. Of all people Christians should be the last to expect life to be easy.

To be sure, in some generations history turns such unexpected corners to such unforeseen consequences that hope and courage are not difficult. As for us, however, I suspect that we are facing troubled times. It looks like it. Our forefathers have bequeathed to us a revolutionary epoch. Yet I am not discouraged. Through all this turmoil sounds an eternal Voice which long ago the prophet Ezekiel heard amid the dismay of his people's exile—"I will overturn, overturn, overturn it: this also shall be no more, until he come whose right it is; and I will give it him." Said Thomas Edison once, "When everybody else is quitting on a problem, that is the time when I begin." Christian faith should produce *that* attitude.

Again, a Christian ought not to be so easily fooled as others are by slick, swift schemes of external reformation, superficial panaceas, as though by changing a few circumstances we could guarantee Utopia. This seems to me one of the major dangers of the left-wing radicals. They habitually oversimplify the situation. They pick out a single devil—capitalism, let us say—as though, if only we could abolish *that*, Utopia would be just beyond. I do not speak as a sponsor of capitalism. Capitalism is very sick and no one should know that better than the capitalists. Profound changes must take place in it if it is to survive at all, and if in the long run another system altogether should emerge to displace it, that would be only what has happened to other economic systems in the past and nothing strange at all. But when a radical friend of mine pontifically announces that all wars are caused by capitalism, I say, How come? Were there then no wars under the feudal system? Were there no wars under the ancient agricultural system when Egypt and Assyria slaughterously wrecked the world? Such naïve selection of a single devil, in the form of an economic organization, as though all human evils came from that alone, is gross oversimplification of the problem, false in fact and dangerous in consequence. For the problem of war, like every other human problem, is far more complicated and profound than such naïve simplicity can cover.

If a drama is going wrong because the actors are not good enough, you cannot solve the problem simply by changing the scenery. So human perversity can bedevil any governmental or economic setup which the wit of man can devise, and to forget that, to forget that external reformation of circumstance without interior regeneration of character leads only to disillusionment, is to invite a dangerous debacle. Christians more than others ought to have a serious realistic apprehension of the power of personal perversity, selfishness, and sin to spoil any outward device of social organization, and therefore a deeper understanding of the profound, interior spiritual needs of men.

Again, Christians, more than others, ought to stand against violence as an agency of social change. Alas, how many in this country now are meditating violence! On the one side comes the shocking news from a Senatorial investigation, with detailed evidence that seems convincing, concerning certain American manufacturers who had been laying in large stocks of war munitions to be used in case of need against American workingmen, and on the other side is the constant preaching of revolutionary violence by the left-wing radicals. A class war in this country, however, can bring us nothing good. A young radical friend of mine said in my presence that while, of course, international war was ugly and wicked, class war was something different, a new kind of war indispensable in the coming revolution and full of moral possibilities. But class war is not new. Class war is civil war. That is old, the ugliest kind of war man has ever fought. How long did it take us after the Great War to cease hating the Germans? We ceased almost immediately, thankful for the chance. Only a few months ago, however, a young friend of mine, trying to sell goods in an out-of-the-way village in the deep South, was told that none of his Yankee stock was wanted there. "But," he said, "I thought the Civil War was over." "Not yet," was the answer, "not down here." The angers of foreign war can swiftly abate but the rankling hatreds of civil war dig in and hang on. It is the ugliest kind of war there is. We ought to know that in this country. Psychologically we in America are still a pioneer people and violence is close under the surface with us. But everything we care for most—democracy, liberty, fraternity—will be swamped in a class war and nothing but dictatorship can rise on the ruins. We Christians more than others ought to see that.

Again, we Christians, more than others, ought to have at least a general idea of the direction in which social development should move. Two major factors are in our modern Western world: on the one side, the old Christian ideal of love, friendship, goodwill, cooperation, being members one of another; and on the other side the new inventions and techniques which make us live together, constrain us to do things together, force us into such contacts and interdependencies as mankind has never had before. These two things belong together and require each other. For our new interdependencies will ruin us without Christian goodwill, and Christian goodwill is vague and socially ineffective until it is implemented by the new techniques. How to get the two together? How to build a cooperative society with the new scientific techniques mastered by the old Christian ideals?

In this regard I fear communism, but not as some of my friends do. They fear it as a possible conqueror of America. I think that a needless dread. The totalitarian-state system of communism has little if any chance in this country. Everything in our psychology and our tradition is antagonistic to it. Our danger is not so much communism as fascism. I fear the ideas behind communism, not as the conqueror of my country but as the competitor with my Christianity. For I am convinced that, say a century from now, mankind will look back on the Russian Revolution a good deal as we look back upon the French Revolution. It was terrible. The tumbrils rolling down the city streets to feed the falling guillotine were the terror of the world; the actress lifted to the high altar of the Cathedral of Notre Dame in Paris by a *régime* that would defame and destroy religion was the horror of Christendom. Yet underneath that terror the French people

[117]

were desperately at work on ideas of liberty, fraternity, equality, which afterwards Christians had to recognize as belonging in their realm and had to confess they should have achieved by their endeavors.

So the Russian Revolution has been terrible. Its cruelty, its ruthless tyranny, its violent suppressions of liberty, its dogmatic atheism have shocked the world. We here in America are rightly determined to have none of it. Yet, underneath all that, the Russian people are desperately at work upon experiments in doing things together in a world of new techniques. Never mind if you do not like the special methods which they employ. Neither do I. It will not do, however, to minimize the importance of their aim. Either in their way or in another, we must build a more coöperative society, in which we are members one of another. That is a Christian ideal and always has been, and to have men who call themselves atheists care more about that and work more tirelessly for that than we care and work is one of the most dangerous things, in the world at large, confronting Christianity. I fear communism because I know that in this country we ought as Christians to be building a more coöperative, more fraternal, more equalitarian and classless society in which we shall be members one of another. That is the goal both of Christianity and of democracy. More than others we Christians ought to see that aim and serve it.

It is not going to be easy in these days ahead to be really Christian. To be sure, one can be partially Christian, for Christianity means many things. It can be to us like music, to which from the raucous discords of the world we flee to bathe ourselves in harmony and peace. It can be to us like nature, to which we retreat from the city's strident clamor to be led in green pastures and beside the still waters, restoring our souls. Christianity can mean prayer, the sinking of deep wells within the soul, which the droughts of earth cannot dry up nor the vicissitudes of circumstance make stale.

But always, from such meanings of Christianity, a man returns perforce to face the world's social struggle, immense, imperative, unescapable. In the end we will be judged by our attitude toward that. So a contemporary described a minister of state of Louis XVI as "a good, easy kind of man, one who would make an excellent peace minister in quiet times." Aye, but those were not quiet times. His ancestors had bequeathed to him a revolution. So is it with us. It is not enough, profoundly important though it is, to be a good man. What about our social attitudes? Do the publicans the same?

The Peril of Privilege

THE more one reads the Gospels the more one confronts the fact that Jesus had his main difficulty with privileged people like ourselves. Here lay the secret of his conflict with the Pharisees. Of all the parties in the Judaism of his day he belonged most intimately with them—not with the Zealots, who were fiery militarists, nor with the Sadducees, who were worldly-wise priests, but with the Pharisees. They were the religious party. They believed in God the Father, taught a noble ethic, were convinced of life eternal. Jesus was spiritually of their kin. Yet with them he had his sharpest conflicts, as sharpest conflicts commonly arise between members of the same family.

The point of the conflict lay in the fact that the Pharisees were a privileged class and that Jesus was outraged at the consequence. In his denunciation of them he put this first: "They . . . love the chief place at feasts, and the chief seats in the synagogues, and the salutations in the marketplaces, and to be called of men, Rabbi." This pride of position Jesus could not abide. So far as the religious doctrines of the Pharisees were concerned, scholars commonly agree that for the most part he was at one with them, and he even said to his followers, "Whatsoever they bid you observe, that observe and do." The nub of their offense was their attitude toward their position of privilege. It made them proud; it built walls around them, shutting them out from sympathy with plain folk. They condescended to common people, saying, as John's Gospel represents them, "This multitude that knoweth not the law are accursed." On that point Jesus broke with them, saying: "Whosoever shall exalt himself shall be humbled;

and whosoever shall humble himself shall be exalted. But woe unto you, scribes and Pharisees, hypocrites!"

Indeed, who can read the Gospels anywhere and not see Jesus' ethical discontent rising most sharply in the presence of class-conscious privilege? Not only the Pharisee who went up to the temple to pray and thanked God he was not as other men are, but the rich man who fared sumptuously every day while the poor man ate the crumbs that fell from his table, were gall and wormwood to the spirit of Jesus, and sometimes he put the case so strongly that he seems unfairly class-conscious himself. "Woe unto you that are rich!" he cried; "Blessed are ye poor"; "It is easier for a camel to go through a needle's eye, than for a rich man to enter into the kingdom of God"; "This poor widow cast in more than all they that are casting into the treasury."

So it stands written in the record, and here, week after week, in our thought and worship, we imply our devotion to the ideals of Jesus. Are we willing with humility and penitence honestly to face this characteristic emphasis of his?

It is typical of our American money-mindedness that we think of privilege mainly in terms of wealth. Now, economic advantage in some degree is at the basis of every other kind of advantage, and Jesus surely did not neglect that fact. Yet, after all, the Pharisees taken as a class were not rich. The privilege that they represented swept a far wider circumference than that. They were the educated, the learned people of their time, holding positions of prestige in school and synagogue. I am solicitous that no one here this morning enjoying any kind of special favor, even that of a college education, should escape the impact of the truth we are trying to present. Jesus seemed to think that the most difficult problem ethically for any man to face is in a place of privilege.

Why should he have felt that way? What was the trouble with the Pharisees?

For one thing, Jesus may have felt as he did about privileged people because a man occupying a favored position is almost irresistibly tempted to estimate himself on the basis of *that*, regardless of the kind of man he is inside. It is extraordinarily difficult for a privileged person to get a true view of himself. A favored place gives us standing, frontage, and setting for our lives. It furnishes us with a show window on the street for all to see, and almost inevitably a man is tempted to think of himself in terms of *that* when his privilege may be merely an extraneous inheritance and acquisition, not truly representative of what he really is.

James M. Barrie depicted this truth dramatically in his play, "The Admirable Crichton." The scene shifts, you recall, from London, with its rankings and discriminations of social class, to a shipwrecked company on a South Sea island, where all special favors are stripped away and the persons of the drama depend each on his own quality. What is a man worth now in himself? As it turns out, it is not the lord but the butler who is the real man—far and away the real man. The lord and his daughters had been getting by on something extraneous to their intrinsic quality. When a man is habitually set in the jewelry of favorable circumstance, he almost irresistibly comes to think that he must be a jewel, when in fact he may be paste.

Because in this country some kinds of social classes do not exist and no chorus of coroneted earls sings, as in a Gilbert and Sullivan opera, "Bow, bow, ye lower middle classes!" we must not suppose that we have escaped this abiding spiritual problem. The protection furnished by an advantageous situation against true self-appraisal and self-judgment troubled Jesus in the Pharisees and it would trouble him in us. The Pharisees had the marks of honor and prestige belonging to their class. They were set in jewelry and thought themselves jewels. That is why Jesus called them hypocrites, not so much because they were consciously trying to deceive others as because they were so deceived about themselves—

all dressed up in external privilege while within they were such people that, with outward trappings removed, they would be shown up as shams. Such self-deceit is the inevitable temptation of a privileged class.

Read again Carlyle's philosophy of clothes in *Sartor Resartus*. If a man could only see himself naked, stripped of adventitious advantage, reduced to his native estate, "a poor forked Radish with a head fantastically carved," then he might see the truth about himself. But these clothes of outward advantage are not ourselves. These acquired and inherited circumstances hide us from ourselves until, as Jesus said, at the great Judgment when men stand face to face with God—high and low, rich and poor, educated and uneducated, white and black—the appraisals of earth will be completely reversed and the last shall be first and the first last. Today we are trying to antedate and forestall that judgment with a private Judgment Day of our own.

For another reason Jesus may have estimated the peril of privilege as he did because a man in an advantageous position, protected by comparatively comfortable circumstance, finds it hard keenly to feel what is wrong with the world. Fortunate folk do not know where the social shoe pinches as the man underneath knows it. They may be better qualified intellectually to analyze it but they do not feel it. There is no wall so high and thick to shut out the poignant and crying hurts of mankind as a privileged position.

Do not, I beg of you, suppose that as from afar I am proclaiming this to you. I am saying this most of all to myself. I was not born into economic affluence—far from it!—but I was born into a schoolmaster's family and all my life I have lived in the atmosphere of schools and books. That is a privileged position and because it is I do not know how the worst inequities and wrongs of our present society hurt some people. There are a quarter of a million bedrooms in New York City into which no direct breath of air or ray of sunshine has come since they were built. I never had to sleep in one of those and, what is more, I have never been compelled, no matter how hard I worked, to see my children sleep in them. I do not know what that means. Sociologists tell us that our criminal population in jails and prisons increased alarmingly during the decade 1924-34 and that the increase came mainly from young boys born and reared in certain well-known slum areas in our great cities. I never had to live under conditions which so like a mill grind out the inevitable consequence of criminality. I do not know what that means. In New York City are hundreds of thousands of people, honest, self-respecting, industrious, loving their families as I love mine, who, working their hardest at menial and drudgerous tasks, can do no more than support their homes on the bare level of a meager subsistence. I have read about that in books, I see the fringes of it with my eyes, but I do not know what it means.

If some one says, You ought not to blame yourself for that, I say, No, but it is of first-rate importance that I should recognize it, that I should say to myself, You have been privileged and so probably you are blind, blind as an owl at noonday to what is going on in society and what ultimately ought to go on, socially blind, as privileged people of all generations have been from the days of the Pharisees until now, so that it is a safe historical generalization to say that in the great social movements of mankind not the privileged but the underdogs have commonly had the right objective.

Of course, if I were speaking to the underprivileged, I would talk to them about their temptations. Every estate has its own problems and moral perils. Many of the underprivileged are such because of their own laziness and self-indulgence. Essential human nature is much the same wherever it is found, and it is as false and dangerous to glorify the proletariat as it is to play sycophant to the privileged. Sin, too, is "no respecter of persons." Its demonic, corrupting power runs through all classes, and no realistic mind can suppose virtue to be preponderant in any special group, even the downtrodden. Today, however, I am talking to *us*—and we need to be reminded, do we not? that the major movements of social progress in history have commonly had their source and sustentation in people who were being hurt. They felt the intolerable social wrongs, not with their wits but with their pulses. Whatever may be true, for example, about the rights and wrongs of the contemporary conflict over the tenant-farmer situation in the South, it is a safe affirmation, backed by long history, that a century from now the social historian, looking back, will see plainly that not those on top but those underneath were right. And that will be true, not because those on top are bad and those underneath are good, but because those on top are on top. They do not feel where the wrong is as does the man beneath. Whatever may be the detailed rights and wrongs of the American laboring man's present struggle for a larger share in the products of industry, it is a safe affirmation, confirmed by long history, that a century from now the social historian in retrospect will say that in his main objective the laboring man was right—that is to say, he did deserve a larger share of the product of industry and he did have a right to collective bargaining on a scale that was being denied him. William Ewart Gladstone, who was certainly privileged, said, while campaigning for Irish home rule, that during the preceding half century the privileged classes, the aristocratic classes, the educated classes, had been on the wrong side of every great social issue and, if their opinion had prevailed, it "would have been to the detriment, or even the ruin of the country."

You see, we are pleading for the Christian virtue of humility on the part of the privileged, and it is not easy to plead for. Privilege does not naturally lead to humility. Favored folk are almost inevitably tempted to think that their privilege is something they have earned, that they deserve it, that it is an outward and visible sign of their superiority. Friends, very little of our privilege have we earned. In this country now, as compared with our colored friends, a white man occupies a privileged position. Is the white man then white because he earned it? Was he not born so? Most of our privilege is not of our earning. Take out of the situation the sacrifices of generations before we were born, the background of our nation, the contribution of our families, what came to us because we were born where we happened to be born, and how little is left of our privilege that we earned ourselves alone! Most of our privilege is a gift. Privilege is something to be humble about.

Especially we need to be humble about what it commonly does to us, how it builds walls around us so that we are shut out from the understanding of our fellows, how it hardens our hearts when we do not know it, so that we do not feel what life means to some people, how it blinds our eyes to the real significance of the major social movements of our time. What I am saying today is Biblical, so Biblical that, were we to take this message out of the two Testaments, what would be left would be like a forest after a fire has swept through it. From prophets like Amos, crying, "Woe to them that are at ease in Zion, and to them that are secure in the mountain of Samaria, the notable men of the chief of the nations . . . they are not grieved for the affliction of Joseph," to Jesus himself, in his parable of the Last Judgment, saying, "Inasmuch as ye did it unto one of these my brethren, even these least, ye did it unto me," this message is the Bible's.

Jesus may have felt as he did about privileged people for the further reason that they have such a tremendous stake in the *status quo*. They do not want the *status quo* changed. It is treating them very well and, comfortably entwined, as they are, like a vine about its trellis, they shrink from disturbing alterations. So throughout history the privileged classes have struggled to maintain outmoded social orders and have resisted those salutary changes which afterward were applauded as the will of God.

We Americans commonly wince at phrases like "class privilege." We do not want classes in this country or any talk about class consciousness. Well, I wish there were nothing in our lives with which such phrases corresponded, but there is no use playing ostrich. We are not talking about class consciousness in Marxian terms but we need to see how prodigious a psychological and spiritual factor class consciousness is. Rich and poor, educated and uneducated, collegiate and non-collegiate, employer and employee, white and black— we all live in classes and, far more than we commonly acknowledge to ourselves, the way we look at things and pass judgment on them, the way we shape our attitudes and make our choices, is determined by our class interests and prejudices. If any man here looks honestly into his own life, he must see that. Have we not long since learned that in the face of almost any public question we can expect a practically unanimous reaction from special social groups and economic classes?

This is one of the most serious facts in our lives. It is our class position that does most of our thinking for us. Here in a great university center dedicated to the training of men in objective, impersonal, scientific deliberation, I still say *that*, for it is a towering fact. Especially on subjects affecting our interest it is our class position that does most of our thinking for us. And in particular, when our class is favored, when it receives support and distinction from the *status quo*, we are almost irresistibly tempted to mass and marshal our thought in support of it. *Most of our thinking about social questions is done, not individually or rationally, but by pressure of our class interests.*

I am far too realistic to suppose that we can altogether escape that. We cannot. But I salute certain men and women who are doing the best they know how. They are privileged. They have almost everything that gives life advantage and prestige but they know their peril. They understand that they are in danger of being imprisoned, shut up within the thoughts and attitudes that their class interests dictate. Seeing that danger, they do not propose tamely to submit to it, so you find them continually trying to put themselves into other people's places, to outflank and overpass the limitations of their class consciousness, to see the honest-to-goodness truth about social situations from an objective standpoint higher than their class prejudice affords, saying to themselves, Whatever happens to my group, let me get at the facts. That is one of the hardest things in the world for any man to do, whether he is a trades-union official or a corporation president or a college student. And any man or woman who does that even a little deserves to be saluted as one of the best citizens of the republic.

Alas, how common is the contrary attitude in history! All too typical is the scene described in our Scripture lesson!* Who were these people who, hours on end, filled the amphitheater in Ephesus with the cry, "Great is Diana of the Ephesians"? They were a special economic class, the silversmiths of the city, with their henchmen and hangers-on. They made the shrines of Diana and therefore liked the *status quo*. They did not want the worship of their goddess disturbed. All the thinking they were doing on the great question of Diana versus Christ was being done by them not as individuals but as a class, not with their minds but with their prejudices, not on the objective merits of the question but in accordance with the selfish interests of their group. How typical that is and how disastrous the consequences!

In recent years we have constantly emphasized the devastating moral results of underprivileged conditions. They can be terrific. But as one looks at history as a whole it is not the underprivileged, the whipped and beaten, who have

* Acts 19:23-41.

brought on the world its greatest evils. No! Privilege is power, and privilege consolidated in a social class is prodigious power, and the misuse of *that*, especially to sustain an unjust *status quo* grown obsolete, has been, I suspect, responsible for the worst wrongs that have cursed mankind. "He that hath ears to hear, let him hear."

These, then, I take it, were the main offenses which Jesus found in the Pharisees. We have made those Pharisees so the butt of our denunciation that we may well try to see where their fault lay. They estimated themselves on the basis of their privilege and did not see what kind of folk they really were. Protected by fortunate position, they enjoyed, said Jesus, long prayers, while widows' houses were being robbed through extortionate rents in which they profited, and they were so comfortable that they did not understand what that meant. And, finding the *status quo* friendly to their distinction and prestige, they wanted no such changes as Jesus called for. They would back up his crucifixion before permitting *that*. Do not suppose I like to put it this way. It makes the Pharisees too numerous.

Nevertheless, while this sermon may have seemed mainly negative and accusatory, at the heart of it is a great and positive philosophy of life, the ethical core of Christianity. Privilege, humbly possessed, unselfishly dedicated, perchance sacrificially renounced, is about the noblest thing in human history. Indeed, the man whom we call the Father of our country was highly privileged. It is said he had to travel seven hundred miles to encircle his vast estates, and that he left half a million dollars in his will. He was, I suspect, the most privileged person in the Colonies. In the tradition of America, Abraham Lincoln stands for what an underprivileged man can do, Washington for what can be done by privilege when it is dedicated. The Washingtons, however, are rare. To handle privilege in such a spirit is, I think, the most difficult task a son of man ever undertakes. Is there any one here who does not need to be humble and penitent about his failure in that respect? This, I take it, is indeed the ethical core of Christianity: "He that is greatest among you shall be your servant. And whosoever shall exalt himself shall be humbled; and whosoever shall humble himself shall be exalted."

When Each Man Cleans Up His Own Life

SOME one has said of Jesus that, whenever he met any one, it was as though that person were an island around which Jesus sailed until he saw where the real problem was—and then he landed. He did that with the rich young ruler and landed on the money question. He did that with the woman of Samaria and landed on the family question. He did that with Zacchæus and landed on the problem of honesty. There was a personal penetration in Jesus' dealing, a clairvoyant realism in getting at what was really the matter with the individuals he touched, which made him terrible to any one who did not wish to be brought face to face with himself.

This personal dealing one misses in many a modern church. A great setting the church may have, and numerous companies of people may come and go, but one knows that if Jesus were there one thing would immediately begin happening which is not so noticeably happening now. Were Jesus dealing with us here today, for example, we would cease being a multitude and would become individuals. He would so look at us as individuals that we could not forbear so looking at ourselves. We might resent and resist it—we probably would—but unless we ran away from him we could not escape him. Again and again he would sail around our lives until he saw where the real problem was and then he would land.

If this penetrating personal dealing is not the central business of vital religion, then what is vital religion all about? Yet for at least two reasons we habitually resent and resist it. For one thing, we do not like to be brought to grips with ourselves. An interesting revelation of human nature is presented in the chronological order in which the great sciences developed. Which science came first? Astronomy. Our first scientific knowledge concerned the things farthest away. And after that came Geology, a little closer in, the story of the ancient background of our earth; and after that Biology, somewhat closer in, the story of the world of life which has preceded us; and after that Sociology—in any scientific sense—still closer in, the story of the human setting into which our lives are born. And, last of all, emerging only yesterday, postponed for centuries by our emotions and prejudices about ourselves, making us unable or unwilling honestly to face ourselves, came Psychology. The realm farthest off came first, the realm nearest at hand—ourselves—came last. It is as though even in science men for centuries had fought against coming to grips with themselves. Look inside your own life and see if this is not a true parable of human experience. The last man any of us wants to meet, so clairvoyantly seen that his real problems stand plainly out, is himself.

For another reason we resist the penetrating personal dealing which is involved in vital religion. We often find it easier to center attention on the social applications of Christianity. That is our contemporary alibi. Our problems today, we say, are social. I can remember the time when the distinctive Christian message was intensely, unhealthily individualistic, presenting to souls a personal gospel of salvation from the world with no corresponding social gospel for the world itself. Now the shoe is on the other foot. Then it was as much as a man could do to get a hearing for the social gospel; now in some quarters it is as much as a man can do to get a hearing for the kind of personal dealing that the Master practised when he sailed around a man's life until he saw where the real problem was and then came ashore, as though to say, Whatever other responsibilities you may have, your own life is primary. I should not dare to preach the sermon I am going to preach today if you had not many times heard here the social gospel, the responsibility of Christians not only for the souls but for the societies of men, with their monstrous evils which damn souls by millions. But, my friends, Christianity is not simply a wholesale business. It is a retail business too.

Charles Kingsley was one of the pioneers and prophets of the social gospel in the nineteenth century, but once, when he was asked what kind of character he disliked most, he immediately answered, "My own." For such honest dealing with oneself, and for the cleaning up of one's own life that should come in consequence, I plead today.

If a text is called for, one is waiting in the initial and continuing message of the Master as he came into Galilee, saying, "Repent ye; for the kingdom of heaven is at hand." That is to say, just because God's kingdom is at hand, because we are at the end of an era and are living in wracked and troubled days, therefore let each man look to himself. Repent —change your mind—clean up your own life.

Consider, in the first place, the backing this emphasis receives from the obvious fact that the first responsibility of every man is himself. Whatever other responsibility John Smith has been entrusted with, first of all comes John Smith. Indeed, I venture today to preach in this regard a kind of healthy egoism. Who has not seen an unhealthy and exaggerated altruism which makes a man feel responsible for almost everybody on earth except himself? Such a man thinks he is generously caring for the world, whereas, by one of the most familiar tricks the mind plays upon itself, he really is using his care for the world at large as a place of escape from the far more exacting task of resolutely and effectively taking charge of himself.

When the Bible, Old Testament or New, proclaims healthy altruism, it couples with it healthy egoism. "Thou shalt love thy neighbor as thyself"—that is, care for yourself first; take charge of yourself first; then you have a place to start from and a standard of judgment concerning your care for your neighbor. When, on the contrary, one watches people who in their far-reaching altruism are fooling themselves, one sees that, whether or not charity begins at home, certainly character does, and that, whether or not the world at large needs to be changed, certainly these altruists need to be changed.

Ibsen, the dramatist, was interested in Brandes, the novelist, when Brandes was a youth, and Ibsen wrote to his young friend a letter with a ringing message in it which any youth might take to heart. "What I chiefly desire for you," said Ibsen, "is a genuine, full-blooded egoism, which shall force you for a time to regard what concerns you yourself as the only thing of any consequence, and everything else as non-existent. . . . There is no way in which you can benefit society more than by coining the metal you have in yourself." So!

This becomes intimately personal as I see the young men and women here. Probably no one sails around a life and sees where its real problems are more constantly than a mother. That is her chief preoccupation. When childhood is past and, with the arrival of young manhood or womanhood, you come to New York, still she goes on sailing around your life and, by intuition if she is a wise mother, knows before you do where the real problem is. Sometimes she writes me about it. She hears me over the air and, because I am in New York and you are also, she writes to me about you, and her concern is always like Ibsen's for his friend—about what is happening inside you, about what you are doing with yourself.

I had a letter recently from a man who in his youth had sailed a fishing schooner with his father in the North Atlantic. One night, he says, near the Arctic Circle, the dark came down, the fog closed in, and the seas ran high. "I was at the wheel," he writes, "doing my best to keep her on her course and my father was standing close by. He knew that we were in for a bad night. 'Well,' said my father, 'about this time the little woman at home is offering up her prayer for us to the God who holds the waves in the hollow of his hand,' and then, after a pause, he cried, 'All hands on deck, put a close reef in the mainsail and let run the jib, we have got to get that prayer answered.' "

I happen to know that prayers are being offered for some of you—parents for children, wives for husbands, husbands for wives, sometimes children for fathers and mothers—about what you are doing to yourself. I want some personal decisions made here concerning that, each man saying to his own soul, We have got to get that prayer answered!

Consider, again, the backing given to this emphasis by the fact that there is no social sin whose central responsibility is not inside individuals. Much nonsense is talked these days about social sin, as though society were a kind of organism or personality that could be of itself moral or immoral apart from the persons who compose it, whereas the fact is that all goodness and badness are first of all inside individuals and only secondarily in their relationships.

Indeed, let a sociologist speak to us about this. Professor Henry Pratt Fairchild is a progressive—I do not know that he would mind being called a radical—sociologist, and when he tries to tell us what *the* social problem is, with *the* italicized, this is what he says: "To bring such influence to bear upon every individual that he will submit tractably to the regulation that is necessary for all, and display the kind of behavior that is requisite of all, is the greatest problem that society has to face—it is *the* social problem." So, even to a sociologist the social problem concerns the kind of personal intelligence, character, and behavior we can depend upon. To be sure, we know what is meant by social sin. War is social sin, so like a tidal wave when it arises that it seems to be ordained by some evil god, but war is the outcome of the way multitudes of individuals behave. Economic evil is social sin, which like the driving dust upon the Western prairies, blasts multitudes of lives, but, after all, economic evil springs from the way multitudes of individuals behave and think.

This does not mean, of course, that, if every individual were what is called a good character, that by itself alone would solve our social problem. On the contrary, while every stone in this church is a good stone, still those stones had to be put together on right structural lines to make the church. Even if every individual on earth were a good character, we still should face the huge, exacting task of economic and international organization. In society, however, it is the living stones that must *organize themselves*, so that we are back again at our primary dependence on personal intelligence and character. Any way you get at it, Professor Fairchild is right—the social problem inheres in begetting in individuals the kind of behavior that is requisite for all.

The full recognition of this fact would demolish one of the favorite alibis of our times. Many people today look at society as though it were an organism apart from themselves, and they blame on it their personal moral failure. Were Jesus here, however, he would sail around the individual until he saw the real problem, and then would land, saying, Here and here in you are the ideas, attitudes, and immoralities, that, pooled and massed together, make every social sin there is.

Over against our contemporary alibi, which sometimes seems to say, Society is very bad and we as individuals would be lovely characters if only society would let us, I venture to paint another picture altogether. Society is not all bad. Taken as a whole, society has made amazing progress. Said one man to another, "Things are not as they used to be." "No," was the answer, "and they never were." Any one who knows history must understand that even now more individuals in America have an opportunity for a fulfilled life than probably ever was true anywhere at any time before. In Queen Elizabeth's day the average length of human life was twenty years; now the average white man of twenty has an even chance to live to be sixty-nine. That is only a parable of the way society as a whole has forged ahead and presented enlarged opportunities for life and self-fulfilment. If, therefore, one is going to personalize society at all, I would picture society as trying to struggle ahead, while the massed interior attitudes of multitudes of individuals hold it back.

Society, for example, is forging ahead toward a world community. Physically we have a world community now. Scientific inventions bind us together. Intercommunications link us into an interdependent neighborhood. Every day, more and more, mankind becomes an intermeshed and reticulated nervous system in which what happens anywhere is felt everywhere. If you ask what is keeping society back as it struggles toward a world community, the answer should be plain—the massed interior attitudes of individuals. Physically we are a neighborhood; psychologically we are not neighborly. Society has crowded us together before, as individuals, we have become fit to live together. The limits of the world community are no longer physical; they are psychological. The trouble is inside ourselves. Listen to people talk and note the littleness, the prejudice, the cynicism, the racial hatred, the nationalism. These are the barriers to a world community. Get that picture, I beseech you: society struggling to move forward and held back by the multiplied attitudes of individuals.

I cannot do for you in this regard what the Master would do if he were here. I wish I could. He came preaching the kingdom of God on earth, but he had an uncanny insight, which antedated by centuries the kind of things sociologists are learnedly saying now. Moreover, he had a strange magnetic power so that, wherever he went, he left behind him trails of individuals who had been forced to come face to face with themselves and repent because the kingdom of God was coming. I dare to hope that here today he may so deal with the consciences of some of us that we will have what our fathers used to call conviction of personal sin and conversion of personal character. If he should sail around your life, do you know where he would land?

Once more, consider the backing this emphasis receives from the fact that no social order can ever come that will relieve individuals from the necessity of cleaning up their own lives. In Thackeray's novel, *Vanity Fair,* Becky Sharp thinks that she could be a good woman on five thousand pounds a year. Many people so fool themselves, whereas any one knowing Becky Sharp would know that, put her anywhere with any income in any heavenly circumstances, and her moral problem still would be the need of a profound, radical transformation of character.

One of the earliest recollections of my boyhood is being taken by my family on a gala day to what was then called a Wonderland. I can see myself yet walking down that corridor, watching a young boy coming toward me from the other end —suspiciously wondering who he was, what he was doing there, and why he kept heading in toward me—till with a crash I ran into myself in a mirror. I have been doing that ever since, no matter what the circumstances have been— sometimes troublous and difficult, sometimes prosperous and full of opportunity—always running into myself as the decisive factor in the case. Every one does that. It is the unescapable determinant of a man's destiny, unpopular though it is to say so now.

I am not forgetting that there are millions on earth with no fair chance in life. You have often heard me talk about that aspect of the matter. Like creeping sands of the desert, which, when once they are on the move, crawl with inexorable deadliness to blot out all beauty and hope, some social situations exist against which the individual strives in vain. Such conditions one finds in city slums, but we are not in city slums. Such conditions one finds among the share-croppers, but we are not share-croppers. I am not talking to people who are absent; I am talking to people who are here. And so far as we are concerned, I venture that, taking human history on the average, not one man in a million in mankind's record has ever had any fairer chance at life than we have had. The trouble with most of us is that we keep running into ourselves in a mirror.

Many people who come to see the minister are cynical about the world. What a world! they say. How do you expect anybody to be decent or courageous or hopeful or devoted to high aims in a world like this? And as they pour out their cynicism and disgust about the world it is necessary in all honesty to say to them this unpalatable thing: You think you are telling me something about the world; you are telling me nothing about the world; the world is what it is, in some ways better, in some ways worse, than it used to be, probably in general more promising; but you are telling me a lot about yourself, about the kind of person you are and about what you are letting the world do to you because you are that kind of person. If people understood that cynicism about the world carries no news about the world at all but tells a lot of news about the cynic, they would not talk so much. As every psychologist knows, disillusioned denunciation is mostly self-revelation.

Indeed, let our imaginations run out now for a moment to that better social order in which we think it would be easier to be good. There are Utopias of escape amid whose fantasies men run away from life's reality, but there are Utopias of reconstruction, which to the builder of a better day are like the vision of the perfected statue to the sculptor as he chips the stone, or as the yet unheard harmonies of the symphony to the composer as he toils. What, then, is the distinctive quality of the better day for society of which you dream, when it will be easier to be good? Surely the essence of it is the coöperative spirit. Some day, we think, we will have a friendlier world, a finer family life, more neighborly cities, an economic order where dog-eat-dog competition will be replaced by coöperation, and no more war, because the nations will have learned to live at peace together. Is not that spirit, however you formulate its details, the essence of all our Utopias of reconstruction?

So, we think, in such a world it would be easier to be good. To be sure it would. There are souls going all to pieces now that there would have their chance. There are frustrated personalities who never get out of themselves now the best that is in them, who there would coin their precious metal into currency. There are millions of spirits crushed now who there would rise and shine. This is true. But it is only half the truth. The other half is that a world like that, so kind, so neighborly, so coöperative, would not automatically run itself, as though it were a machine. It would take marvelous personal character in multitudes of individuals—devoted, unselfish, disciplined, free from littleness and prejudice—to sustain a world like that. *The better the social order we achieve, the finer personal character will be demanded to sustain it.* As society improves, mark it, not less but more farseeing, all-inclusive, profoundly loving character will be demanded, the kind of character, that is, which you cannot get anywhere, at any time, save as individuals grapple with their own lives.

Perhaps the commonest message we hear today in this realm is that if we change circumstances we change persons. That is true but it is only half the truth. Not only is it true that if we change circumstances we change persons; it is also true that if we change persons we change circumstances. Today I am not talking to circumstances as though to say, O Circumstances, change yourselves and so change persons; but I am talking to persons, living persons, so that there is some fair chance of getting effective consequence from our meeting here, if we will take the latter half of that truth in earnest—change persons and you change circumstances.

I want some personal conversions here this morning. May the spirit of Christ, as he sails around our lives, with clairvoyant eye seeing where the problem is, be welcome when he lands!

What Christians Have Done to Christ

THROUGH Christian thought and worship in their most typical expressions runs a note of gratitude for all that Christ has done for us. Our emphasis is naturally on that. We see him as the giver, ourselves as the recipients, him as the actor, ourselves as acted on. But dare we face the other side of the story—not what Christ has done for us but what we Christians, all these centuries since he was here, have been doing to him?

What is more helpless than a man, however great he may have been, who has lived and taught and died and passed from the seen into the unseen? No sooner has he gone than, as it were, men fall upon him, the very men who were his friends and devotees. They use his name for things he never would have used it for. They represent him as thinking what he never thought. They claim his sponsorship for causes he would not have sponsored. They clothe him in garments of language and idea he would not have chosen. And what can he do? He has gone, and his memory and influence are at the mercy of those who are alive—who can use his name, while he cannot talk back, who can claim his sponsorship, while he cannot deny it. To talk, therefore, about what Christ has done for us is hardly half the story. Think what we Christians have done to him!

This process started even while he was here on earth. His contemporaries tried to make him out to be what he was not. They pictured him as a Messiah after the model of their own nationalistic expectations, and he was not that at all. They foisted on him the reputation of a miracle man, a wonder-worker, whereas he begged them to be silent even about his healings and let him be known as the teacher of spiritual life he really was. According to John's Gospel they tried to crown him as though he were an earthly king, and that was the last thing he would have chosen. Even while he lived, men tried to twist him to their purposes and claim his sponsorship for their ideas and aims. A living man can protest against such treatment and in some measure can guard against it, but when a man has passed into the unseen how helpless he is!

Remember the scene in the Prætorium when the Roman soldiers mocked him before they took him out to crucify him. Some of the items in that scene we all recall—the crown of thorns, the spitting in the face, the beating with a rod. But another item, which many forget, may well have been the cruelest of all to Christ: they "put on him a scarlet robe." What was that scarlet robe? Surely, part of the uniform of a Roman officer. They put *that* on him. Somewhere in the Prætorium they picked up the scarlet robe of a military chieftain and, putting it on the Prince of Peace, saluted him and mocked him. That was bad enough when his enemies did it, but look across the centuries and see his friends! How often they have dressed him in scarlet robes he never would have chosen!

This process springs naturally from the deep need in man's life for what the psychologists call defense mechanisms. That is to say, we choose a course of action, associate ourselves with a cause, proclaim a creed, and then, wishing to defend our position, we find that of all defenses none is more satisfying than the support of a great name. Now, of all names in the Western world, none is so potent as that of Jesus. Despite the deterioration of religion's influence, it still remains true that no name is so powerful in sponsorship as his. Everybody, therefore, has been after it. All the creeds of Christendom, bitterly irreconcilable as they are, have been proclaimed in his name. His sponsorship has been used for slavery and against it, for the divine right of kings and

against it, for superstitions like witchcraft and against them
—yes, for the liquor traffic and against it. It has been the
voucher for feudalism, for capitalism, for socialism, for an-
archism, for fascism. Pacifists put his name on their banners
and yet nineteen years ago one of the most forward-looking
of the Protestant leaders was crying: "Jesus Christ calls
his followers to the colors and . . . their response to the
call constitutes a triumph for Christianity such as the world
has never before known." One might almost say that the
sponsorship of Jesus has been used on both sides of all
questions that have arisen since he was here. It is the most
dreadful thing that has happened to him.

To be sure, in a sense it is complimentary. How incredible it seems that the little babe whose humble birth in a
manger in Palestine we celebrate at Christmas time should
today have a name so potent that all causes want it. But
while it is marvelous it is a sorry marvel, and while it is
complimentary it is a sad compliment. To what wild lengths
has this process not gone! Even the Nazis, with their bitter
anti-Semitism, must somehow claim Jesus' name, and so they
teach the doctrine that Jesus was not even by race a Jew but
an Aryan. In how many strange garments has he been forced
to walk the centuries!

A process of thought so deep-seated, springing from such
natural human motives and exhibited in so many realms,
cannot be altogether alien to us. We must be tempted to
act so too.

For one thing, consider how Christians have made of
Jesus a kind of God he never would have chosen to be.
They have dressed him in the scarlet robe of metaphysical
concepts of Deity; they have pushed him off, as in the By-
zantine frescoes, into a distant heaven, until Christ, the real
Christ who grew up in Nazareth, who taught beside the
lake, who challenged the bigotry of the priests, refused to
bend before the power of Rome, prayed in an agony of need

in the garden, and died courageously on Calvary, has been covered up in theological silks and satins. It is not his enemies who have done to him this dreadful thing; it is his friends.

Do not misunderstand me to be speaking lightly of that profound and vital matter, finding the Divine in Jesus. That is something else altogether. Indeed, one would wish to put that great matter into words not easily forgotten. Life constantly presents itself to us as a dualism, no matter what words we use to describe it by: material versus nonmaterial, physical versus spiritual, the seen versus the unseen, the metric—things, that can be weighed and measured —versus values, which no rod can measure and no scales can weigh. Behind this dualism there may be a monism. I think there is. I believe in an eternal Unity. In actual experience, however, life presents itself to us in two aspects, and when a man decides on which side of that dualism he will find the main highroad to the ultimate reality in this universe, the Creator, the Determiner of destiny, he has made the great choice in his philosophy. On it depends whether he will be a materialist, regarding all spiritual life as the fortuitous by-product of the physical, or will find in the spiritual the revelation of the eternal Unity.

On this point the choice of the New Testament is clear: "God is love; and he that abideth in love abideth in God, and God abideth in him." That is to say, God is not first of all to be thought of as throned in a distant heaven; he is disclosed here and now wherever spiritual life is present in beauty and power. Where love is, God is; where goodness is, God is. What is highest in man is deepest in the universe. On that basis of course the New Testament Christians found the Divine in Jesus. How could they help it? Where else has the spiritual life been revealed in such glory? They never said, Jesus *is* God—never. They did say, "We beheld his glory, glory as of an only begotten from a father, full of grace and truth." So say I.

Even so, Jesus was himself so human and so humble that one wonders what he would have thought had he been told the things people would some day say of him. "Why callest thou me good? none is good, save one, even God" —he said *that* once to a man who, so he thought, was over-praising him. "Not every one that saith unto me, Lord, Lord, shall enter into the kingdom of heaven; but he that doeth the will of my Father who is in heaven"—he said *that* once to those who were substituting sentimental worship for ethical fidelity. That is the sort of person he was. He never would have wanted to be the kind of God Christian theology has often made of him.

How dreadful some of it has been! If ever there was a friend of little children it was Jesus. It is no accident that Christmas is a children's festival. He made it so, not simply by his own babyhood but by his attitude toward children all his life. Yet one Christian theologian, believing in the damnation of non-elect infants, said that he doubted not there were infants not a span long crawling about the floor of hell. Think of twisting the name of Jesus to sponsor that!

If some one says that things like that are ancient history, I answer, Yes, but still we manage to get rid of the real Jesus by dressing him in ideas alien to his spirit. Statisticians reckon that there are about 682,000,000 Christians on the planet. Commenting on a similar figure, a secular journalist remarked once that he wondered where they lived. I wonder, not only where they live but how they manage to get rid of the real Jesus and to escape his ethical demands on life. Not by crucifying him! They would not do that. Not by denying him! They would not do that. Strange anomaly! They get rid of him by adoring him, by making him God, by pushing him off to some distant heaven, by thinking of him mainly over the high altar of the church, safely distant from their daily lives, by putting him into magnificent creeds the words of which Jesus himself would not know the meaning of—anything, except to face him and his demand, "Follow me." Ah, Christ, this is the saddest thing that ever happened to you and it is your friends who have done it.

Phillips Brooks once told of a missionary in Africa who, on a furlough home, bought a sundial that it might help his folk in the African village to tell the time of day. So he set it up in the midst of the village, but his people were so filled with admiration and wonder that straightway they built a roof over it to protect it from the sun and rain. Well, Christ came to help us tell the time of day, to be the revealer of what the everlasting sun is doing, that we might guide our lives thereby, and, lo! under the guise of honoring him we have built a theological roof over him. Millions of Christians could do nothing better than to get that sundial back into use again.

Consider, further, how often Christians have made Christ sponsor for social causes which he never would have sponsored. Here we must take literally that scarlet robe the soldiers put on him in the Prætorium. How they must have enjoyed that jest! He seemed to them such a whipped and beaten Jew. If any echoes of his teaching had come to them, they were full of peace and love, goodwill and humility. Doubtless he looked the part, quiet and resigned amid the boisterous soldiery. A large half of humor lies in unexpected contrast and they saw the humor of *that* scene—such a person in the scarlet robe of a Roman officer. If only we could leave the matter so, with his enemies doing that to him! But look at the centuries and see his friends putting on him a military uniform, putting his cross on their battle-flags, using his name in their battle-cries, bespeaking his sponsorship on their slaughter, until in our own lifetime we have seen that done and some of us have had a hand in it.

At first, Christians did not do that. Until well on in the

second century, to be a Christian and to be a soldier were mutually exclusive terms. There is good documentation for that statement. Was it because those earlier Christians were so near Jesus that they could not bring themselves to caricature him as a military leader? Or was it that, harshly treated under the Roman Empire, they themselves had no personal interest in fighting in its defense and so no temptation to militarize their Christ? As Christians became politically powerful, however, especially after Constantine had made the empire officially Christian, they had an interest. War became advantageous—they would have said, necessary. So they did that incredible yet inevitable thing, they made Christ the sponsor of their wars, they dragged his name over to bless their slaughterous crusades, and ever since he has been forced to march in his scarlet robe with the armies of Christendom. O Christ, your crucifixion on Calvary was nothing compared with that!

What we are thinking of now is not simply a moral but an intellectual matter. We are concerned not simply with what is right but what is true. No individual ever is healthy-minded until he gets back behind his defense mechanisms, his rationalizations, and faces reality. Neither is any church healthy-minded until it does that. And the realistic fact is that to picture Jesus in the scarlet robe of militarism is a gross misrepresentation.

The first message to the church, then, on the war question is, Take that scarlet robe off Jesus! If you say that sometimes we must go to war, very well, but take that scarlet robe off Jesus! Find, if you can, some semblance of honest argument to support your position, but do not drag his name over as sponsor of that hideous thing, all of whose causes, processes, and consequences are the utter denial of everything he stood for. Stop pretending that he is a militaristic patriot.

This thing we are trying to say, not simply about war

but about many social questions, seems to me of first-rate importance. Jesus is the great tradition in our spiritual heritage. He is to us the ideal. The sacredest memories in our personal lives are associated with his name. So, if we are capitalists we want him to be a capitalist; if we are socialists we want him to be a socialist; if we go to war we want him to go to war with us; if we have a great stake in the *status quo* we want him to sponsor the *status quo*. A strange paradox—we honor him so much that we drag him along with us to vouch for what we think and do; we adore him so highly that we make of him a rubber stamp. That is the cruelest paradox in history.

To what mad lengths it has gone! In our grandfathers' day slavery was a vested interest in the economic order. Men at one and the same time were slave owners and devout Christians. So they did that incredible thing—which yet is so inevitable that even the preacher wonders whether it is of any use to tell people not to do the like—they made Christ sponsor slavery. Listen to one of them. It is the mildest kind of thing they said. "American slavery is not only not a sin, but especially commanded by God through Moses, and approved by Christ through his Apostles."

That kind of thing is habitually going on. Throughout this congregation it is going on. Here is a person, for example, who says that he thinks Jesus has nothing to do with social questions. In view of what the real Jesus in the Gospels did and said, that seems incredible. But after long acquaintance with that type of mind, I think I see the course of thought by which the strange conclusion is arrived at. Almost always the man who thinks that Jesus has nothing to do with social questions is privileged; almost always he sits in a cushioned seat in the *status quo;* he wants what *is* made secure much more than he wants change. But, as well, he is often a devoutly earnest Christian. So he wants Christ to be the sponsor of his *status quo.* How natural that is! To that end he spiritualizes Christ until Jesus becomes in his eyes a teacher concerned only with the inner matters of the soul, with one's moods and attitudes, with one's personal virtues, with the deep resources of spiritual power, the strengthening fellowships with God, and the eternal hope. That Christ he adores. That Christ suits his personal interests. That Christ leaves undisturbed what he does not wish disturbed. How easy it is to start by adoring Christ and to end by appointing him chairman of the board of sponsors of our special interests!

Of course the realistic fact is that the Jesus of the Gospels, caring tremendously about the soul, cared in consequence tremendously about the body, which vitally affects the soul, and about social circumstances, which terribly impinge upon the soul. He made practical service to the hungry, the naked, the sick, the very test of the Judgment; he healed the ills of the body; he rose in indignation against injustice to the poor; he made what happens to personality, the whole personality, the test of any social situation he faced, and when personality was hurt he spoke out against the offender; and at the center of his gospel was the kingdom of God on earth, which, whatever else it may mean, involves another kind of social order than we have now. Were Jesus here in person—we know it well enough when we are honest with ourselves—we couldn't keep him out of the slums or stop his tongue as he spoke against our inequities and wars. Friends, we never can make the real Christ the sponsor of our special class interests.

I would almost say that the first prerequisite of a genuine revival of spiritual and ethical religion in the church is to see this and, in consequence, to stop the use of Jesus as a lay figure which we dress up in our own clothes. We need to disentangle him from the sponsorship of our accursed *status quo*, to take from him the scarlet robes we have put on him and let him be what he ought to be, the judge of our inequities, the light that shows up our darkness, our very disturbing, very challenging Lord. Were that to be done, the number of Christians would be less but their quality would be real.

Once more, consider how often we Christians have claimed Jesus as sponsor of partisanships he never would have sponsored. Even in an inclusive, interdenominational church like this, when a preacher speaks against the nationalism that splits up the world and in favor of one mankind under one God, he feels a hollowness in his own words. For the church provides a poor sounding board from which to speak of belief in a united world. The churches themselves are not united. The churches are as dissevered as are the nations. How easily the world can say to the church, "Physician, heal thyself." In the United States alone there are about two hundred different kinds of Christians, each one claiming the name of Jesus. That is the tragedy of our wretched sectarianism, not simply that it is stupid, the miserable left-over of a bygone day, or that it is wickedly wasteful, but that it maltreats the name of Jesus. It drags his name about— Baptist here, Presbyterian there, Methodist yonder, and heaven knows what else—when the realistic fact is that were he here in person he would first look on these sectarian peculiarities with bewilderment, unable to make head or tail out of them, and then, I think, would visit on them that holy scorn he poured on the ecclesiastical peccadilloes of his time.

John Wilkes was a dashing English liberal, very popular with wide areas of the people. Soon, however, his followers, calling themselves Wilkites, got out of hand and went wild, and John Wilkes had to explain, as, for example, to George III, that, as for him, he was not a Wilkite. To think we have reduced Jesus to that! For were he here, looking on our sectarian Christianity, he would say, If that is Christianity, I am not a Christian. We may not be able at once to realize our prayer for a united church but one thing we can do, we can take off from Jesus the scarlet robe of our ecclesiasticisms, we can stop identifying him with our sects. For he stands outside them all, above them all, alien to them all, lamenting over them all, praying still that they may be one.

To be sure, this temptation to twist Jesus into the support of anything which we may think or do is so strong that I suspect no Christian altogether escapes it. So Dean Sperry of Harvard says concerning Renan's *Life of Jesus* that it "is patently three parts Renan and one part Jesus." How difficult it is for any one to avoid such egoism in thinking of Christ! For we start by taking him as supremely great; therefore we wish to agree with him. When, however, we start by wanting to agree with an historic personage, it is dangerously easy to end by making him agree with us. So Carlyle, who thought of greatness in terms of heroes, made Jesus his supreme hero. So Matthew Arnold found in him the embodiment of the sweetness and light he loved at Oxford. So Tom Hughes, with his pugnacious masculinity, wrote about *The Manliness of Christ*, while Voltaire made him a supreme humanitarian after the eighteenth century model and Harnack portrayed him as a rather typical liberal Protestant of the late nineteenth century variety. How easy it is thus to look in the mirror and think we see Jesus, until, despite our protestations of faith in him, we are up to the same old game—three parts Renan, one part Jesus!

Yet there is something to be said on behalf of presenting this matter to our minds and consciences. If we really see that this is our temptation, if we recognize the ruinous consequence of it in history, we can do something to stop the worst of this twisting of Jesus to our purposes. We never would have crucified him—so we think. When Clovis, king of the Franks, first heard the story of the crucifixion, he was so moved that he cried, "If I had been there with my Franks

I would have avenged his wrong." We sympathize with that. But, friends, the crucifixion did Jesus no harm. He handled that magnificently. He made that the most impressive spiritual force in human history. What has well-nigh spoiled what Jesus tried to do is not the cross. It is the way his friends have misused his name. Remember Shakespeare's lines:

Who steals my purse steals trash; 'tis something, nothing;
'Twas mine, 'tis his, and has been slave to thousands;
But he that filches from me my good name
Robs me of that which not enriches him
And makes me poor indeed.

My soul, discover, if you can, the real Christ. Take that scarlet robe off him. Even of the soldiers in the Prætorium it is written that after they had mocked him they put his own raiment on him. If his friends would do as much, then men might see his quality of spirit, his way of life, his vision of truth, for the lack of which the world is sick and to bring which to the world the church was founded.

The Church Must Go Beyond Modernism

IF WE are successfully to maintain the thesis that the
church must go beyond modernism, we must start by
seeing that the church had to go as far as modernism.
Fifty years ago, a boy seven years of age was crying himself to
sleep at night in terror lest, dying, he should go to hell, and
his solicitous mother, out of all patience with the fearful
teachings which brought such apparitions to the mind, was
trying in vain to comfort him. That boy is preaching to you
today and you may be sure that to him the achievements of
Christian modernism in the last half century seem not only
important but indispensable.

Fifty years ago the intellectual portion of Western civilization had turned one of the most significant mental corners in
history and was looking out on a new view of the world.
The church, however, was utterly unfitted for the appreciation of that view. Protestant Christianity had been officially
formulated in prescientific days. The Augsburg Confession
was a notable statement but the men who drew it up, in-
cluding Luther himself, did not even believe that the earth
goes round the sun. The Westminster Confession, for the
rigorous acceptance of which the Presbyterian rear-guard
still contends, was a memorable document but it was written
forty years before Newton published his work on the law of
gravitation. Moreover, not only were the mental patterns of
Protestant Christianity officially formulated in prescientific
days but, as is always true of religion, those patterns were
sacred to their believers and the changes forced by the new
science seemed impious and sacrilegious.

Youths like myself, therefore, a half century ago faced an
appalling lag between our generation's intellect on one side

and its religion on the other, with religion asking us to believe incredible things. Behind his playfulness the author of *Through the Looking Glass* had this serious matter in mind when he represented the White Queen as saying to Alice, "I'm just one hundred and one, five months and a day." Said Alice, "I can't believe *that!*" Said the Queen pityingly, "Can't you? Try again: draw a long breath, and shut your eyes." So the church seemed to be speaking to us.

Modernism, therefore, came as a desperately needed way of thinking. It insisted that the deep and vital experiences of the Christian soul with itself, with its fellows, with its God, could be carried over into this new world and understood in the light of the new knowledge. We refused to live bifurcated lives, our intellect in the late nineteenth century and our religion in the early sixteenth. God, we said, is a living God who has never uttered his final word on any subject; why, therefore, should prescientific frameworks of thought be so sacred that forever through them man must seek the Eternal and the Eternal seek man? So we said, and, thanks to modernism, it became true of many an anxious and troubled soul in our time that, as Sam Walter Foss expressed it,

> He saw the boundless scheme dilate,
> In star and blossom, sky and clod;
> And as the universe grew great,
> He dreamed for it a greater God.

The church thus had to go as far as modernism but now the church must go beyond it. For even this brief rehearsal of its history reveals modernism's essential nature; it is primarily an adaptation, an adjustment, an accommodation of Christian faith to contemporary scientific thinking. It started by taking the intellectual culture of a particular period as its criterion and then adjusted Christian teaching to that standard. Herein lies modernism's tendency toward shallowness and transiency; arising out of a temporary intellectual crisis, it took a special type of scientific thinking as standard and became an adaptation to, a harmonization with, the intellectual culture of a particular generation. That, however, is no adequate religion to represent the Eternal and claim the allegiance of the soul. Let it be a modernist who says that to you! Unless the church can go deeper and reach higher than that it will fail indeed.

In the first place, modernism has been excessively preoccupied with intellectualism. Its chosen problem has been somehow to adjust Christian faith to the modern intellect so that a man could be a Christian without throwing his reason away. Modernism's message to the church has been after this fashion: When, long ago, the new music came, far from clinging to old sackbuts and psalteries, you welcomed the full orchestra and such composers as Palestrina, Bach, Beethoven, to the glory of God; when the new art came you did not refuse it but welcomed Cimabue, Giotto, Raphael, and Michelangelo, to the enrichment of your faith; when the new architecture came, far from clinging to primitive catacombs or the old Romanesque, you greeted the Gothic with its expanded spaces and aspiring altitudes; so now, when the new science comes, take that in too, and, however painful the adaptations, adjust your faith to it and assimilate its truths into your Christian thinking.

Surely, that has been a necessary appeal but it centers attention on one problem only—intellectual adjustment to modern science. It approaches the vast field of man's experience and need head first, whereas the deepest experiences of man's soul, whether in religion or out of it, cannot be approached head first. List as you will the soul's deepest experiences and needs—friendship, the love that makes a home, the enjoyment of music, delight in nature, devotion to moral causes, the practise of the presence of God—it is obvious that, whereas, if we are wise, we use our heads on them, nevertheless we do not approach them mainly head first, but

[155]

heart first, conscience first, imagination first. A man is vastly greater than his logic, and the sweep and ambit of his spiritual experience and need are incalculably wider than his rational processes. So modernism, as such, covers only a segment of the spiritual field and does not nearly compass the range of religion's meaning.

Indeed, the critical need of overpassing modernism is evident in the fact that our personal spiritual problems do not lie there any more. When I was a student in the seminary, the classrooms where the atmosphere grew tense with excitement concerned the higher criticism of the Bible and the harmonization of science and religion. That, however, is no longer the case. The classrooms in the seminary where the atmosphere grows tense today concern Christian ethics and the towering question whether Christ has a moral challenge that can shake this contemporary culture to its foundations and save us from our deadly personal and social sins. So the world has moved far to a place where mere Christian harmonizers, absorbed with the intellectual attempt to adapt faith to science and accommodate Christ to prevalent culture, seem trivial and out of date. Our modern world, as a whole, cries out not so much for souls intellectually adjusted to it as for souls morally maladjusted to it, not most of all for accommodators and adjusters but for intellectual and ethical challengers.

When Paul wrote his first letter to the Corinthians, he said that he had become a Jew to the Jews that he might win the Jews, and he intimated that he had become a Greek to the Greeks that he might win the Greeks. "I am become," he said, "all things to all men, that I may by all means save some." That is a modernistic passage of adjustment and accommodation. But that is not all Paul said. Had it been all, Paul would have sunk from sight in an indistinguishable blend with the Greco-Roman culture of his day and we should never have heard of him. When he wrote the second time to the Corinthians he said something else:

> Come ye out from among them, and be ye separate,
> saith the Lord,
> And touch no unclean thing.

Church of Christ, take that to yourself now! Stop this endeavor to harmonize yourself with modern culture and customs as though they were a standard and criterion. Rather, come out from among them. Only an independent standing-ground from which to challenge modern culture can save either it or you.

In the second place, not only has modernism been thus predominantly intellectualistic and therefore partial, but, strange to say, at the same time it has been dangerously sentimental. The reason for this is easy to explain. One of the predominant elements in the intellectual culture of the late nineteenth and early twentieth centuries, to which modernism adjusted itself, was illusory belief in inevitable progress. So many hopeful and promising things were afoot that two whole generations were fairly bewitched into thinking that every day in every way man was growing better and better. Scientific discovery, exploration and invention, the rising tide of economic welfare, the spread of democracy, the increase of humanitarianism, the doctrine of evolution itself, twisted to mean that automatically today has to be better than yesterday and tomorrow better than today—how many elements seduced us in those romantic days into thinking that all was right with the world!

In the intellectual culture to which modernistic Christianity adapted itself, such lush optimism was a powerful factor, and the consequences are everywhere present in the natural predispositions of our thought today. In the little village of Selborne, England, the visitor is shown some trees planted by a former minister near his dwelling, so that he might be spared the view of the village slaughter-house. Those trees are suggestive and symbolic of the sentimental illusions we plant to hide from our eyes the ugly facts of life. Especially we modernistic Christians, dealing, as we were, with thoughts of a kindly God by evolution lifting everything and everybody up, were deeply tempted to live in a fool's paradise behind our lovely trees!

For example, modernistic Christianity largely eliminated from its faith the God of moral judgment. To be sure, in the old theology, the God of moral judgment had been terribly presented so that little children did cry themselves to sleep at night for fear of him and of his hell. Modernism, however, not content with eliminating the excrescences of a harsh theology, became softer yet and created the general impression that there is nothing here to fear at all. One of the most characteristic religious movements of the nineteenth century heralded this summary of faith:

> The Fatherhood of God.
> The Brotherhood of Man.
> The Leadership of Jesus.
> Salvation by Character.
> The Progress of Mankind—
> onward and upward forever.

Well, if that is the whole creed, this is a lovely world with nothing here to dread at all.

But there *are* things here to dread. Ask the physicians. They will tell us that in a law-abiding world are stern conditions whose fulfilment or non-fulfilment involve bodily destiny. Ask the novelists and dramatists, and at their best they are not lying to us as they reveal the inexorable fatality with which character and conduct work out their implied consequence. Ask the economists. They will tell us there are things to dread which lead to an inevitable economic hell. Ask even the historians and they will talk at times like old preachers about the God of moral judgment, as James

Anthony Froude did when he said, "One lesson, and only one, history may be said to repeat with distinctness: that the world is built somehow on moral foundations; that, in the long run, it is well with the good; in the long run, it is ill with the wicked."

Indeed, cannot we use our own eyes to see that there are things here to fear? For this is no longer the late nineteenth and early twentieth centuries. This is the epoch after the first world war shook the earth to its foundations, and the God of judgment has spoken. My soul, what a world, which the gentle modernism of my younger ministry, with its kindly sentiments and limitless optimism, does not fit at all! We must go beyond that. Because I know that I am speaking here to many minds powerfully affected by modernism, I say to you as to myself: Come out of these intellectual cubicles and sentimental retreats which we built by adapting Christian faith to an optimistic era. Underline this: *Sin is real.* Personal and social sin is as terribly real as our forefathers said it was, no matter how we change their way of saying so. And it leads men and nations to damnation as they said it did, no matter how we change their way of picturing it. For these are times, real times, of the kind out of which man's great exploits have commonly been won, in which, if a man is to have a real faith he must gain it from the very teeth of dismay; if he is to have real hope, it must shine, like a Rembrandt portrait, from the dark background of fearful apprehension; if he is to have real character, he must achieve it against the terrific down-drag of an antagonistic world; and if he is to have a real church, it must stand out from the world and challenge it, not be harmonized with it.

In the third place, modernism has even watered down and thinned out the central message and distinctive truth of religion, the reality of God. One does not mean by that, of course, that modernists are atheists. One does mean, however, that the intellectual culture of the late nineteenth and

[159]

early twentieth centuries, to which modernism adjusted itself, was predominantly man-centered. Man was blowing on
his hands and doing such things at such a rate as never had
been done or dreamed on earth before. Man was pioneering
new truth and building a new social order. You young people
who were not here then can hardly imagine with what cheer-
ful and confident trust we confided to man the saving of the
world. So the temptation was to relegate God to an advisory
capacity, as a kind of chairman of the board of sponsors of
our highly successful human enterprise. A poet like Swinburne could even put the prevailing mood into candid words:

Thou art smitten, thou God, thou art smitten; thy death is upon
  thee, O Lord.
And the love-song of earth as thou diest resounds through the
  wind of her wings—
Glory to Man in the highest! for Man is the master of things.

Look out on the world today and try, if you can, to repeat
those words of Swinburne and still keep your face straight!
At any rate, if ever I needed something deeper to go on
than Swinburne's sentimental humanism, with man as the
master of things, it is now—a philosophy, namely, a profound philosophy about what is ultimately and eternally real
in this universe. We modernists were so disgusted with the
absurdities of the old supernaturalistic theology that we
were commonly tempted to visit our distaste on theology as
a whole and throw it away. But theology means thinking about
the central problem of existence—what is ultimately and
eternally real in this universe. And in the lurid light of days
like these it becomes clearer, as an increasing number of
atheists are honestly saying, that if the eternally real is merely
material, if the cosmos is a physical fortuity and the earth
an accident, if there is no profounder reason for mankind's
being here than just that at one stage in the planet's cooling
the heat happened to be right, and if we ourselves are "the
disease of the agglutinated dust," then to stand on this tem-

porary and accidental earth in the face of this vast cosmos and try lyrically to sing,

> Glory to Man in the highest! for Man is the master of things,

is an absurd piece of sentimental tomfoolery. And because I have been and am a modernist it is proper that I should confess that often the modernistic movement, adjusting itself to a man-centered culture, has encouraged this mood, watered down the thought of the Divine, and, may we be forgiven for this, left souls standing, like the ancient Athenians, before an altar to an Unknown God!

On that point the church must go beyond modernism. We have been all things to all men long enough. We have adapted and adjusted and accommodated and conceded long enough. We have at times gotten so low down that we talked as though the highest compliment that could be paid Almighty God was that a few scientists believed in him. Yet all the time, by right, we had an independent standing-ground and a message of our own in which alone is there hope for humankind. The eternally real is the spiritual. The highest in us comes from the deepest in the universe. Goodness and truth and beauty are not accidents but revelations of creative reality. God is! On that point come out from among them and be ye separate! As the poet imagined Paul saying:

> Whoso has felt the Spirit of the Highest
> cannot confound nor doubt Him nor deny:
> yea with one voice, o world, tho' thou deniest,
> Stand thou on that side, for on this am I.

Finally, modernism has too commonly lost its ethical standing-ground and its power of moral attack. It is a dangerous thing for a great religion to begin adjusting itself to the culture of a special generation. Harmonizing slips easily into compromising. To adjust Christian faith to the new astronomy, the new geology, the new biology, is absolutely indispensable. But suppose that this modernizing process, well started, goes on and Christianity adapts itself to contemporary nationalism, contemporary imperialism, contemporary capitalism, contemporary racialism—harmonizing itself, that is, with the prevailing social *status quo* and the common moral judgments of our time—what then has become of religion, so sunk and submerged in undifferentiated identity with this world?

This lamentable end of a modernizing process, starting with indispensable adaptations and slipping into concession and compromise, is a familiar phenomenon in religious history. For the word "modernism" may not be exclusively identified with the adjustment of Christian faith and practise to the culture of a single era. Modernization is a recurrent habit in every living religion. Early Protestantism, itself, emerging along with a new nationalism and a new capitalism, was in its day modernism, involving itself and us in entanglements and compliances with political and economic ideas in whose presence we still are tempted to be servile. Every era with powerful originative factors in it evokes from religion indispensable adaptations, followed by further concessive acquiescences, which in time must be superseded and outgrown. Early Christianity went out from an old Jewish setting into a new Greek culture and never would have survived if it had not assimilated into its faith the profound insights of Greek philosophy. So in the classic creeds, like that of Nicæa, we have a blending of the old faith with the new philosophy, and in that process John and Paul themselves had already played a part. But, alas, early Christianity in its adjustment of its faith to Greek culture did not stop with adaptation to the insights of philosophy. At last it adapted itself to Constantine, to the licentious court, to war, to the lucrative enjoyment of imperial favors, to the use of bloody persecutions to coerce belief. One after another, it threw away the holiest things that had been entrusted to it by its Lord until, often hardly distinguishable from the culture it lived in, it nearly modernized itself into moral futility. Lift up that history, as it were a mirror, in which to see the peril of our American churches.

It is not in Germany alone that the church stands in danger of being enslaved by society. There the enslavement is outward, deliberate, explicit, organized. Here it is secret, quiet, pervasive, insidious. A powerful culture—social, economic, nationalistic, militaristic—impinging from every side upon the church, cries with persuasive voices, backed by all the sanctions and motives most urgent to the self-interest of man, Adjust yourself, adapt yourself, accommodate yourself!

When Great Britain was as mad about the Boer War as Italy is mad today about the Ethiopian War and all the forces of propaganda had whipped up the frenzy of the people to a fever heat, John Morley one night in Manchester faced an indignant, antagonistic crowd, and pleaded with his countrymen against the war. This in part is what he said: "You may carry fire and sword into the midst of peace and industry: it will be wrong. A war of the strongest government in the world with untold wealth and inexhaustible reserves against this little republic will bring you no glory: it will be wrong. You may make thousands of women widows and thousands of children fatherless: it will be wrong. It may add a new province to your empire: *it will still be wrong.*" John Morley did not call himself a Christian. He called himself an agnostic. But he was far nearer standing where Christ intended his church to stand than the church has often been.

We modernists had better talk to ourselves like this. So had the fundamentalists—but that is not our affair. We have already largely won the battle we started out to win; we have adjusted the Christian faith to the best intelligence of our day and have won the strongest minds and the best abilities of the churches to our side. Fundamentalism is still with us but mostly in the backwaters. The future of the

[163]

churches, if we will have it so, is in the hands of modernism. Therefore let all modernists lift a new battle cry: We must go beyond modernism! And in that new enterprise the watchword will be not, Accommodate yourself to the prevailing culture! but, Stand out from it and challenge it! For this unescapable fact, which again and again in Christian history has called modernism to its senses, we face: we cannot harmonize Christ himself with modern culture. What Christ does to modern culture is to challenge it.

Why Worship?

TO BEGIN with, here are two or three quotations from prominent modern intellectuals, which, to say the least, strike one as queer. Professor Wieman of the University of Chicago says about worship, "There is no other form of human endeavor by which so much can be accomplished." Professor Hocking of Harvard, speaking of the finest things in human experience, such as recreation, friendship, love, beauty, says in italics, *"Worship is the whole which includes them all."* And Professor Tawney of the University of Illinois exclaims about worship, "It is indeed so important that one finds oneself sometimes wondering how any of us can afford to do anything but educate ourselves in this art." Even here in a service of Christian devotion, such words from philosophers sound extreme and strange. Can it be that worship is as important as all this?

To be sure, the Bible is full of it, from the Old Testament's typical call, "O magnify the Lord with me, and let us exalt his name together," to great passages in the New Testament proclaiming God as Spirit, so that "they that worship him must worship in spirit and in truth." Moreover, man everywhere appears as a worshiping creature. Some of us have prayed with Buddhists in their temples, bowed with Confucianists in their shrines, knelt with Moslems in their mosques, worshiped many a time in synagogues, and with all sorts of Christians have shared devotion. What does all this mean? Why do people worship? What does it do? It must do something.

Thinking of worship in its primitive forms, one may give it a primitive explanation and with the skeptical Latins say, *Timor deos fecit*—Fear made the gods. That, however, does not cover the case. Worship is like agriculture, in primitive days primitively carried on but so universal and indispensable that the most modern and sophisticated societies cannot outgrow it. "Fear made the gods" may explain some worshipers, but not President Eliot of Harvard, remembering the days when Phillips Brooks conducted worship in the university chapel and saying, "Prayer is the greatest achievement of the human soul." Can it be that worship is as important as that?

We do not treat it so. We Christians, who occasionally or even customarily are found in the sanctuary, do not take worship so seriously as *that*. As for the world outside, few practises seem to the average man farther from the vital centers of human need or less applicable to the critical problems of mankind's peril. Yet, here today we are worshiping, while men of intellectual light and leading say that there is no other form of human endeavor by which so much can be accomplished. How can this be?

Let us confess that many people, some of whom are doubtless here, get little or nothing out of worshiping. The reasons are not far to seek. For one thing, while such folk come to church, they may not worship. A prevalent American disease has been called "spectatoritis." We go to see football games played, but do not play ourselves; to hear dramas performed, but do not share in the performance. In one realm after another we are only spectators. So in church we watch the ministers and the choir indulge in prayer and praise. Thus to go to church is an external act, but genuinely to worship—to be lifted by the companionship of kindred and aspiring souls until the spiritual tides rise within, and reefs and sandbars which lower moods could not surmount are overpassed and the soul sails out into God's great deep—is an inward, creative experience. Many receive little or nothing from their formal devotions because they suffer from spectatoritis.

Others receive little from what they call worshiping because they do not fulfil the serious conditions for receiving anything. They saunter in, saunter through, saunter out. Great things, however, are greatly arrived at. We cannot saunter in to a Beethoven symphony, saunter through, and saunter out, or, if we do, it will amount to nothing. One of our leading psychologists tells of a country boy, unversed in music, who, coming to live in Boston, early in his stay attended a concert by the Symphony Orchestra. It meant nothing to him. It might as well have been produced by tom-toms and harmonicas for all he received from it. Yet around him he saw people to whom such music was like the breath of life, and he determined that if music could mean so much to others he would find the secret of it for himself. For a full season, therefore, he attended the concerts of the orchestra, each evening taking with him a musical friend. Gradually the light began to break, some here, some there, until a new world opened up before that youth, a marvelous world of which he is now the grateful citizen, and which he might easily have missed. He took music seriously enough to fulfil the conditions of understanding and of enjoying it. Do we suppose that we can worship the Most High God in spirit and in truth on lesser terms?

Furthermore, many receive little from their worshiping and are discouraged concerning it because they expect a unanimous record of success. That, however, is too much to expect. James Russell Lowell once entered a European cathedral and had a high experience there, which in his poem, "The Cathedral," he has made immortal. Even to James Russell Lowell, however, that did not always happen. Once in Switzerland I climbed the Rigi. It was a foggy day upon the summit; we could not see fifty feet. Is the Rigi, then, a failure? If you have ever been there when the day was clear and the vast horizons opened up their unforgettable panorama of majesty and beauty, you know that it is worth climbing the Rigi many times to get that view once. So to any soul worship is not always a success, but he who knows what can happen when the great hours come and the amplitudes of the spiritual life are open to one's vision, knows that its consequence is worth habitual continuance and patient waiting.

Well, this is the question: Is worship a realm of experience so supremely important? What is it, indeed, that we are looking for in worship? With multitudes of people the very nub of the problem lies there—they do not even know what they are looking for when they are worshiping.

In the first place, in worship we are reminded of values that the world makes us forget. The word itself means worthship, the recognition and appreciation of real worth. In this sense we all do inevitably and habitually worship, but see what the casual secular world does to this process in us! It puts first things last and last things first, makes the great seem small and the small great, often holds a penny so close to the eye that we cannot see the sun, and every day magnifies the transient and carnal at the expense of the abiding and spiritual, until our sense of worth is twisted and awry. Often in hours like that, when one can hardly tell what one is living for, one knows why the Psalmist cried, "My soul longeth, yea, even fainteth for the courts of the Lord." We do desperately need to be brought face to face with the Most High and there reminded of the real worths that this world makes us forget.

All this has been specially vivid to me since, some years ago, I visited the Orient. At home I had taken services of Christian worship for granted. They were as much a part of life as the hills and trees. In the Orient, however, I reached places where one could not take for granted an assembly of Christian people, meeting together in kindling aspiration and praise. I never shall forget, after returning home, the first stirring service of great worship. I felt like a branch, long fallen from a bonfire and well-nigh gone out, that now had been thrown back into the community of conflagration and had caught fire again. On a recent Sunday morning a missionary family spoke with me here. They had been seven years on a lonely outpost station and now, home on furlough, they had been attending their first service of worship. They were in tears. Once more to feel the assembly of the church around them and the "joy of united reverence," once more in a fellowship to be reminded of the high things that a man ought not to forget, was to them a renewing experience.

Recently one of our city's clergymen created a sensation by suggesting a moratorium on preaching. Probably he will not get it. It may be he would not like it if he did, but I think I know what he is driving at. He is concerned because the great multitude of our Christian people do not really worship. They must have some one forever talking to them. They do not know how to make high use of the power and joy of united reverence. His concern was justified.

Here in this church we are at work seven days and nights a week. On an average, ten thousand people enter our doors each week. We have only one sermon. That is not overdoing preaching—thirty-five minutes of it in a week. I am not sure, however, that we are getting what we planned to get when we so arranged it—the worship of the people in the services where there is no preaching. I am concerned about you. Do not try to tell me that you do not need to worship. I know you too well. I know this city too well. You deeply need to be reminded of high and Christian things that the world makes you commonly forget.

In the second place, in worship one is carried far enough away from the close-ups of daily life so that one can see the horizons around his living and thus, reorienting himself, regain his sense of direction. Canon Streeter of Oxford said recently, "The greatest need of mankind today—socially and individually—is a true sense of direction." One does not go about achieving that merely by working harder, as though,

[169]

lost in a fog, a boat tried to get its bearings by driving about more furiously. Nor does one get it by thinking more meticulously, as though, faced out of countenance already by the immediacies of this troubled time, we put our minds still more closely on them and analyzed them further. If we are lost in the woods, the one thing we must seek first is altitude. We must find a hill, if we can, and on it a high tree, but somehow we must get altitude so that around the confusing close-up of the woods we can see horizons and perspectives. Recovering the sense of direction is always a matter of elevation and vision.

Who does not need *that* today in his spiritual life? The canyons of these city streets sometimes become to us unbearable; the pressure and tension of their noisy restlessness we cannot endure. We must away where there are distance and altitude, sky and horizon. So one lives with the terrific problems of our time—personal and social, economic and international—until the whole world seems mad and all its ways incoherently insane. But coming, it may be, into a service of great worship, see what may happen to a spirit so confused! "O God, who art, and wast, and art to come, before whose face the generations rise and pass away"— what a world of long distances and vast horizons this is! The world speaks no such language.

> Before the mountains were brought forth,
> Or ever thou hadst formed the earth and the world,
> Even from everlasting to everlasting, thou art God!

So the transient and temporal are not all; the insanities of man many a time have reared themselves against the Most High, and still the Most High he is. "While we look not at the things which are seen, but at the things which are not seen: for the things which are seen are temporal; but the things which are not seen are eternal." So one can know the east from the west and the north from the south and take up his way again. "Strengthened with power through his Spirit in the inward man"—so there are resources which can enable one to carry on.

Forgive me if I make the matter seem easier than it really is. I know that effectively entering into worship and getting from it large consequence is not simple. There are many difficulties, theoretical and practical, in the conduct of public worship, which keep even the intelligent from understanding and the spiritual from profiting. We have to use symbolism, for example, and symbolism becomes obsolete and for many loses meaning. Nevertheless, do not miss a major matter because of a minor difficulty. You need spiritual altitude. Almost more than anything else in the world, for your living, day by day, you need spiritual altitude. And the casual secular world does not supply it, but rather bears you down with its externalisms and vicissitudes. As you care for your soul, therefore, have a hill to climb—a familiar hill habitually climbed—from which returning, to face once more the wrath of devils and the scorn of men, the great affirmations of the faith echo in your heart: "Therefore will not we fear, though the earth be removed, and though the mountains be carried into the midst of the sea. . . . The Lord of hosts is with us; the God of Jacob is our refuge."

In the third place, worship is an experience that rebukes the evil in one's life. Out in the world it is dangerously easy to get by with one's conscience. There are plenty of other people living worse lives than we are. There is ample moral darkness in which the gray shades of our compromises and surrenders do not show up. We are pretty good out in the world. But let a man really worship and his worse self comes face to face with his better self, and his better self comes face to face with something better still. That is a humbling experience without which there is no spiritual health. No man can be his best unless he stands over and over again in the presence of that which is superior to his best.

To be sure, the relationship of worship to the good life is not simple. Worship has often been used as a substitute for righteousness, as though God could be placated by pious observances and flattering praise. Alongside those passages in the Bible, therefore, where worship is exalted, one must in all honesty put others where it is vehemently condemned: Isaiah, crying against his people's ritual observances amid their cruel social injustices, and, saying in the name of God, "Who hath required this at your hand, to trample my courts?"; Micah, drawing his appalling picture of the worship of his day, saying in contrast, "What doth the Lord require of thee, but to do justly, and to love kindness, and to walk humbly with thy God?"; Jesus, saying, "If therefore thou art offering thy gift at the altar, and there rememberest that thy brother hath aught against thee, leave there thy gift before the altar, and go thy way, first be reconciled to thy brother, and then come and offer thy gift."

If any one here needs that kind of message, let him take it! Of all substitutes for a good life, worship is the most superstitious and hypocritical. "Be not deceived; God is not mocked" by empty hymns, anthems, and prayers. I suspect, however, that that kind of message is not the prime need of most of us. Who here commonly practises worship as a substitute for a good life? The realistic fact is that the modern man does not worship much at all.

At times, therefore, I should like to appeal to Jesus against the universal application of his own words. I think he would understand my meaning. Lord, I would plead, you say that if I come to worship at the altar and there remember that my brother hath aught against me, I am to leave my worshiping, first go be reconciled with my brother, and then come and worship. But I beg of you, let me worship a little first! For this man you call my brother I do not like. I am not sure I wish to be reconciled with him. He has wronged me, and I hate him. I cannot blow on my hands and go out to be reconciled with him. Something transforming must happen within me before I can do that. Let me worship a little first! For if I could worship until I saw myself so needing to be forgiven that I should be willing to forgive, if I could worship until I saw you upon your cross, even there forgiving, if I could be lifted a little above the rancor and vindictiveness of common moods, until pity for our kindred human frailty grew real to me and the love of God were shed abroad in my heart, then I might go out and be reconciled to my brother. Let me worship a little first!

The other day a man sent $12,000 to the United States Government in payment of duty on goods he had smuggled in. Why did he do that after he had gotten safely away with his theft? I happen to know about that—he had been worshiping. Once a journalist in this city checked out on a Sunday morning from his hotel with only a little money in his pocket, and, buying a deadly poison at a drugstore, started for the park to take it and die. But passing a church and seeing a crowd waiting, his journalistic curiosity was so aroused that he entered, and, to his astonishment, found himself being lifted by the worship of the congregation. When he went out he poured the poison down the nearest manhole, took a new grip on life, and a week later, his battle for a new character and a new career well started, he came to tell me about it. As he went out from that rememberable interview, I recall thinking that, after all, the poets are often wiser than the cynics, and that more things are wrought by prayer than this world dreams of.

Finally, worship is an experience that rededicates life and so releases its power. You must have felt, as I have, that such a theme as we are dealing with runs so counter to the powerful drift and tendency of our time that it is hard to make headway with it in our thinking, and harder yet in our living. All the more because of this powerful, antagonistic drift, we need to apprehend the import of our truth. Professor Hocking is right in saying that all man's life can be reduced to two aspects, work and worship—what we do ourselves, and what we let the higher than ourselves do to us; what we actively labor at, and what we receptively are enriched by, what we are aggressive about, and what we are spiritually hospitable to; what belongs to us because we achieve it, and what we belong to because it has mastered our loyalties. This boat of human life is rowed with two oars—work and worship—and the trouble with many of us is that we are rowing with one oar, and, going around in circles in consequence, are getting nowhere.

If any of us are finding in life radiant meaning and clear direction, then somewhere, somehow, we have found values, greater than ourselves, to which we belong and our loyalty to which emancipates our powers. If some one says that this experience came to him outside the church, very well! The church's worship is the endeavor to make easily and habitually available to all the people the liberating experience for which we plead, and while Isaiah had his in the temple, Jesus had his alike in the temple and on Galilean hillsides. Be sure of this, however, he who knows only the work side of life is a slave; it is worship, wherever you find it, that gives life elevation, emancipation, and release.

When we deal with the physical world, we grow great by the things we master. We say to this material power, Go, and it goes; and to that, Come, and it comes; and we grow powerful thereby. But when we deal with the spiritual world, we grow great by the things that master us, by the goodness, beauty, and truth that lay hold on us and to which we loyally belong. That experience is the essence of worship.

To be sure, there are modern endeavors to explain worshiping in terms of pathological psychology. When men grow weary of the gross and realistic world, so this explanation runs, they escape to the imagination of a superearthly world where all is right and God is love and goodness is triumphant, and in that visionary world of fiction and fantasy they find retreat from the too hard realism of their actual existence. To this I say in answer, Granted that worship, like everything else, can be perverted; granted that it can be pathologically misused. The Bible often grows fiery with blazing denunciations of that. But when a man like Isaiah goes into the temple, sees the Lord there high and lifted up, finds there the great loyalty to which his life belongs, and, saying, "Here am I; send me," comes out again to live one of the supreme lives of history, that and the reduplication of that across the centuries, in the supreme characters and careers of service, cannot be explained in terms of pathology—or, if it can, then may God make us all sick, for there is nothing this world needs much more! We verily are sick for the lack of this thing we have been pleading for, sick with complacency over things, sick with satisfaction concerning our technological mastery of material, sick for the lack of reverence toward things that ought to be revered, of adoration toward things that should be adored, of loyalty toward things alone worth living for.

Can it be that still this truth of which we have been speaking seems irrelevant to some? Some of us cannot live without great music, but there are others to whom it is irrelevant. Some of us cannot live without great books and the magnificence and loveliness of nature, but there are others to whom they are irrelevant. Some of us cannot live without great worship, but there are others to whom that is irrelevant too. Yet what a commentary such irrelevances are! "O magnify the Lord with me, and let us exalt his name together."

Putting Great Horizons Around Christianity

FIVE words in the New Testament especially demand the attention of Christians in our day—"The field is the world." They are among the most astonishing words ever ascribed to Jesus. For he was reared in a humble home in the small town of Nazareth, in his lifetime he had no wide influence, he was permitted only a few months of public ministry, and he was slain at thirty-three. Yet here stands his affirmation that the world needs his message and, what is more, that his message needs the world in which to operate. It is astonishing.

Astonishing also is the history of these words across the centuries. When first they were spoken, the world in view was the Roman Empire and Christianity took that as its field. Then came the barbarian invasions. The heathen hordes became terribly real and Christianity took up the challenge. Columba, Ansgar, Boniface, Augustine, Patrick went north with the gospel, and our fathers in the forests heard for the first time the story of Christ, until all Europe was covered with the institutions of Christianity. There, however, the expansion of the Christian movement paused. Mohammedanism had thrust its adamantine barrier across all the trade routes into Asia, and there was no way through. Then suddenly, as with a magic key, the mariner's compass unlocked the long closed doors. All Christendom waked up. Columbus sailed west; Vasco da Gama rounded the Cape of Good Hope to India. "The field is the world," said the Jesuits, pioneering America. "The field is the world," said Saint Francis Xavier as, in one of the most adventurous lives in history, he carried the gospel, as he understood it, to India and Japan.

That same Francis Xavier and John Calvin had been students at the University of Paris at the same time, and when Xavier, the Catholic, went to the Orient, John Calvin, the Protestant, went to Geneva and helped to turn Europe upside down with his reforming doctrine. At first Protestantism was completely preoccupied at home. The struggle for self-preservation was so furious that there was no strength left for distant propagation. But at last Protestantism had standing-ground under it and before it stretched the world untouched by its message. The first voices of the new day were few and hesitant, almost drowned out, but they gathered power and volume until, with an inward propulsion not to be denied, the missionary expansion of Protestantism started and Carey went to India, Judson to Burma, Paton to the New Hebrides, Morrison to China, Livingstone to Africa, and the field was indeed the world.

In our day, however, there has come another pause in the expansion of world-wide Christianity. Millions of people in our Protestant churches no longer feel the force of the old challenge. What is the use? they say; is it worth while? who are we to carry our religion to the ends of the world? So criticism mounts, enthusiasm wanes, resources dwindle, and the outward expansion of the Christian movement pauses. Nowhere more than in a liberal congregation would I expect that mood to be prevalent.

This sermon is based on the frank acknowledgment that this era of criticism and pause in the expansion of Christianity is amply justified. For example, 139 different foreign missionary agencies in this country are collecting funds for the support of their enterprises. What an absurd, not to say wicked, situation that is! What possible relevance to the world-wide field have the peculiarities of these sectarian denominations? What possible excuse is there for the appalling wastage of 139 overheads? An immense amount of practical, sensible, financial criticism of the whole setup of our missionary enterprise is amply justified.

Deeper yet, the whole picture of the world that once motivated the missionary enterprise—Europe and America in general Christian, Asia and Africa in general pagan—will not do any more. Even the missionary maps used so to present the case—the West white, the East black. Who in my generation cannot remember the military metaphors used, as, moving out from the high privilege and enlightenment of the West to lands afar, we were urged to batter the citadels of darkness down and capture the strongholds of the enemy? To no intelligent man today would that idea of the world appeal. Indeed, see the West, still dripping with the blood of the last war and suicidally preparing for another, the West, whose science has produced the most outrageous instruments of mutual slaughter that the imagination of the race ever has conceived, the West with its imperialisms, its militarisms, its appalling social and economic wrongs, and imagine it marching to the East singing its misssionary hymn,

> Can we, whose souls are lighted
> With wisdom from on high,
> Can we to men benighted
> The lamp of life deny?

That whole basis and background of the missionary enterprise has gone. No wonder that Gandhi said, "Why should you self-styled whites get it into your heads that Christianity is your special largesse to distribute and interpret? You have made a mess of it yourselves."

Now, this church has taken the intolerableness of the present missionary situation so deeply to heart that we have definitely broken with it. That is to say, once we gave our funds mainly through a single denominational board, but we do so no longer, first, because we are not interested in denominationalism here or anywhere, and, second, because we know that, if our gifts were to go into any single denominational pool, some of them would be used for kinds of work in the world field that the people of this church would not approve. What we are giving, therefore, to Asia, Africa, and the islands of the sea—and it is all too little—is given precisely as we give in New York City, to causes and types of work individually investigated and vouched for without regard to denominational backing or lack of it. That is our present policy and I mention it as a guarantee of our sincerity in recognizing that the whole missionary enterprise needs to be rethought, restated, and reorganized.

Today, however, I am trying to clear my conscience with you about the deeper matter that the field is the world. Say what we will about the old denominationalism, it did at least keep *that* fact in the center of attention. The least member of the littlest sectarian church in this country knew that he was part of a world-wide movement and the claims of that planetary enterprise were habitually urged on his attention. When I was seven years old, in a little Baptist church in a small village in western New York, I heard a presentation of the world field so thrilling that then and there I made up my mind to be a foreign missionary. That little church stood for a type of Baptist sectarianism that I would not for a moment consent to now, but at least it was big enough to keep a map of the world before the eyes of its people.

In our days, however, with denominational interest and devotion everywhere going to pieces, see the consequence. Many people, surrendering their narrow denominationalism, have nothing left in their outlook on the church beyond the local congregation. I venture that that is true of many of us here and it is a strange, ironical anticlimax. To give up denominationalism because it is narrow and to end with no vision of the Christian field except the local congregation— *that* is narrower than the old denominationalism ever was. I am concerned about our churches in this regard and I ask you conscientiously to face with me those five words, to for-

get which is to surrender something essential to Christianity—
The field is the world.

In the first place, how can one face those words without
at least being grateful that we had some Christian forefathers
who believed them? For the ancestors of some of us of Anglo-
Saxon and Celtic origin were primitive barbarians, if there
ever were any, in the forests of Britain. Listen, for example,
to Saint Jerome, a great Christian scholar of the fourth century: "Why should I speak of other nations when I myself,
a youth on a visit to Gaul, heard that the Atticoti, a British
tribe, eat human flesh, and that although they find herds of
swine, and droves of large or small cattle in the woods, it is
their custom to cut off the buttocks of the shepherds and the
breasts of their women, and to regard them as the greatest
delicacies?" Who were those reputed cannibals? Friends, they
were among our ancestors in ancient Britain. I suspect that
this is a right and honest place to start, with the recognition
of the fact that some of the finest things in our lives go back
to Christians who could not keep their Christianity within
local limitations but, girding up their faith and courage,
headed north even to distant and barbarous Britain, saying,
"The field is the world."

Again look at those five words and see how true to fact
they have become in modern times. Say, if you will, that it
is strange that Jesus should have said them, but, surely, none
of us can fail to see now the reticulated, intermeshed, indi-
visible unity of the world.

Even a generation ago there might have been arguments
against that but not now. About 1831 a prominent citizen of
Boston, a great optimist, making a speech in Faneuil Hall,
said that if they could get a railroad between Springfield and
Boston that would make the trip in five hours, he actually
thought that on an average there would be nine people a
day wishing to make the trip. Boston laughed that off as
preposterously exaggerated. But look at our world today!

I am working here in New York while my sister is teaching in a Christian college in Istanbul, Turkey. What is the difference? Istanbul is a fascinating city—fine character, noble family life, glorious art, earnest religion. And Istanbul is a dreadful city—vice, corruption, superstition, ignorance, greed, poverty. That is to say, Istanbul is a great deal like New York. What is the difference? In reality there is no such thing as foreign missions any more. The name is a misnomer. What we are talking about is service, Christian service, wherever it is needed, and it belongs as much in Istanbul, Calcutta, Shanghai, and Tokyo as in New York. Where will you begin to draw the line? Of course the field is the world.

If anybody proposes artificially and arbitrarily to set the national boundary line as the limit of our outlook and responsibility, and, concerning the regions beyond, to say, Let them alone! the answer is almost too simple to deserve enlargement. What do you mean, Let them alone! "A cigarette in the mouth of every Chinese man, woman and child, in ten years" has been the slogan of a great tobacco company. And you are saying we should not have slogans like, Scientific medicine for every life in China! That seems strange. Or listen to this: "Open a schoolgirl's desk, and you will find on top of her books a movie magazine with pictures of Hollywood stars." Guess where that was said. The natural answer is, a city in the United States. No, that was in Baghdad. That was said by the principal of a girls' high school in Baghdad, Mesopotamia. Yet people still are saying, Let them alone.

We are not letting them alone with anything else of importance in the Western world, so why should we let them alone with our best? How can we let them alone with our best? We Protestants are operating eight hundred hospitals in the non-Christian field. Shall we let them alone with that? Some of those hospitals represent the only access to scientific medicine among three million people. Let your imagination play around that. My personal friend, Dr. Berry of Worcester, Massachusetts, now fallen on sleep, was the first man in history to introduce to Japan the profession of nursing. Shall we let them alone with that? Around the world we have a great cordon of colleges, many of which I personally have seen, in the Near East, in Egypt, in China, and Japan. Shall we let them alone with that? Once it required vision and faith to see the world field. Now I should suppose it took only realism. Of course the field is the world.

Again, look at those five words and see how inevitably in our reaction to them is revealed our judgment upon Jesus Christ himself. We have two kinds of possessions. Some of them are local, limited, peculiar to ourselves. I once heard a group of American college women asked if they thought Chinese women ought to adopt our American styles of feminine apparel, and they unanimously voted, No. I suspect they were unanimously right. We do have possessions that are peculiar to ourselves. But some are not. Scientific discoveries are not. When the new telescope with its two-hundred-inch reflector reveals fresh truth about the stellar cosmos, every one will feel that that truth by its very nature belongs to all mankind. What pertinence have national and racial boundaries to that? Some lives in this congregation have been saved by insulin. Is that, along with other scientific medical discoveries, local? The need is universal; can the remedy be provincial? So we do have two kinds of possessions, some peculiar to ourselves, some, by their very nature, belonging to the world.

Now, the question is, In which class do we propose to put the spirit of Jesus? Is he one of our localisms, one of our Western or American peculiarities? But he was not even a Westerner; he was an Oriental. Moreover, growing up in a nationalistic and racialistic religion with tight restrictions, in one of the greatest religious reformations of all history he broke free into a kind of religion so profound in its faith, so universal in its ethical demands, that any one, Jew or Gentile, Greek or Roman, Scythian, barbarian, bond or free, could be his follower.

One of my learned colleagues at the seminary says that Jesus was the first man in history to take monotheism with complete moral seriousness. That is to say, others before him had believed in one God but he first did so with complete ethical seriousness—one God, one Father of all, one family of men therefore, no racial distinctions, no national distinctions, one brotherhood of man under one God. In a deep sense he was

> . . . the first that ever burst
> Into that silent sea.

On what basis, then, shall we localize the spirit of Jesus? "Thou shalt love the Lord thy God with all thy heart, and with all thy soul, and with all thy mind. This is the great and first commandment. And a second like unto it is this, Thou shalt love thy neighbor as thyself"—what is there local about that? "Blessed are the pure in heart: for they shall see God"; "Whatsoever ye would that men should do unto you, even so do ye also unto them"; "Inasmuch as ye did it unto one of these my brethren, even these least, ye did it unto me"—what is local about that? The story of the Good Samaritan, the story of the Prodigal Son, any significant utterance characteristic of the essential style of Jesus—what is local about that? Christ belongs to the world, and as a man sees today the increasing unity of the world—not political, for that lags behind, but the real unity—ideas passing over all barriers, scientific inventions becoming homogeneously the possession of all mankind, and an inevitably emerging cultural blend that, like the sea, will lave every shore and affect every life, how can a man who cares for Christ at all not want Christ to have a dominant influence on that world culture? Christ essentially belongs to all mankind.

Again, however, look at those five words and see, in the

light of them, how radically the local Christianity of our Western churches needs to be reformed. For while it is true that the spirit of Jesus rightly claims a world field, the local Christianity of our Western churches is not fit to be propagated, and no man feels that as he should until he sees it against the background of the world.

For example, we could muddle along with our sectarian denominationalism here at home, where at least we know the history of it, can give excuses for its existence, and have become accustomed to its disadvantages. But we cannot muddle along with our sectarian denominationalism in the world field, where it is a ridiculous laughingstock and a hopeless handicap. This month of February, the Christians of America are remembering the centenary of Dwight L. Moody's birth. I commend to you one thing that Moody said—"If I thought I had one drop of sectarian blood in my veins, I would let it out before I went to bed; if I had one sectarian hair in my head, I would pull it out." One feels *that* even when one looks at the home field. One feels that more deeply when one thinks of the world. There is much more interdenominationalism on the world field than there is at home. For whenever Christianity intelligently faces the world, it has at least to try to be big enough for the world—not small, petty, parochial, trivial, but large, inclusive, catholic, universal. The healthiest and most enlarging influence that could be brought to bear upon our home churches and our home Christianity would be a real vision of the world.

Recall the spirited description which E. Stanley Jones has given of the influence on his life of his missionary experience in India. When he went out to India first, he says, he was holding a long line of defense that stretched all the way from Genesis to Revelation and on to Western civilization and the Western Christian churches, and he went bobbing up and down along that line, fighting behind Moses and Paul and Western civilization and the Western churches, until he was worried and played out. Then it dawned on him that he had no business to defend that long line. Why should he force the Old Testament on India when in Hinduism and Buddhism India had its own Old Testament, some of it very fine indeed? Why should he try to defend Western civilization when Western civilization is quite indefensible? What business of his was it to transport to the Orient the provincialisms of Western creed and custom, which to the Orient were an intrusive offense? So he stopped defending that long line and came in to one point, Christ, the spirit of Christ. "I saw," he says, "that the gospel lies in the person of Jesus, that he himself is the Good News, that my one task was to live and to present him." So today it is E. Stanley Jones and people like him who come to us from the world field with the most passionate, withering attacks on our denominational sectarianism that any one is making. They are fighting for their lives, you see, for a world Christianity, not petty, mean, sectarian, trivial, but large, catholic, inclusive, universal.

See what we are saying. The preacher generally proclaims that the world needs Christianity. What I am saying now is that Christianity needs the world. Whenever we try to coop Christianity up in a locality it gets little and nothing can keep it large and catholic except the world.

Once more, consider those five words and see if you do not think that in our time, perhaps above all times in history, we need an international, interracial Christian fellowship out of every tongue and tribe and people and nation. I have hardly used the phrase "foreign missions" this morning. That phrase is less and less at home in our vocabulary. But "international Christianity," across all boundaries of race and people—put it *that* way and who that cares for Christ at all does not feel the need of it? Is it not important to the world that Kagawa is a Christian? You remember how he himself put it: "We want to ask Christ to take out his first and second naturalization papers in Japan!" Well, don't we want that?

One evening in Tokyo I sat at dinner next to Kawaii San. For forty generations her ancestors had been priests at the Shinto shrine at Ise. It is the most honored of all the shrines of Shinto in Japan, and for forty generations the forbears of Kawaii San had there been priests. Then disaster fell upon their household. One of the members of the clan went into the far country of dissipation. He disgraced the family. But through the influence of a Christian missionary the power of Christ was brought to bear upon him. Christ made a man out of a moral wreck. So Kawaii San's father, deeply moved by his brother's reformation, turned his back on the honor and prestige of Ise and became a Christian. And that evening, as I sat next to her at dinner, I learned that Kawaii San was president of the Young Women's Christian Association of Japan. Wasn't that worth while?

Yes, far beyond the boundaries of the organized Christian fellowship, isn't it worth while that the influence of Jesus should be world-wide? Gandhi in a formal sense is not a Christian. We quoted a few minutes ago one of his vehement attacks on Western Christianity. But listen to Gandhi talking to the boys in his college in India: "I say to the 75 per cent of Hindus receiving instruction in this college that your lives also will be incomplete unless you reverently study the teachings of Jesus. . . . The message of Jesus is contained in the Sermon on the Mount, unadulterated and taken as a whole. . . . If, then, I had to face only the Sermon on the Mount and my own interpretation of it, I should not hesitate to say, 'Oh yes, I am a Christian.' " Isn't that worth while?

Yet I know well that when I have said all this it is highly probable that some here will be estopped from seeing it, believing it, and acting on the basis of it, by their ideas of what missionaries are like, formulated from unfortunate specimens they may have seen or caricatures of missionaries on the public stage, or through realistic portraitures of some old fanatic like Pearl Buck's father, The Fighting Angel. Well,

I have been on the foreign field, too, and I would say that some of the work there is dreadful—little men and women, bigots, fanatics, busybodies, trying to transfer the peculiarities of Western creed and custom into lands where they are offensive intruders. But some of it I should call magnificent—about the ablest, most strategic, most statesmanlike, most potentially influential investment of life and money being made on earth today. As for the missionaries, I agree with Robert Louis Stevenson, viewing the matter as he did from Samoa in the mid-Pacific. Once in a while he would let loose his indignation on a feeble missionary but it was for a missionary that he reserved the highest praise of all—"the most attractive, simple, brave, and interesting man in the whole Pacific."

Go to how many lands today and ask, Who first brought in scientific medicine? and the answer is, The missionaries! Who first brought in scientific agriculture? The missionaries. Who first reduced the spoken language to writing so that there could be books? The missionaries. Who first brought in schools? The missionaries.

I am concerned about ourselves in this regard, because some of us are leaving out something. Just because we are liberals we are leaving out something that one might suppose the liberals would not leave out, leaving out of our Christianity—think of it!—the map of the world.

On Being Indifferent to Religion

THE popular attitude toward Christianity, which causes anxiety to Christian people today, is not so much hostility as indifference. Hostility at least treats religion as sufficiently important to be withstood, but indifference passes it by as negligible. The ultimate disgrace of anything is to become an affair of apathy. Yet all around us are people apathetic to religion. They do not deny or defy it; they treat it as irrelevant. It is nothing to them. So prevalent is this attitude that even here in a Christian church there must be many to whom it would be fair to say, You are neither strongly religious nor defiantly anti-religious but, rather, neutral, unconcerned. Indeed, all of us fall at times into moods concerning religion that Dean Sperry of Harvard has described as "the listless consent, more deadly than doubt, which we give to a platitude."

There is nothing new in this. We commonly think of Jesus as meeting either loyal acceptance or vehement hostility. The people who deeply loved him and deeply hated him stand out in our imagination. But the population of Palestine was not so divided. To the mass of the people he did not matter at all. They went about their secular pursuits and trivial pleasures with no concern to waste on him. Some of the saddest words ever used concerning Jesus were picked by John Stainer from the book of Lamentations and, in his oratorio, "The Crucifixion," applied to the crowds that watched Christ's suffering on the cross: "Is it nothing to you, all ye that pass by?"

Let us today, then, study some of the causes, meanings, and results of our religious indifference.

Some people are indifferent because they have been disgusted by trivial forms and expressions of religion. So Gallio, the Roman proconsul in Corinth before whom Paul's enemies dragged the apostle and then fell into a heated argument about their religious opinions, endured the spectacle as long as he could and then cried, "If indeed it were a matter of wrong or of wicked villany, O ye Jews, reason would that I should bear with you: but if they are questions about words and names and your own law, look to it yourselves." Many today, observing our creedal trivialities and ecclesiastical peccadilloes, lift against the churches and the religion for which they stand a similar cry of boredom and disgust, "words and names . . . look to it yourselves." Who can blame them? The most disastrous things done to religion are done not by its enemies but by its friends, who, when little themselves, make littleness of great matters.

At the World Conference on Faith and Order, held a decade ago at Lausanne, Switzerland, a representative of youth said this: "It has been my privilege to feel the pulse of youth and study the attitude of youth towards ecclesiasticism in some fifteen countries of the world, and it is stating it mildly to say that youth is plainly apathetic, indifferent toward much of the credal emphasis of the Church, and is chafing under the restrictions that these inherited forms impose." Surely that is obvious. While, however, one sympathizes with youth in this regard, it is never wise to exclude from our experience a great matter because it is caricatured. Everything has been caricatured. Education, music, love, home life—everything suffers from the appalling capacity of small people to belittle great matters. In this situation I commend to you one of the underlying principles of Aristotle's philosophy as Dr. Rufus Jones has paraphrased it: "The true nature of a thing is the highest that it can become." We do not think of trees in terms of whipped and beaten shrubs. There are magnificent trees. We do not at our best think of homes in terms of loveless and embittered households. There are great homes in which the real nature of home life comes to glorious flower.

When, therefore, we thrust into the forefront of our thought and imagination the caricatures of Christianity, we miss the point. There is great Christianity. That is the point. It is a profound philosophy of life, a conviction that the ultimate reality, the determiner of destiny, is not materialistic but spiritual. That is a great matter. It is a profound way of living life, the noblest ethic that mankind has ever tried to follow. That is a great matter. It is a profound resource in life, deep wells from which to draw peace and poise, fortitude and power. That is a great matter. It is a profound hope ahead of life, both for society on earth and for each of us, when "the shadows lengthen and the evening comes, and the busy world is hushed, and the fever of life is over, and our work is done." And that is a great matter. Moreover, we have seen this great religion gloriously exhibited in radiant and serviceable lives. How can a man be indifferent to that?

There are two ways of revolting against the trivialities of religion. One is to identify the reality with the caricature, to let the belittling work of small men shut one out from a great field of experience. That is cheap and easy. The other is Jesus' way. He, too, revolted against the trivialities in his people's faith. He revolted vehemently and his attacks were unremitting and merciless. But always he was in revolt against the trivialities of religion in the name and for the sake of great religion. When he went out against the Pharisees, these words might have been upon his banner—"The true nature of a thing is the highest that it can become."

In the Goethe-Schiller epigrams we read: "You ask me which of the religions I profess. None of all that you name to me. And why none? Because of my religion."

Other people are indifferent to religion not so much because they are alienated by the churches' trivialities as because they have substitutes for religion. In a certain community a surgeon commonly regarded as irreligious, not to say atheistic, resented being called so. One day, cornered by his friends as to what his faith was, he said, "If you want to know what my religion is *come and see me operate.*" One feels sincere respect for that. As between the formalities of conventional religion and such delight in craft and skill bestowed on useful service, by all means give us the second. Jesus would regard that surgeon with affection and respect. Jesus was always strong for the humane and serviceable deed. There is a religion of science, of music, of art, of any spiritual realm, where a man is carried out of himself by something greater than himself and says, If you want to know what my religion is, come and see me operate.

Religion is not confined to the churches, is not cooped up in any creedal or ecclesiastical cubby-hole. This is what the doctrine of the Holy Spirit means: wherever spiritual quality rises into strength and beauty, wherever integrity, kindliness, love, truth are, there is the presence of the Eternal Spirit, there is God. To use Beecher's illustration, as walking down the street one hears through an open window a snatch of music and says, That is Beethoven, not all of him but enough so that I can recognize him, so one, walking through life, hears out of the casual living of common days the notes of integrity, kindliness, love, truth, and says, That is God, not all of him but enough so that one can recognize him, that is God. In medicine and music, therefore, in social service and philanthropy, in every fine and serviceable spiritual realm, the New Testament would support this attitude—if you want to know what my religion is, come and see me operate. Is it not written there, "Pure religion and undefiled before our God and Father is this, to visit the fatherless and widows in their affliction, and to keep oneself unspotted from the world"?

Nevertheless, having granted this to the surgeon, I should wish to talk further with him thus: You do not want us to coop our religion up in our cubby-holes. Why, then, do you coop your religion up in yours? Why have a religion that exhibits itself only when you operate? That is too small a place to confine great religion in. You know it is. It is you who are shutting religion up in a small place, your own particular craft and skill, and neglecting its wide meanings and exhibitions. It is a profound philosophy of life, a profound faith in God, a great personal and social ethic, a deep resource for living, an eternal hope. Even the churches have a greater religion than you have. Trivial as they sometimes are, yet in their Scriptures, in the great tradition and heritage of their prayers, in their noblest hymns, in their outreach of care to the ends of the earth, in spite of themselves they strike a universal note. "In the beginning God . . ."—at least their Bible starts with that. "The field is the world"—at least their Christ said that. "Strengthened with power through his Spirit in the inward man"—at least they face that elemental need. "I saw, and behold, a great multitude, which no man could number, out of every nation and of all tribes and peoples and tongues, standing before the throne"—at least they cherish that all-inclusive hope. "For this corruptible must put on incorruption, and this mortal must put on immortality"—at least they face that eternal problem. There is more hope for a great and universal religion in the churches, even as they are today, than in these substitutes which constrict religion to the place where an individual says, Come and see me operate.

So, I would say to that fine surgeon, you tell us to come out of our cubby-holes and we agree. Some of us have been trying to do that for years. Now we say to you, Come out of your cubby-hole and meet us. For a religion based on a profound philosophy, nurtured from spiritual depths, overflowing into humble service, leaving the soul at last face to face with the Eternal, crying, "O death, where is thy sting?" is too great a matter for any man to be indifferent to.

[192]

Would that the churches could make that more evident! A bishop sometime since was invited by one of his clergy to come out to the parish and conduct devotions on their "quiet day." The bishop declined, saying, "Your parish does not need a quiet day; it needs an earthquake." I wonder how many of us need that? Was there ever a time when the church faced a more critical need in the world and a more imperative opportunity to present great religion greatly?

At this point, however, one runs into a third group, indifferent to religion for this very reason—they think religion too great, too serious, too solemn, too demanding. They turn to another kind of life altogether, more trivial, more sensational, titillated by the externalities and immediacies of existence, getting what they want when they want it without troubling to resist temptation. Of such are a multitude of the indifferent. They are indifferent because they are preoccupied with lesser living.

A similar phenomenon appears in every realm—in science, for example. They are making now a great new telescope whose two-hundred-inch reflector will surely bring amazing news from the frontiers of the cosmos. Some of us are so interested we can hardly wait, but many are indifferent. It is nothing to them. For all they deeply care, they might as well be living on the old, flat earth, and a man could almost throw a stone and reach the boundaries of their poignant concerns. Their interest never gets far beyond their pleasure. If that is true about cosmology, which, after all, puts no ethical demands on us, no wonder it is true about great religion, which is tremendously serious and demanding! It is too big for some people. *That* is not the scale they wish to build their lives upon. I see too many, coming even from the university circle, indifferent to religion because they do not wish to live the kind of life it represents, to doubt the presence of some such here today.

Is it not fair to say that a man apathetic to religion for that

[193]

reason is passing judgment on himself? That is the kind of person he is. I have tried to be fair in facing justifiable criticism against the churches for belittling religion, but there are multitudes of people indifferent to religion not at all because the churches have belittled it but because they themselves are developing a kind of character and are living a quality of life utterly antagonistic to great religion. They are not bothering with Christianity because they do not want Christianity to bother them. There are few more important measures of a man's character than the things he is indifferent to. In a world where great music is, if a man say, It is nothing to me, give me merely jazz, he is passing judgment on himself. In a world where there is great literature, if a man say, What do I care? give me a tabloid, he is passing judgment on himself. And in a world where there is great religion, where Christ has come and his spirit has been gloriously reproduced in radiant and useful lives, for a man to say, What difference does that make to me? give me this other kind of life, undisciplined, undedicated, careless of life's ultimate meaning and destiny, passes judgment on his own quality. That is the kind of person he is. As the New Testament says, "This is the judgment, that the light is come into the world, and men loved the darkness rather than the light; for their works were evil." I wish I could pierce the defensive armor of some one here and make unmistakably evident that we are commonly indifferent to religion not at all because of the excuses we give but because we do not wish to live the kind of life it stands for.

Is it not true also to say that, if we are that kind of person, we still do not escape the haunting apprehension of a higher world to which we know we have no right to be indifferent? Is there a soul so superficial or so wayward that he altogether avoids the intimations and surmises of that higher spiritual world impinging on him, to which his life rightfully belongs? Sometimes in nature we, like Wordsworth, feel a Presence that disturbs us with the joy of elevated thoughts, as though all the things we see were the signs and tokens of a world invisible and real. Sometimes within ourselves a Presence rises, not to be denied, as though some Self greater than ourselves were seeking to win our allegiance from the selves we actually are. Sometimes among our friends we see troubles conquered, handicaps surmounted, spiritual victories won, until a soul that the world seemed about to conquer rises conqueror instead, strange, invisible resources coming to his help. And sometimes we see friends face death and, lo! the world invisible appears to welcome them

> . . . as if some fair city were one voice
> Around a king returning from his wars.

Who escapes these surmises and intimations of the soul? They are the witnesses of our spiritual nature, our kinship with the Divine. How can a man be indifferent to that?

Moreover, is it not fair to say that if we are indifferent we never escape the penalty? Our forefathers used to try to force men out of their religious indifference by preaching hell. They too saw multitudes insensitive, apathetic, unconcerned, so in dreadful wise they preached hell. Men could not be indifferent to that, they thought. But so fearful a cure of spiritual unconcern is not for us. Nevertheless, I think there is a hell on earth for those who, indifferent to life's deepest meanings, careless of its noblest faiths and hopes and loyalties, try to live out the measure of their years with no better food than a trivial philosophy about life and an undisciplined, undedicated spirit in living it. As a man grows older, what is it he most needs for the undergirding of his years? Meaning in life—deep meaning in life—that the world should not be

> . . . a tale
> Told by an idiot, full of sound and fury,
> Signifying nothing,

but should have meaning in it, as though the whole cosmos would at last make sense and the man's life be part of the significance. If a man have such undergirding, he can stand anything that happens to him. If a man lack it, what dust and ashes does this strange business of existence come to at the last!

I see young people turning their backs on great religion because they think it too deep, too solemn, too serious, too demanding. Friends, the Christian faith is the most radiant philosophy of life men ever had opportunity to believe in. It puts meaning into life. Even if it takes a man to the cross it does this basic and indispensable thing—it keeps profound meaning in life. Granted Christianity's truth, life comes from somewhere, signifies something, is going somewhither, and we can be part of its significance. So futility, cynicism, aimlessness, those three great curses of a man's soul as he grows older, need not afflict us. Christian faith solemn and demanding? I grant it is majestic and awesome but it is the most radiant and sustaining faith a man can have. How can a man be indifferent to that?

Finally, many in our time are indifferent to religion because they do not think it important to the world. At any rate, they have other causes and movements which they think so much more important that they pass religion by. Science, education, economic reform, the fine arts—they matter. You can put your finger on what such things do, but religion is more subjective, more vague. They are apathetic to it.

To such a person I would put the question thus: If you do not think that religion in general is important to the world, do you or do you not think that bad religion—unintelligent, unethical, reactionary religion—is important to the world? There is plenty of that. The kind of religion that sanctifies the obsolete, that writes anti-evolutional laws, that makes bigots, or, as Jesus said, tithes mint, anise, and cummin, and neglects the weightier matters of the law, the kind of religion that embitters men, imprisons men, frightens men—do you or do you not think that such bad religion is momentous for the world? You know it is. It is one of the most disastrous forces ever let loose in human life.

Religion, then, is not a matter of indifference. Professor Shotwell of Columbia University is right when, speaking as a historian, he says: "Religion moves, vast and potent, in the world to-day. One must be blind, indeed, not to see the evidences of its power in both the structure and the movement of our modern world." How can a man, then, seeing that bad religion is so powerful a force for evil, think that great religion is of no moment? We never will displace bad religion except by great religion—we may be sure of that. Great religion in the souls of men around the world would elevate everything, as though a rising tide lifted man over ancient sandbars long insuperable. Many a thing science can never do for us, nor education, nor economic reform, without great religion in the lives of men. How can one who cares about the world at all be indifferent to that?

I can understand the positive antagonists of religion, the valiant atheists who attack religion because they honestly think it untrue. One can respect them. Thomas Hardy, for example, was an atheist but looking upon his Christian fellows, he said,

> That with this bright believing band
> I have no claim to be,
> That faiths by which my comrades stand
> Seem fantasies to me,
> And mirage-mist their Shining Land,
> Is a strange destiny.

Though he was an atheist, he was not indifferent to religion.

I can understand men who bitterly fight religion because of an antagonistic social philosophy. Professor Ernst Bergmann, the Nazi, calls what we would regard as normal Christianity "sheer brain disease of the human race, a mental affliction." Of course he says that. He is out for a thoroughly nationalistic philosophy of society, based on blood and soil, and he knows that, with all its faults, Christianity is incurably internationalistic and that he must fight it as one of the most powerful foes of everything he stands for. One can understand that.

But the indifferentists, who act as though Christianity did not matter at all, as though the towering question whether bad religion or great religion is to prevail on earth were an affair of unconcern—what intellectual or moral standing-ground have they?

Yet all through this congregation are moods, attitudes, habits of thought and life, which in effect express indifference to Christian faith. I am not trying now to convict us of our sins so much as to convict us of our possibilities. A great religion could have tremendous meaning to us. It could make our lives all over. *It,* did I say? *He!* For great religion has been personified; it has been exhibited in the most glorious spiritual life man ever had the chance to believe in, be loyal to, and follow. How can a man be listless about Christ?

Six Paradoxes Concerning Trouble

NOTHING more deeply influences the quality of our lives than the way we handle trouble. Certainly in many people the most powerful factor in determining character is their attitude toward hardship. Here, then, are six paradoxes concerning trouble, not exhortations about it, as though saying, Be brave! Bear up! Have faith! but six truths which people, I suspect, often miss because they are so paradoxical.

The first paradox is that if we would be happy we had better take trouble for granted and accept life as essentially difficult and tragic. Many people make impossible the constructive handling of adversity because they start by thinking that an untroubled life is the ideal, so that all their disasters become intruders to be resented. Beginning thus with a picture of life embowered in pleasure and quite weedless, they soon discover they cannot get on well with it. For hardship outwits them, adversity climbs their stoutest walls, and their ideals of an untroubled life go to pieces in disillusionment. They started wrong.

Let us, then, begin with the alternative proposition that life is essentially difficult and tragic. It begins in painful birth and ends in painful death, and its fabric in between has dark threads running through. That is why a great tragedy like Hamlet lives on and, generation after generation, holds a mirror up to nature. Life is essentially difficult.

Concerning this proposal many will feel at once that it presents a gloomy view of life. No, my friends, not gloomy, but the only basis for happiness. If we start by thinking that the ideal is an untroubled life, then adversity seems a wretched intruder to be resented, a miserable trespasser that has no business here. But if we start by accepting life as difficult and tragic, then our blessings, the joy, beauty, and love that enrich us, will appear so marvelous that it will seem a miracle to have them.

Here is a man who starts with the ideal of pleasure only— no disaster, no difficulty, only pleasantness and peace. Well, he is preparing to be miserable. For he begins by thinking that ideal weather involves a cloudless sky, and every cloud will be an insult to him. But here is Paul who began with a profound and realistic world view: "The whole creation groaneth and travaileth in pain together until now." That is the tragic truth, with no silly fooling. Was Paul, then, unhappy? Rather, he lived one of the most radiant lives in history. Stone him, pile intolerable burdens on him, shipwreck him, imprison him, and still he says, "Rejoice in the Lord always: again I will say, Rejoice." He started with life as trouble and against that dark background, as in a Rembrandt portrait, his blessings shone like a revelation. As between Paul, with this profound and realistic philosophy, and these wretched hedonists, with their cheap ideas about life and their cynical results in living it, I choose Paul, alike for truth and consequence.

Indeed, does happiness really lie in an untroubled life? Of course it doesn't. Some of the most tingling happiness we know is victory over opposition. Give us a hard task, a towering difficulty, and strength to win the day—there is the secret of our realest happiness. Happiness is not mostly pleasure, it is mostly victory. So said the Greeks—"The best things are the most difficult." Does a good sailor always want a calm sea? Rather, give him a gale that he may try his powers against the adverse elements until he feels his heart sing in the storm.

To be sure, there is a quieter happiness, as when lovely sunsets come and we sit and look, but no man worth his salt can be content with such passive pleasure only. Great happiness takes off like an able aviator against a head wind. When happiness grows too scarce in pleasant places, men fly the Atlantic or explore Antarctica to find it, or, like Shakespeare's soldier, seek

> . . . the bubble reputation
> Even in the cannon's mouth.

Great happiness often has difficulty for its setting and adventure for its strength. Even when heavy griefs come, there is a radiance in those who transcend and transmute them and find "some soul of goodness in things evil" that all the hedonists on earth cannot achieve.

This, then, is the first paradox, that if we would be happy we had best accept life as essentially difficult and tragic.

The second paradox says that it is a cosmic honor to be able to suffer. How many people we meet to whom their trouble seems disgrace, as though God were punishing them for some unknown sin of theirs! Rather, the capacity to suffer is the mark of noble rank in nature.

Long ago some creatures, like the oysters, put their skeletons on the outside and their nerves on the inside, that they might not suffer. But that was a blind alley; that offered no way through for evolution. So a new experiment was tried in creatures who put their skeletons on the inside and their nerves on the outside. What consequence has come from that! All man's goodness, truth, beauty, love would have been impossible without that—nerves on the outside, so that we can sensitively feel and greatly suffer. For sensitivity is the basis of all nobility in man. It is alike the glory and the terror of the world. Without it no fine thing is ever done and yet by it all man's trouble is made possible. *The capacity to suffer is the mark of noble rank in nature*.

Would we have great poetry? Then we must have great sensitivity, some John Keats, crying,

> O what a wild and harmonized tune
> My spirit struck from all the beautiful!

But if we have such sensitivity we have a great sufferer, to whom Shelley's words apply:

> . . . a nerve o'er which do creep
> The else unfelt oppressions of this earth.

So sensitivity and creativity involve each other. A stout ruffian cannot suffer as Mozart did but he cannot create as Mozart did. Samson could not suffer as Jesus did but, then, he could not do what Jesus did. As we move up the scale of life, we find not less sensitivity but more, and so not less suffering, as modern sentimental cultists try to beguile us into thinking, but more suffering. It is as though when the cosmos wanted to crown a man it gave him for his coronation the capacity to suffer greatly.

Long before the evolutionary basis for this was known, the New Testament was full of it. The central figure there was the great sufferer, so sensitive that he said whatever happened to the least of his brethren happened to him, so sensitive that his followers said he had borne their griefs and carried their sorrows. We well may pray to be forgiven for the way we have dishonored and misused trouble, when the fact is that the capacity to suffer is the mark of rank in nature.

The third paradox is that, much as we hate trouble, without it our best never comes out—no hardship, no hardihood; no fight, no fortitude; no suffering, no sympathy; no pain, no patience. We may not like that kind of world but that is the kind of world we live in. Behind every great virtue stands a corresponding trouble.

If one should go through this congregation inquiring in what kind of experience we have learned the most profound and meaningful lessons about life, how often it would turn out that great trouble has been our teacher!

> I walked a mile with Pleasure.
> She chattered all the way,
> But left me none the wiser
> For all she had to say.

> I walked a mile with Sorrow,
>   And ne'er a word said she;
> But, oh, the things I learned from her
>   When Sorrow walked with me!*

Do not misunderstand my meaning. I am not saying I like trouble. I hate it. I am not being a preacher this morning and forgetting I am a man. I hate trouble and would do much to avoid it. But that is the point of the paradox: these things we hate, shrink from, and try to escape, often turn out, when handled handsomely, to be the source of the best in our lives. So runs the proverb of our forefathers: "No pains, no gains."

When one looks at human history as a whole, this truth is clear. The great insights of mankind have not come commonly from smooth and easy days. When Solomon sat upon the throne of Judah and the Hebrew realm reached the climax of its prosperity, we have no record of great thinking. But in the Exile, when the nation was broken and in agony, lo, an upthrust of creative thinking such as Judaism never had produced! So, as another put it, all thinking begins with a pain.

It is when something hurts us, like a dread disease or intolerable distress, that we begin to think in science. In social life it is when something hurts that we ponder the way out. There is more thinking going on in this nation now about the possibilities of a decent economic order than ever before in our history. We have been having a pain in our economy.

As for ourselves, we may well say, Ah, Trouble, we hate you but what would we be without you? Put us in a lotus land of pleasure and no pain, and what mean, selfish creatures we would be—no heroism, no courage, no self-sacrifice, no great love, no great endeavor! The finest qualities in human life are like those of Wordsworth's "happy warrior,"

* By Robert Browning Hamilton.

Who, doomed to go in company with Pain,
And Fear, and Bloodshed, miserable train!
Turns his necessity to glorious gain;
In face of these doth exercise a power
Which is our human nature's highest dower;
Controls them and subdues, transmutes, bereaves
Of their bad influence, and their good receives.

Thus to handle trouble is one of the central problems of life. You here in difficulty and distress, this adversity that has befallen you is no intruder. This is the very stuff of life, the innermost test of our right to be alive at all—can we handle trouble constructively?

The fourth paradox is that one of the best things about this world is its injustice. That looks like a hard nut to crack but there is meat in it. Some people feel so badly about having an unjust world that they try to make it seem just. But it isn't—not by a long way, not, at any rate, to all individuals here and now. A world where Socrates drinks the hemlock and Christ is crucified and saints are boiled in oil and Joan of Arc, who thought her voices called her to save France, perishes in flames—that is not just. See the innocent, bearing on their scarred lives the miseries they never have deserved. That is not just. Before we are through with this sermon we will say that we could make this a far juster world if we humans behaved ourselves, but we are saying now that in the popular idea of what justice means it would not do to have this world perfectly just.

For people commonly mean by justice that every time a man does good he should be paid for it by corresponding happiness and every time he does wrong he should be punished for it by corresponding pain. So all life would be reduced to a commercial transaction, *quid pro quo,* so much pleasure for so much goodness and so much pain for so much sin. A world like that, where God paid wages every Saturday, would never do. In such a world there would be no such thing as moral risk, no Esther going up before the king saying, "If I perish, I perish." All life would be a commercial *quid pro quo*. But the finest thing you and I have ever done has been to take moral risks, to say about some important matter: This seems to me right and true; God helping me, I cannot see it otherwise, and whatever comes of it I will stand for this, in scorn of consequence, although the heavens fall. That is the finest thing we have ever done. At that point, as when Christ went to the cross, character reaches its climax, and that would be impossible in a world which in the popular sense could be called just.

Obviously, this universe is not built on the neat, small principle of *quid pro quo*. It is vastly greater than that, more creative, more adventurous. For see the fourfold structure of this tremendous universe.

It is law-abiding, so that any one whether bad or good, who disobeys so much as the law of gravitation suffers terribly!

And the universe is evolutionary, starting the race in evil places—in primitiveness, savagery, illiteracy, tribalism, strife —forcing us to fight our way up, if we want a better world, at what cost to innocent and guilty alike, who can measure!

And the universe is intermeshed, so that what happens to any one overflows on others, the goodness of the good upon the evil and the badness of the evil on the good, at what tremendous cost!

And this universe has personal initiative at the very center, so that, free to choose right, we are also free to choose wrong and so can bring tragedy upon ourselves and our fellows.

So stands the mighty structure of this universe, and I am sure it is vaster, deeper, more adventurous, more creative, with more hope in it, than any neat, commercial *quid pro quo* could make it.

Do not understand me to say I never rebel. I do. O God,

I sometimes say, a little suffering from the structure of your universe might help but why this wild excess and superfluity of it? Some rain is nourishing, but why a flood? What good does cancer do or cholera or infantile paralysis or typhoons or earthquakes? O God, your cosmos overdoes trouble until suffering becomes so vast and insurmountable that millions are submerged and ruined in it. So I complain and hurl at the Most High my unanswered questions, as did my Lord upon the cross—"My God, my God, why . . . ?" But in profounder hours of deeper insight I am certain that this universe—law-abiding, evolutionary, intermeshed, with personal initiative in it—is more creative, more adventurous, than *quid pro quo* could make it. Sometimes it may seem mad, but I tell you there is method in it.

The fifth paradox is that, much as we hate trouble, it is one of the most valuable trusts committed to our care. When a man has great wealth, great ability, or great position, we all say, That is a trust; do not waste it. But how seldom we think of saying that about trouble! Yet it should be said. Trouble is a trust. Some of the most splendid things in history have been done with it. Do not squander it!

Here, for example, is a man who for over twenty-five years has been a shut-in. Before his calamity befell he was a vivid person. He was preparing for a horseback ride across the South American continent when the disease came on him that ever since has been his companion. Now, after a quarter of a century of constant invalidism he writes a book called *Shut-In*. Listen to these simple, modest words: "As the most barren regions of the Earth yield something to the botanist and the geologist, the most desolate aspects of life are not wholly without interest to the philosopher." So! As though life had exiled him to the Gobi Desert, he has taken trouble as a trust and has turned botanist and geologist to see how much in that strange region he can learn. Believe me, he has learned a lot!

Ah, Christ, we call you Lord and Master, yet how little we learn this lesson from you! You took trouble as a trust. That is a hard lesson for us to learn. We take it as a curse and resent it. You took it as a trust. You used every bit of it. You made it the most impressive spiritual force in human history. They handed you the cross as a disgrace and you took it as an opportunity, saying, "I, if I be lifted up from the earth, will draw all men unto myself."

Do not take this as piety because we are talking of it in a church. It is the very stuff of daily life. Watch your child as he begins to face his first calamities, and as you note his emotional reactions, his outbursts of resentment, his retreat into sullenness, his self-pity, his escape into wishful thinking, or his radiance and good sportsmanship, you are seeing a major process in life building at its very center. And during all the years that follow, his response to trouble still is the pith and marrow of life building. Treat your troubles constructively as an opportunity. If we could make that philosophy real and implement it with spiritual techniques, we could save this world a large proportion of its human wreckage.

The final paradox is that, far from driving man away from religion, trouble constrains him to it. How often we find people who still think that the tragic trouble of life is a denial of the Christian faith! But that is absurd. No one can think *that* unless he has so sentimentalized the Christian faith that he has made a soft and saccharine caricature of it. The New Testament is built on trouble. Even amid the loveliness of Christmastide we must recall the massacre of the innocents. The austere faith of the New Testament takes tragedy for its background and at the very center of the gospel is the cross, so cruel a calamity that I think the most damning thing to be said about this world is that it is the kind of place where that sort of thing could happen. The New Testament and trouble are not antagonists; they are twins. They were born into the same cradle. Paul made a magnificent statement of

New Testament philosophy when he said, "The whole creation groaneth and travaileth in pain together until now," "For the earnest expectation of the creation waiteth for the revealing of the sons of God." Aye, travail, but something being born out of it! That is a magnificent world view, profoundly realistic but involving also faith and hope and love.

If some one says, But how could a good God make a world with so much suffering in it, I answer, How could *no* God make a world with so much good in it? We never escape mystery by denying God. If God is, then, to be sure, much of the tragedy we see is a mystery. But if there is no God, if all comes from an accidental collocation of atoms, then all good, all beauty, truth, love, and creativity are insoluble mysteries. No, we little people on this wandering island in the sky cannot escape mystery in so vast a universe. But it is, I think, a solid, realistic fact that here before our very eyes is a conflict in which we must take part. All qualities have opposites—beauty and ugliness, love and hate, good and evil, justice and injustice. All qualities have opposites, and the Christian faith means at its center our alliance with the right against the wrong in the high faith that that right has backing in the very character of the Eternal.

Do you mean to say that life's trouble drives you away from that faith? It so constrains me to such faith that without it I should think existence not desirable and real life not possible. This, indeed, is the paradoxical conclusion of all our paradoxes. Do not center all your thought on the trouble which comes from the universe as such. That is not what most embitters us. It is man's inhumanity to man that embitters life. The stars in their courses are not responsible for that. Man is responsible. The universe is vast, objective, and its clean calamities come without malice and without partiality. It is man's inhumanity to man that embitters life. See then! To have a deep inward religion so that one transcends

[208]

and transmutes his trouble into good, and then to have an ethical religion so that man's inhumanity to man shall be less because he has lived—who in a world like this would not cry out for such a faith? Never let trouble drive you away from God. Let it constrain you to him.

The Cross and the Ordinary Man*

TODAY, beginning a week at whose center stands the cross and at whose end comes Easter, our chief danger is unreality. Coerced by the calendar to think about the cross—that in itself tempts us to insincerity. The event which this week commemorates was terribly real. A young Prince of Glory, loving life and doubtless praying for more years in which to do his fuller work, walked out instead, with a cross upon his back, toward Calvary and its horrors. Gethsemane and the crucifixion were terribly real.

Just because Calvary was so dreadfully real to Jesus, however, it is likely to be unreal to us. It is too great for us, too terrific and too great, that bloody cross on Golgotha with the figure there broken in bleak agony and crying, "My God, my God." Look at our lives in comparison, their ordinary preoccupations, their familiar burdens and sins. What kinship is there between us and Calvary?

The classic story runs that young Themistocles, avid of glory, fascinated by the heroic days when Miltiades withstood the hosts of the invading Persians, and anxiously fearful that Europe was not yet saved from the inundations of Asia, was stirred to emulation and said that the trophies of Miltiades would not suffer him to sleep. I suppose there are such souls who cannot rest till they have equalled or surpassed the most heroic and sacrificial deeds they have ever heard about. But most of us are not like that—not on ordinary days.

Sometimes I think that days might come, with fascism triumphant in America, with concentration camps and death against a blank wall the penalty for standing out as a Chris-

* A Palm Sunday Sermon.

[210]

tian in opposition to the coercions of a totalitarian state—
the days might come, as they have come elsewhere, with the
choice plain between conscience and death, when the cross
of Christ would grow very real to me. In such an hour the
sight of him, hanging there, might summon all one's powers
to dare to follow him. But that is not the case on ordinary
days.

This morning, therefore, we seek some element in the experience of the cross so universal that it must be real to us in
our daily life. Note, then, that what Jesus did when he went
to the cross was something that no one could have required
of him. No laws could be passed coercing a man to sacrifice
himself like that, and were such laws passed they could not
be enforced. In going to the cross Jesus was taking on himself something that no one could demand. He was moving,
that is, in the great realm of unenforceable obligations.

How great a realm it is and how much of the glory of life
is there! When the steamship Morro Castle burned, the chief
wireless operator was George W. Rogers. With the conflagration all around him, the floor so hot he could not keep
his feet on it, the flames so close he breathed through a wet
towel, when the last limit of legal or customary or enforceable obligation had been long overpassed he was urged to
escape, but his answer was, "I intend to stand by my post."
He did what no one could have demanded of him.

Even our ordinary life is pretty much made up of two
things, enforceable and unenforceable obligations—on the one
side, conduct that the laws of court or custom can demand,
and, on the other, the ways of living that no laws and no codes
of custom ever can require. Even within the family some
things can be lawfully demanded, but all great motherhood,
great fatherhood, and beautiful family life move in the realm
of the unenforceable obligations. Moreover, in the nation
this is true. A friend of mine once heard the late Lord
Moulton make what he still remembers as a notable speech.

And this was the theme of Lord Moulton's appeal to the English people: The greatness of a nation lies in the number of its citizens who can be trusted to obey self-imposed law.

At the present time in America, the importance of this may be obscured by the fact that we suffer from such outrageous lawlessness that we think we should be well off and happy, if only all the people would keep the laws already on the statute books. We are told that out of every forty-two persons in the American population one has had a prison record. Obviously, we should be much better off if all the people were law-abiding. That, however, by itself alone would not make a great nation. The greatness of a nation lies in the higher realm where men and women in every relationship of life do far more than can be demanded. This is true, even about basic matters like common honesty. An American farmer wrote to his senator urging his vote for a pure-food bill then before the Legislature. The senator knew that farmer as a man who was adulterating the syrup he was marketing, so that the pure-food law, if passed, would bear heavily upon him. Accordingly the senator wrote to him in surprise and received this frank reply: "Yes, I am accused of adding brown sugar to the syrup. That is why I want you to vote for that law. I want you to pass a law to stop me from doing it." There is revealed one of the profound problems of human life—the inner difficulty of acquiring the kind of character that will yield obedience to the unenforceable obligations.

Ah, Cross of Christ, only a moment ago you seemed too tragic and terrible, too high and lifted up, to be comprehensible to us, but now you touch our lives at every point. For this is what Christ was doing that last week, reduced to its simplest and most universal terms—he was voluntarily taking on himself what no one possibly could have demanded.

In the first place, consider our public need of this kind of character. If with canny eyes one watches people, one sees them falling into three general classes: first, lawless folk; second, law-abiding folk whose standard of conduct comes mainly from without, from the codes, customs, requirements of society; third, those other folk who get their criteria of character and standards of behavior mainly from within. They have an inner Sinai nobler than the outer one, and, in Shakespeare's fine phrase about Desdemona, they hold it a vice in their goodness not to do more than is requested.

Perilous to society as lawless folk are, the second class is our greater danger. There are many more of them; every one of us is tempted to belong with them—the barely good, who get by on the conduct that is required. And our first thesis now is that no great society can be sustained by such character, that Lord Moulton is right: the greatness of a nation lies in the number of its citizens who yield obedience to the unenforceable laws.

The true artists of a nation belong in this class. "The artist's conscience is a fearful thing." Indeed it is. The artist must satisfy an inner criterion or else be miserable. What Toscanini does is something that no one could demand of him but that he demands of himself. The true scientists of a nation belong in this class. They are bound by an inner loyalty to the disinterested love of truth. On that point they have a conscience which, as Huckleberry Finn said, takes up more room than all the rest of their insides put together. True public servants of a nation belong in this class. No laws ever can demand what men like Washington and Lincoln endured and did.

Especially today, however, we are trying to say that all true Christians belong in this class. The essence of Christian living lies in breaking free from, and rising above, all legalism and doing far more than any law can exact or any person can require. This is the nub and marrow of Jesus' spirit and teaching. "Whosoever shall compel thee to go one mile, go with him two"—that is his philosophy in a nutshell, the ex-

[213]

cess and extra gift of an overflowing goodwill. "If ye love them that love you, what reward have ye? do not even the publicans the same?" "Love your enemies"—that is something over and above all that enforceable law can require. "When ye shall have done all the things that are commanded you, say, We are unprofitable servants; we have done that which it was our duty to do." So! To have done what can be required is only the starting point of life. "How oft shall my brother sin against me, and I forgive him?" said Peter, "until seven times?" "I say not unto thee, Until seven times," said Jesus, "but, Until seventy times seven." Thus the privilege of generosity begins where the requirements of law end. This is essential in Jesus' teaching, so that when, that last week, he faced the cross, which no one could have demanded that he bear, his acceptance of it was but the climactic expression of everything he had taught and done in more ordinary days.

One knows well the natural reaction of some to this idea of Christian living. It's an extravagance of goodness, they think, a superfine ethical filigree, not fitted to the rough-and-tumble of daily business life. Yet when it really is put into daily business life we never forget it. Mark Twain was involved in a financial failure and saw his publishing house forced into bankruptcy, with large outstanding debts. He had no legal responsibility. He was free from his burden. But voluntarily Mark Twain shouldered those debts and at sixty years of age started on a heartbreaking lecture tour, saying, "I am confident that if I live I can pay off the last debt within four years, after which, at the age of sixty-four, I can make a fresh and unincumbered start in life." And he said also, "Honor is a harder master than the law."

That phrase is worthy to be inscribed on the banners of a man's conscience. Who here would not be the better for taking it to heart? It is not excess goodness and ethical filigree. It is the substance of character, which alone makes any society great. "Honor is a harder master than the law."

In the second place, consider not only our public need of such character but the impressive influence it wields when it appears. We commonly estimate the worth of characters like David Livingstone, going to Africa, or Sir Wilfred Grenfell, going to Labrador, in terms of the practical service they render to Africa or Labrador. But that is hardly half the story. Probably the greater thing such men and women do lies in their powerful influence upon our whole philosophy of life. They shake our self-complacency to pieces, they challenge and subdue us by the simple fact that they voluntarily undertake to do what no one could possibly demand of them. The sight of some one thus moving grandly off into the realm of unenforceable obligation is the most impressive thing in the moral world.

This powerful influence begins with our mothers. Many of us would agree with Emerson—"Men are what their mothers made them." My mother was a young girl, standing beside a syringa bush on a village street in the Chautauqua hills, when my father, coming home from college, first saw and loved her. Many years ago she passed into the unseen, but how vivid yet she is in my imagination and how powerful in her influence upon my life! She was to me what no one could have expected or required. Her love moved always in the "second mile." I can without irreverence paraphrase Paul's words: What the law could not do, God, sending my mother, did for me. How powerful a grip this extra quality in love and life gets on a man!

Moreover, it gets a powerful grip on the world. One of the most influential men in our time is Gandhi of India, and the secret of his potent life obviously lies in his selfless care for his people, of a kind that no one ever has any right to demand of another. Once Gandhi was beaten into insensibility by brutal attackers. When he recovered consciousness, an eye witness says, he was helpless and bleeding. The doctor was cleansing his wounds and the police officers were watching beside him, while he used what small strength he had to insist that no action should be taken to punish his would-be murderers. "They thought they were doing right," he said, "and I have no desire to prosecute them." At first the old Adam in me protests against that. That's carrying it too far, I say. To be beaten up and then make excuses for the attackers, to be crucified and still pray, "Father, forgive them; for they know not what they do"—that is an extravagance of goodness beyond all earthly need. But when the old Adam in me is through protesting, I find my eyes inevitably wandering back to that amazing thing, that haunting, fascinating, incredible thing, that most impressive sight in the moral world, the kind of life which goes so far beyond what any one can possibly demand.

A new biography has just been written of Elizabeth Fry. Strange, a new life of her after a hundred years! She was a lovely Quaker woman. She had beauty and quiet gaiety and charm, intelligence and wealth. She was the mother of eleven children. One would think she had enough to occupy her life. But there were the women prisoners in Newgate, living under conditions such that even our modern prisons, wretched as they are, seem paradise in comparison. She had no responsibility for them. No one could expect or require her to care about them. But there were the women prisoners in Newgate and because she was Elizabeth Fry she went to Newgate and put her amazing personality at their disposal. So the Parliament in England began to consult her about prisons, and the Republic of France asked for her help concerning women in prisons, and one government after another in Europe sat on her doorsill, and a century afterwards we are still fascinated by the miracle she wrought, doing what nobody could possibly have demanded.

That is the essential spirit of the cross in its simplest, most universal meaning, and when I see the cross in that light I cannot get away from it even on ordinary days. Every boy or girl here, every day in home and school, can do something beyond what anybody could have demanded. Every man or woman here every day can do for some one more than any one could have expected. This amazing spiritual power, the most elevating and impressive in the world, is in our hands even in our ordinary hours. At the beginning of this sermon the message of the cross seemed vague and general, like a program coming from a distance over the radio— public, not personal. But now I am startled, as though I had heard my own name mentioned over the air. This cross means me, ordinary me on ordinary days. Every day I can do something beyond what any one has a right to demand.

Finally, note that the consideration of this quality of life leads us straight to the need of personal Christianity, the kind, that is, which gets at a man not from without but from within. The motives and sanctions for obedience to enforceable laws are obvious. The penalties of governmental or of social displeasure fall heavily upon us unless we live up to certain external standards. But if a man is going to move over into the realm of unenforceable obligation, something must happen inside him. He must have a potent philosophy of life within, an interior criterion of conduct, a deep and inward propulsion of the spirit. He must fall in love with something from within so that he does not stintingly measure what he does for it. No one can hire, or bribe, or compel a man to live a life like Paul's, but Christ got him to do it. There is no telling how far a man will go when he loses his heart to something or some one worth following to the limit.

Professor Palmer of Harvard used to tell of a boy lying in bed very late in the morning and being called by his mother. "Aren't you ashamed to be lying here so late?" said the mother, and the boy answered, "Yes, mother, I am ashamed, but I had rather be ashamed than get up!" How familiar that mood is! All through this congregation there must be people, ashamed of things they are doing, who would rather be ashamed than get up. And that crucial, decisive next step will never be taken until something important happens inside. Recall James M. Barrie's putting of it in his play, "Dear Brutus." Says Purdie, "It isn't accident that shapes our lives," and Joanna answers, "No, it's Fate." And Purdie says, "It's not Fate, Joanna. Fate is something outside us. What really plays the dickens with us is something in ourselves. Something that makes us go on doing the same sort of fool things, however many chances we get." So! Something in ourselves! And the only cure for that is something else within ourselves, something we deeply believe in, fall in love with, give ourselves to, so that for it we will do more than any one could possibly demand. The most significant day in a man's life comes when that experience begins.

Now, this inward experience can exist in many fashions and degrees, but its highest and most potent form comes, I think, when a man feels that something has been done for him so great that he never can pay back the debt. His life no longer is his own. It does not belong to him. He is bought with a price. Some of life is cruelly unjust to us, but that is not the major element. Some of life is an earned reward, a commercial transaction, *quid pro quo,* so much for so much, but that is not the major element. The major element arrives when we feel some beauty, goodness, love, truth poured out on us by the sacrifices of others beyond our merit and deserving. Mothers and martyrs, seers, prophets and friends put us under an obligation we can never pay. So at last we stand before the cross of Christ and see that it is not solitary and unique. It is a symbol of one of the most towering facts in life, the realm of grace, the sacrificial gifts bought and paid for by those who did what we had no right to ask.

> Were the whole realm of nature mine,
> That were a present far too small;
> Love so amazing, so divine,
> Demands my soul, my life, my all.

At that point a man moves over into the realm of unenforceable obligation.

Every preacher has his dreams and this is mine, that not only will many of us ordinary men and women have this spirit of the cross in our common days but that there may be here some special boy or girl, a youth of distinguished possibility, for whom God is particularly looking. When out into his generation such a youth moves, ready to do what nobody has any right to expect, the whole world is changed. So the doors of history's new eras are opened to mankind. O Youth like that, remember that the greatest things have not yet been done; the greatest music has not been composed; the greatest books have not been written; the greatest discoveries in science have not been made; the greatest advances in social life have not been achieved; the greatest triumphs of the spirit have not been won. They wait the coming of the right men and women, distinguished by a common characteristic—they yield obedience to the unenforceable laws.

An Appeal from the Present to the Future

SOME of the greatest books in the world's literature have been written for a curious and suggestive reason: men ahead of their time, facing disbelief and opposition from their contemporaries, knowing that they would not live to see the triumph of the cause they stood for, set their faith down in a book. Thus they have borne witness against the blindness of their own time and have appealed for their vindication from a hostile present to the future.

So Job, facing the contradiction of his friends, cried,

> Oh that my words were now written!
> Oh that they were inscribed in a book!

So Jeremiah, despised and rejected of men, speaking the wisest words uttered in his time on public and spiritual issues, only to be scorned, heard God say to him, "Write thee all the words that I have spoken unto thee in a book." So Isaiah's prophecies came to be preserved. Had his contemporaries believed him and followed his counsel, the chances are we might hardly have heard of him. Constrained, as he was, however, by the antagonism of his own time to make appeal to generations yet unborn, he heard the command, "Now go, write it before them on a tablet, and inscribe it in a book, that it may be for the time to come for a witness for ever."

For such characters one feels instinctive admiration. To see a truth which your contemporaries fail to see, to believe in its victory even when you do not expect to witness it, and to put it in a book as an appeal to future generations, shows moral vigor. I wonder if ever in history there was greater need than now for this type of character.

Such men, whose quality we admire, were not, in the ordinary sense of the word, optimists. Certainly Job, Jeremiah, and Isaiah never had that reputation. Their dire denunciations of their people's sin and their realistic pictures of the consequence of contemporary evil make it impossible to ascribe to such prophetic souls soft and easy attitudes. They did not think that everything was coming out all right. They did not trust in any vague, ameliorative drift. They had not even heard the comfortable and fallacious doctrine of inevitable progress. They were exceptionally hard-headed men, living exceptionally difficult and painful lives, but they were strong in character and the cause they believed in they believed in so much that on its behalf they appealed to the future and fell on sleep leaving their faith in a book for their children's children to see.

Let us note the contrast between that type of character and some of our contemporary attitudes and tempers.

For one thing, in the light of such characters we feel the contrast between strong patience and fretful impatience. One does not mean that these prophetic souls in a cheap sense were patient. Often they were tremendously impatient with the follies, sins, and cruelties of their generation, but in a profound sense a strong patience was part of their character. They did not give up a great matter because it failed to come off successfully all at once. Around their towering souls lesser men rose and fell away—men, that is, who thought that oaks should grow like mushrooms and who, when some great matter failed to take root and flourish, were ready to sign themselves, as one letter coming to me a week ago was signed, "duped, cheated, and embittered."

Isaiah tells us of impatient people in his day saying about God, "Let him make speed, let him hasten his work, that we may see it." Jeremiah in his time described impatient people as saying, "Where is the word of the Lord? let it come now." In Jesus' day, impatient people pressed around him, supposing "that the kingdom of God was immediately to appear." How natural, how familiar, and how contemporary that is! About international peace, a decent economic order, Christian union, and many other great causes, multitudes of people, disappointed with hope deferred, that makes the heart sick, are crying, Let it come now!

Over against such fretful impatience we set today another type of character, which says in effect, Probably I shall not live to see the triumph of my cause; nevertheless, I nail that flag to the masthead; for it I stand, in it I believe, on its behalf I work, and, as for its triumph, I entrust the vindication of my faith to the future—write that in a book.

Characters of such quality realistically fit this kind of universe. Far from being the sentimental optimists they sometimes are accused of being, they are the realists. For a fretful impatience is one of the most unrealistic attitudes a man can take in this kind of world. Leonardo da Vinci, about 1500, foresaw airplanes, drew pictures of them, and put them in a book! Think of the impatient cynics since, laughing that faith to scorn, crying, Let it come now and let us see it! Well, four centuries and more have passed and Leonardo has been vindicated. He was the realist. Always the strong, wise, patient, farseeing people have been the realists.

At this point we run on one of the basic mysteries of the universe, which I do not pretend to understand. If God was going to make the cosmos, why didn't he make it, as Aladdin built his palace, with magical swiftness, finishing it overnight? I do not know. But, obviously, the method of creation in this cosmos is of another kind altogether, so that of every great matter Keats' description of the Grecian urn holds true—"Thou foster-child of Silence and slow Time." That puts on us a heavy strain. We are in a hurry. We think too much of ourselves to wait for the fulfilment of our desires some centuries after we are dead. This universe is not scaled to the short measurements of our desires. It is far too big a task for some of us to live in a world to whose God a thousand years are but as yesterday when it is past, and as a watch in the night.

In some valleys of the Tyrolean Alps it takes four hours for sunrise. Four hours the cosmos works in bringing up the dawn. But a few years ago some cinema men took a moving picture of that sunrise which is run off, they say, in ninety seconds for the delectation of the crowds. That is our way. We say to the universe, Hurry up! How natural it is! Yet we might well seek the wisdom of the long look and the patient mind. After all, not the impatient cynics but Isaiah, Jeremiah, Jesus, and the Leonardo da Vincis have been realistically right.

In the light of such strong characters we feel a contrast, also, between essential belief in the power of right and lack of that belief. Most people, I suspect, think of right as good, beautiful, lovely, ideal, but not as powerful. They leave out of their concept of right one factor which has always been present in the thinking of strong characters. In Victor Hugo's "Hernani" is a splendid passage which we might summarize by saying, Nothing in this world is so powerful as an idea whose time has come. That conviction has always belonged to strong characters. They have been certain that the adjective "mighty" belongs with the word "right" and the adjective "self-defeating" belongs with the word "wrong." Lowell put it,

Truth forever on the scaffold, Wrong forever on the throne,—
Yet that scaffold sways the future, and, behind the dim unknown,
Standeth God within the shadow, keeping watch above his own.

For the time being we may omit the divine guarantee of the victory of right.

Truth forever on the scaffold, Wrong forever on the throne,—
Yet that scaffold sways the future—

stop it there if you will. Even on the basis of observed human fact how often that has been the case!

Can we not, for example, observe the self-defeating nature of wrong in the case of war? War is wrong—that is clear. But something more than that is clear, which was not evident a few years ago—war is self-defeating; it is suicidal; no one can really win a war; the more war flourishes the more it fails; the bigger wars grow, the more intolerable they become; the more we improve the implements of war, the more they ruin those who wield them. War is not simply wrong, it is a *cul de sac;* there is no thoroughfare down that road. If some one says that in the world today war seems very powerful, I answer, Of course, and if, because of that and because a first experiment with a League of Nations has not made the war system collapse like Klingsor's palace before the magic spear in Parsifal's hand, you are out of hope, then you *are* out of hope. But some of us are not. War is self-defeating. War itself makes war on war. The more I watch the accursed thing, the more I echo Carlyle's words, "No Lie can live for ever." I do not expect to see peace splendidly victorious in my lifetime, but if wagering were possible I would wager with you. I would put it in a book. War will be subdued along with torture chambers, religious persecution, slavery, and many another curse that once possessed the earth.

Recall that day when Gladstone allied himself with the Liberal Party in Parliament and, in the face of the bitterest opposition, made his brilliant appeal for Lord Russell's Reform Bill. "You cannot fight against the future," said he. "Time is on our side. The great social forces which move onwards in their might and majesty, and which the tumult of our debates does not for a moment impede or disturb—those great social forces are against you; they are marshalled on our side; and the banner which we now carry in this fight, though perhaps at some moment it may droop over our sinking heads, yet it soon again will float in the eye of heaven . . . perhaps not to an easy, but to a certain and to a not distant victory." He turned out to be realistically right. Lord Russell's party was overturned but the next year an even more sweeping Reform Bill was passed and put into effect.

In the light of such characters, one feels a further contrast between clear insight into the momentous forces in a generation's life and lack of such insight. Almost never has a noisy thing in any generation been the really significant event. In what generation has the future ever belonged to the blatant, the ostentatious, the spectacular? Always the incredible has happened and some idea, some movement so obscure that contemporaries have almost missed it, has turned out to be the major factor in the epoch. Pick out any significant era in human history and it is a safe generalization that the great mass of its people had not the faintest idea what was important there. What turned out in the end to be of world-transforming consequence was so quiet, so unostentatious, that contemporaries well-nigh missed it.

For myself, then, I cannot realistically be a cynic. I cannot believe that this generation is utterly different from every other. I hear the raucous noises which fill the public places of the world, but when I think of what our children's children will say about this age when they look back on it, I am sure we would be utterly astounded could we listen. Always it is what the contemporaries miss that turns out to be important.

So in his time Kepler was content to say that since God had waited thousands of years for an observer of his stars, he, Kepler, could afford to wait a century for a reader. So Spinoza was banished from his home city because he was unorthodox, and after his death it was almost a hundred years before people dared mention his name with respect, much less acknowledge their indebtedness to him. So Milton got a paltry ten pounds for "Paradise Lost," and Mozart, dying in poverty, was buried in a pauper's grave. As for Socrates and Jesus, think what their contemporaries did to them!

Seeing all this, the cynic says, What is the use, then, of

believing or endeavoring great things? To which I answer, Friend, these things that the contemporaries missed were going to be the masterpieces of the world. It takes a long time for a masterpiece to win its way into the acceptation of mankind but when it is there it stays. Ten thousand lesser things rise and pass away but the masterpieces stay. Great things come slowly but they last.

Therefore pray for eyes lest we should miss the really momentous affairs of our day. Be sure of this, they are not spectacular and noisy. They are not in the limelight on the public stage. What if the great thing in our time were not violent nationalism but the slowly emerging idea of a world community? What if the great thing in our time were not economic chaos but the slowly growing idea of a new, amazing technology, socially employed to abolish poverty? What if the great thing in our time were not our miserable religious partisanships but the slowly growing possibility of a more united Christendom? What if our children's children, looking back, should say, This was the creative movement of that age to which the future was to belong? Should *that* be so, our generation would be running true to history. For my part, I am willing to write that in a book.

In the light of such characters we see a still further contrast between deep faith in a divine Coöperator and lack of such faith. In this is involved the essential meaning of belief in God. If the universe were merely materialistic, how could we wager anything on the future? All the dice would be loaded against us. Then we little people, blowing on our hands and trying to do something, would be pitting our small strength against the dead-set and vast indifference of the universe. Even if we won a victory it would be only temporary. We could not ultimately whip an antagonistic universe—be sure of that! But if at the center of creation there is a Spirit and purpose with which we can coöperate and so become in Paul's great phrase, "God's fellow-workers," then we can wager our lives upon the future. Such confidence, I think, is the essential meaning of belief in God.

Some of us as children became aware of a purpose in our home, an underlying intention in the family, that we should be educated and that, thus competently trained for some special work, we should live useful and creative lives. That undergirding purpose in the family did not take responsibility from us; it put responsibility upon us. We worked hard, but always with this stimulating fact in view—we were coöperating with a purpose greater than our own, by which everything we contributed was caught up, backed up, and carried on. We never would have gotten anywhere without *that*. And now in maturity we face a similar situation in the universe. In this age-long and tremendous task of building here a decent earth for men to live upon, are we human beings merely going it alone in a cosmos that cares naught for us and ultimately will wreck our work? Is there not an eternal purpose by which what we sow is caught up, backed up, and carried on?

Let no one here dismiss this profound problem from his philosophy of life as a light matter. Whenever any one becomes socially in earnest so that he finds himself nailing some flag to a masthead, saying, I never expect to see the victory of this cause in my lifetime but I wager my life that the future belongs to it, he faces the need of that philosophy. Every great character in history who has sacrificially appealed from a hostile present to the future has, so far as I know, believed in some kind of cosmic backing, whether he called it "philosophic dialectic" or God.

Who does not need that? Sometimes the human river runs in smooth courses, but then come rapids and cataracts and in the tumult of the time men are tempted to cry, This is the end of the world! Yet commonly such days have been the beginning of new eras, with new prospects and new courses. Suppose you had been a Hebrew in Egypt under Pharaoh, trying to make bricks without straw, when Moses rose in indignation against an intolerable situation and killed a task-master—how could you have guessed what would come of that? Suppose you had been a Jew in Palestine when the great prophets taught, who, far from seeming great to their contemporaries, were derided and scorned; when Jerusalem fell before invading armies and the prophets were powerless to do more than keep a small remnant true to their spiritual heritage—how could you have guessed what would come of that? Suppose you had been at Calvary when the power of the Roman Empire was concentrated on the fearful business of putting a glorious life to a disgraceful end—how could you have foreseen what would come of that? In a thousand troubled eras, when the hearts of men turned to water in them for fear, how could we have previsioned the outcome? Yet always the outcome has been a new epoch with larger prospects, new hopes. Our human life is a river; rapids and cataracts do not stop it—you can put that in a book.

Two travelers, one a veteran and the other a novice, were climbing in the Pyrenees. At night they were caught on one of the peaks and had to sleep upon a ledge. Toward morning a storm came up and the howling wind that the old Latins called *Euroclydon* wailed fiercely among the heights. The frightened novice waked his friend and said, "I think it is the end of the world!" "Oh, no," said the veteran, "this is how the dawn comes in the Pyrenees!"

To be sure, I am almost afraid to preach this sermon. I dread that some may think I mean that everything is coming out all right. Upon the contrary, our whole Western civilization may wreck itself. If it does, it will not be the first civilization gone to ruin, trying to escape the laws of God, in accordance with which what men and nations sow they reap. So Egypt fell and Assyria and Greece and Rome. Yet even that was not the end of the world. It takes more than such rapids and cataracts to stop the river. Modern life has richer hopes and possibilities than Egypt could have guessed or Rome have dreamed. Many a time civilizations have fallen and the fierce *Euroclydon* has howled across the world, but still the dawn was coming up, and the only realists of the time were those who kept their eyes on the things to which the future belonged.

Take a fresh look, then, at the universe! This, I think, is the innermost fact about it: it is built up of and replete with law-abiding conditions, waiting to be fulfilled to bring amazing consequences. This afternoon I shall speak over the air, and then from places like South Africa and Chile, Alaska and Newfoundland, I shall hear from the auditors. Fifty years ago that performance would have been incredible. Yet fifty years ago all the conditions which make that possible were in the cosmos waiting—waiting to be fulfilled to bring the amazing consequence. That kind of universe we inhabit. It is not the dour and dreadful thing discouraged souls suppose. The world is a bundle of potential miracles. The world is a cosmic pipe organ, on only a few of whose stops we have played while hundreds more are waiting. There is no telling what divine surprises are ahead. In any case, the conditions for the divine surprises are waiting. What a universe it is! How unworthy we are to live in it! How it calls for intelligence, for faith, for character—those three—without which it will give us nothing good but with which it will become indeed a bundle of progressive miracles!

The Dignity of Being Up to Date

ONE of the most powerful motives playing on human life today is the desire to be up to date. Advertisers, who understand the secret of persuasive appeal, habitually take this for granted and present their goods to us as the latest thing. Moreover, when we look within ourselves, we see how much we dislike being considered back numbers and how much we desire to be thought of as abreast of the times.

In the last two centuries this motive has greatly deepened its appeal. In the ancient and medieval world man's ideal was located behind him, not ahead. History had started with the garden of Eden and fallen from it; mankind had begun with its golden age and, lapsing through its silver and bronze eras, was now in the iron age and growing worse. So man's highest standards were behind him, not before, and to be up to date was no ideal at all. With the coming of the modern age, however, bringing new discoveries, new inventions, new comforts and conveniences, the golden age was transposed, in man's imagination, from the past to the future, and the psychological effects of that change constitute one of the most extraordinary and radical innovations in human history. Mankind's face was turned toward the front. In every realm tomorrow was almost certain to be more interesting than yesterday. So it came to pass that to be outmoded, old-fashioned, out of date, became one of the most distasteful estates imaginable and to be abreast of the times became a dominant desire.

What we are dealing with today, therefore, is no small matter. We are in the grip of a powerful drift of the human spirit, which none can avoid. The communists tell us that

Marxian communism, set in the totalitarian state, is the new gospel of social organization, come to displace the moss-grown ideas of the past. The fascists tell us that fascism is the great new word in social polity, come at last to triumph over decadent and moribund democracy. And when from such matters, habitually presented, mark you, in terms of being the latest thing, we turn to typical behavior in New York, we see that the Pied Piper, whose captivating tune calls the crowd after him, is always something new, or represented as new, accredited with the grace of being up to date. We parents, almost more than anything beside, fear having our children think us has-beens. You young people, almost more than anything beside, in your ideas and behavior dread being behind the times. Indeed, on the Maine coast is a sign whose existence I hardly would have credited had I not seen it: "Be up to date and buy your antiques at Sawyer's." So! In a world where, even when buying antiques, we must be up to date, it is important to consider with what kind of conduct that motive should be identified.

Religion, say some, is old stuff, but to be irreligious and atheistic is to be modern. Chastity before marriage and fidelity in it are obsolete, say some, but to be as libidinous as desire dictates is up to date. Liberty, say some, is *passé*, but the mass regimentation of the totalitarian state is the latest thing. And from such matters to popular, current vulgarities, what cheap and carnal practise does not win its way under the guise of novelty!

Let us consider whether this identification of moral looseness with modernity is justified. Let us see if we cannot lift this powerful motive to altitudes with which it is not commonly associated. So our Lord himself announced: "It was said to them of old time . . . but I say unto you." He too was pleading that men be up to date, but how many miles away his meaning was from our popular way of thinking!

In the first place, really to be up to date means that in

a contemporary day we see those ideas and causes to which the future belongs and, seeing them clearly, give ourselves to them. *That* is a long way from the moral sag and let-down with which being abreast of the times is commonly identified. Call the roll of those minds and spirits who, generation after generation, have seen a little farther than the rest into the ideas to which the future has belonged, and what intellectual dignity and moral superiority have been theirs! Whether it be Copernicus in science, or Columbus and Magellan in exploration, or Beethoven pioneering in music, or Gutenberg experimenting with movable type, or Francis Bacon, his mind flashing like a beacon from below the skyline of the age that was to be—such spirits have been really abreast of the time. Florence Nightingale with her daring faith in a new profession, Martin Luther writing his essay, "Concerning Christian Liberty," William Tuke, the Quaker, founding the first hospital for the insane in human history, Roger Williams, laying the foundations of a commonwealth where the government should keep its hands off the religious conscience—these have been up to date. Yet see to what trivial and ungodly uses we let this high motive and ambition fall!

Forgive me if, watching the desecration of this motive in our time, I am indignant. For to see people, old and young, going native in unbridled sensuality, following like sheep the drinking customs of the time, accepting sophisticated selfishness as their philosophy of life, and doing this in the name of being up to date, is not only morally but intellectually disgusting. *There is nothing new in sin.* In drunkenness there is nothing new, however modernly we dress it in the garish setting of our cocktail hours. All the motives that lead to it, the sensations involved in it, the consequences that come from it, are thousands of years old. There is nothing new in unbridled sensuality. In the days of the Arabian Nights everything that a modern man can think, feel, say, or do about it had long since been thought, felt, said, and done. There is nothing new in sophisticated selfishness. The motives that lead to it, the excuses that justify it, the consequences that flow from it, are thousands of years old.

It is the evil in life that is old-fashioned, hoary with age, and long since past engendering any fresh or novel thing. But sometimes a soul does visit the earth, pushing past obsolete customs and ideas and crying to his generation, "It was said to them of old time . . . but I say unto you," and, lo! a new day dawns. And always, mark it, these souls, the really up-to-date, move in the high realms of intellect and character. In science, in music, in art, in letters, in morals, in social reform, in religion—there and there only lies any possibility of the creatively new. And to be abreast of the times in these realms calls for the best in a man. It means not following the crowd but being true to one's vision, not letting down but rising up, not license but discipline. There is hardly a higher ideal that any man can have than to follow, even as a humble disciple, the great succession of those pioneers who, age after age, have been truly up to date.

In the second place, it follows from this that our common association of moral looseness with modernity, and moral earnestness with being old-fashioned, is mistaken. In some circles to be genuinely religious dates a man—he is a has-been. To be morally in earnest dates him—he is old-fashioned. But if a man chases the transient fads of the contemporary time, thinking, drinking, gadding, as does the common crowd, then he is accounted worthy of the accolade of modern knighthood—he is up to date.

As a matter of realistic fact, that is preposterous, and no one knowing history can be patient with it. How many, for example, understand that the latest thing in family life is monogamy? To hear the common talk, one would think that promiscuity, practical polygamy, trial marriage—taking a mate, that is, and dropping her if she is not satisfactory—

tandem marriages, and extra-marital relationships, were something new. New! Every one of them is covered with moss. They have been experimented with for centuries. Trial marriage was so firmly established in Jesus' time that a man, to be rid of his wife, needed only to give her a piece of paper and dismiss her from the home. But out of the ancient welter one new idea has come, beginning far back in history, to be sure, but with precarious stance, an idea of the family so high, so demanding, so new, that it has seemed scarcely credible—one man and one woman loving each other so much that they do not wish to love anybody else in the same way at all, and so throwing around their growing children the strong security of an abiding and dependable home. Looked at from the standpoint of history as a whole, that is the latest thing in family life. Out of endless ancient experiments, this has risen to say, It was said to them of old time . . . but I say unto you, *This is a real home*. One does wish there were more people with character enough to be up to date.

Again, how many understand that one of the most distinguishing characteristics of this modern age is faith? To hear the common talk one would suppose faith to be old-fashioned and the contemporary, disllusioned, fatalistic mood to be something new. Set in contrast with the easy-going optimism of the mid-Victorian age, materialistic determinism seems modern, realistic, up to date. Everything is predetermined, it says; we are only the pawns of fate. That sounds sophisticated, *à la mode*. As a matter of fact, however, that is thousands of years old. Age after age it has turned up in one form or another. Astrology was one phrasing of it— we are determined by our stars. Religious fatalism was another phrasing—we are predestinated by God. Materialistic determinism was another, from the days of Lucretius, before Christ, until now, saying, We are only the sport of atoms.

Who was the prize determinist and cynic of them all, calling us

> But helpless Pieces of the Game He plays
> Upon this Chequer-board of Nights and Days;
>   Hither and thither moves, and checks, and slays,
> And one by one back in the Closet lays?

That was Omar Kháyyám, ages ago. Determinism is as old-
fashioned as the Ark. What's new is faith, faith that in a
law-abiding universe, which is itself a new insight, we can
so fulfil conditions, physical, intellectual, and spiritual, that
there is no telling what, by God's grace, may come of it
at last. Few things more clearly distinguish the modern from
the ancient world than this richness and variety of faith
in human possibilities. That is new.

If a man is to be successfully up to date, the first require-
ment is that he should at least know a little concerning history. All about us, minds, innocent of information about
the past, are being invaded by ideas that they think quite
fresh and new, whereas they are mildewed and stale, musty
with age and threadbare with long handling, and what is
really new is something else altogether. I commend to you
our Lord as being abreast of the times. He belonged to the
succession of the pioneers. He was a radical—make no mis-
take about that. When he set the old, which he disregarded,
over against the new, which he accepted, he meant it. He
would not have his gospel, he said, sewed like a new patch
on an old garment or poured like fresh wine into old wine-
skins. He was a radical but he was successful at it and in
part because he started with history. Listen to him talking
about the great spiritual heritage of his people: "I came not
to destroy, but to fulfil."

Thus to begin with the great tradition, to see the emergent
truths there to which the future belongs, and then to unfold
and release them into new meanings and applications, *that*

is to be up to date. It is high and serious business. So Beethoven, the great pioneer in music, knew as much as any other man of his time about the musical heritage. So if a writer is doing something creatively fresh and adventurous with the English language, you may be sure he knows the best that has been done with it already. So if in science there comes a brand-new revelation, you may be sure it is not brand-new at all but that the man who brought it had lived for years with the high tradition of science until he had seen there an emergent truth which he could fulfil. And if in our spiritual life we are to be up to date we had best start by going deep into the great heritage and finding there the abiding truths to which the future belongs.

Young man or woman—for I am thinking most of you —if this thing I am saying is not what you mean by being up to date, then the alternative is plain. You mean chasing contemporary fads. Multitudes mean that. It is, I think, the most contemptible servitude to which the human spirit can subject itself. There is at least some intellectual and moral dignity in a man's saying that while this is the twentieth century he chooses to live upon the best ideas and the best ideals of the thirteenth century. A man might manage to live nobly so. But merely to chase contemporary fads, which for the most part are only the stale follies of the ancient world warmed over and served in new dishes, is the most contemptible tyranny to which the mind can give itself. Lift up, I pray you, this potent motive to a nobler altitude. Get your eyes on those really great truths and causes in our day that stand, like Christ himself, challenging us—It was said to them of old time . . . but I say unto you.

In the third place, let us name a few of these ideas and causes and so help ourselves to elevate our too low conception of what it means to be an inhabitant of the modern world, abreast of the times.

World citizenship is new. To be sure, it comes from the

great tradition. The Second Isaiah glimpsed it; the teachings of Jesus involved it; the early church broke over all national boundaries to reach out toward it; and men like Dante said they were citizens of the world. But tribalism and nationalism have withstood it terribly. And they are old—part of the ancient, savage, primitive origin of the race. Yet today the Hitlers and the Mussolinis come, along with echoing voices in other lands, calling militarized nationalism the new gospel, arrived at last to supersede the world-wide hopes of democracy. So they use one of the most powerful motives in the world to support the revival of one of the most savage and cruel systems of thought in history.

That is what I am trying to straighten out in my thinking. I too want to be up to date. I would hate being a has-been. I want to be abreast of the times. But I do not want to be fooled about it. And there are multitudes of voices trying to fool us. They say that dictatorial, militarized nationalism is new, and that is false; it is one of the most accursed left-overs of man's primitive savagery. What is new is world citizenship, its ideals, its possibilities, its tentative and difficult experiments. God give us grace to be up to date enough to stand for it!

Again, the liberty of the individual mind and spirit, free to think without external constraint, free to speak without fearful subservience, free to believe in God, if one will, or not to believe if one chooses—that is new. Coming though it does from the great heritage, yet up to the very doorsill of our modern time it has been only a dream. Just three centuries ago Roger Williams for the first time in history founded, in Rhode Island, a little community where the government took its hands off the religious conscience. Yet now the dictators come, fascist and communist, the exponents of the regimented and totalitarian state, saying that a completely communized life is the new ideal. Minds of men dragooned by propaganda and coercion, opinions of men penalized by incarceration and death, spirits of men put into uniform and set marching to the goose step—that is new, they say. It is a falsehood. As every sociologist knows, mankind started thousands of years ago with a primitive communism. No one allowed to think heretically on pain of death, every detail of life, within and without, regimented by tribal custom and taboo—that is where we started millennia ago. And the new thing is this struggle to release the mind and spirit of man, to give him air to breathe, to give him liberty to think and speak and live. That is new.

Again, faith in the reality of the spiritual world, sovereign in man's allegiance and supreme as the revelation of the eternal God—that is new. To be sure, it comes from the great heritage, especially from the days of Plato in Greece and the major prophets in Israel, but it has fought its way precariously against the ancient, primitive materialism of man's habits and beliefs. For materialism is where we started ages ago. Yet our modern materialists tell our young people that man's spiritual life is the by-product of matter, as though that idea were new, a modern discovery, now at last illumining the world, philosophy *à la mode* and up to date. That is a falsehood. As every anthropologist knows, the first theory man ever had about himself was materialistic. His life was his blood, his only soul was his breath, his whole self was his body, and there was no life for him here or anywhere save as the function of the flesh. That is where the race started thousands of years ago. The first theory man had about himself was a primitive behaviorism. And the emergent truth, which has been struggling all these centuries to cast off the confinement of thus taking appearances for granted, has been the concept of man as a spiritual being, born with a spiritual heritage, possessing a spiritual nature, intended for a spiritual destiny. That is new.

We modernists, I think, are under special obligation to

emphasize this line of thought because we have accentuated being up to date.

New occasions teach new duties; Time makes ancient good
    uncouth;
They must upward still, and onward, who would keep abreast
    of Truth.

So we have said, and it is true. Indeed, there is hardly a better way to describe what sin is than to say that it means being belated, obsolete, out of date. Banditry was once an all-but-universal principle of action and head-hunting was a road to honor and prestige, so that our modern bandits are simply belated people living in a new world upon an old principle long out of date. Race prejudice was once a necessity to tribal integrity in a world of incessant and bitter war, but now, in our modern world of intermeshed mutuality, it is a monstrous evil and hopelessly belated. Flogging little children was once taken for granted in practically every family but a family that practises that technique now advertises itself a colossal failure, for flogging is out of date. To forgive a man who had wronged you was once considered weakness and brought only derision, but now to be vindictive and vengeful is the sure symptom of a small mind, because in all high-minded morals vindictiveness is out of date. You see, it is a great thing to be up to date if we make a great thing out of it.

The early church did. We Christians have given youth much cause to think of religion as musty, dog's-eared, and old-fashioned. Those first Christians, however, went out from the influence of a Master who said, "It was said . . . but I say." They called their sacred book the New Testament. They said with Paul, "The old things are passed away; behold, they are become new." When they dreamed their fairest hopes of their movement's aim and consequence, they dreamed "new heavens and a new earth, wherein dwelleth righteousness." On every page of the New Testament you can hear the spirit of man saying, Hats off to the past, coats off to the future!

This spirit, whose recovery would do as much as anything to make Christianity come alive again, is dominant there for one basic reason—the early Christians thought the future belonged to Christ. They thought he was not behind but ahead of them. I think he is ahead still, far ahead, the great pioneer. If one would be really abreast of the times, see him there, moving before our souls and our societies, crying still, "It was said . . . but I say."

Giving the Highest a Hearing*

A FTER these many months of comparative seclusion and
quiet, you would hardly expect me on this first Sunday morning of our reunion to speak about the affairs
of the world, with its social upheavals and clamorous problems—you have been living in that world yourselves. You
might, however, expect me to speak about another realm,
where I perforce have been, where one must stop being
active and become receptive, stop being strenuous and become
quiet, stop talking and listen.

Centuries ago Elijah had that experience. In the midst
of a strenuous life, in a turbulent time, an emergency befell
that put a stop to his active social struggle and led him on
a long journey to the wilderness of Sinai. There, as though
to picture his own life to him, the noisiest things in creation
passed before him—a strong wind, an earthquake, a raging
fire, and God in none of them. Then in the narrative come
the words which to succeeding centuries have rightly seemed
among the most significant in the ancient literature of religion: "And after the fire a still small voice. And it was
so, when Elijah heard it, that he wrapped his face in his
mantle, and went out, and stood."

So, long ago, a man came to the place where he gave the
Highest a hearing.

Such is our predisposition that we naturally estimate listening to a still small voice as both more easy and less significant than dealing robustly and effectively with the world's
hurly-burly. But even a moment's serious reflection indi-
cates that giving the Highest a hearing is about as important an event as ever happens in human life.

* The first sermon preached after a long, enforced vacation.

The turning points in scientific progress have been associated with it. One man, compelled by the prevalence of a pestilence to suspend his teaching labors at the University of Cambridge, and forced, like Elijah, to take a vacation in the country, sat in his garden and, seeing an apple fall, listened to a still small voice about what it meant. To scientists as to other people, this noisy world is a stimulating place in which to do things but a poor place in which to hear things. When, therefore, we trace back momentous scientific achievements to their creative origins, we commonly come to secluded and listening minds like Copernicus, or Newton, or Darwin, each in his own realm giving an idea a hearing.

Even more obviously is this experience associated with the turning points of man's spiritual progress. A new idea succeeds in catching the inner ear of some attentive soul and, lo! an era begins. It may be a carpenter who listens until the very flowers on Galilean hillsides speak to him and he is captured and commanded by an inner voice so that he will die on Calvary rather than deny its imperious validity, and centuries afterwards men still know that if they would listen to what he heard they would find the things that belong unto their peace.

This profound, interior experience of sensitive audition to the Highest is not easy, nor is it a mystic matter isolated from the world. It goes to the very quick of life. Of all of us in this audience it is true that sometime or other, in a way large or small, we have had a spiritual disaster; some ethical failure, some moral tragedy has befallen us; and as we carry back our memory to the causative beginning of that lamentable time we know that it need never have happened if we had listened to an inner voice. To be sure, there were urgent clamors persuading us to what we did but there was another kind of voice—our better selves, our finer moods, our common sense, our consciences—divine mentors that al-

most always speak in a quiet tone. In this sense, the most
deplorable tragedies that befall mankind come because we
will not give the Highest a hearing. Even railroad crossings
advertise the warning, "Stop, Look, Listen."

With this much preparation of our thought, let us now
walk about our truth and see it, one aspect at a time. In the
first place, we must take it for granted that the appeal of
the Highest will habitually come to us quietly, modestly,
without obtrusiveness. We might have made this world other
than it is, with the loveliest things shouting at the top of
their voices and evil things shy and retiring, but, as it is,
the actual world behaves far otherwise. When the New Testament presents the divine method of approach to life, it pictures God as saying, "Behold, I stand at the door and knock:
if any man hear my voice and open the door, I will come
in to him, and will sup with him, and he with me." So the
Divine is not obtrusive; he bursts into no man's life unbid-
den; he is reserved and courteous. He knocks at the door
to see if any one, listening there, may care to welcome him.

How true to our experience this picture is becomes evident when we consider the divine voices in detail. Beauty
does not shout at us. The fairest things we know are not
clamorous—the loveliness of flowers, or of woods at sunset
time, or of poems, or of moving symphonies, or of a mountain stream

> In the leafy month of June,
> That to the sleeping woods all night
> Singeth a quiet tune.

Consider how beauty stands upon our doorsills and knocks
to see if some one within may be interested.

Our finest moods are not clamorous. Our worst moods
are. Our tempers, passions, and despairs can blow like howling hurricanes and thunder like Jove, but when the hour

of visitation from on high arrives and a nobler mood is ours, it almost always speaks with a still small voice.

Our consciences commonly are difficult to hear. Especially in the world's continuous din and furious explosions, a man must take heed if he is to hear his conscience speak. The young son of a friend of mine said once to his father, "What is conscience?" to which my friend answered, "I am not quite sure what conscience is, but, son, whenever that telephone bell rings, you take down the receiver and listen."

All the familiar appeals of the Highest speak in calm tones. The admonitions of experience, the reasonableness of common sense, the appeal of a new idea slipping silently into the mind, the call of social need, described by Wordsworth as "the still, sad music of humanity," and even those more tremendous advents of God into select souls, to their own transformation and the shaking of the world—seldom are such approaches of the Highest noisy.

When, then, in such a boisterous world a man tries to keep his soul alive, he finds that one of the central problems is maintaining a sensitive ear for these quiet voices. If to any this fact seems a sweet and gentle thing to say, it shows how little its import is understood. The great characters of history that most have stood like towers of brass against the tumult of the world have so been built. Each of them had an inner voice so imperiously clear that when the pinch came and the cries of the crowd were against him, that voice was more commanding to him than all else. So in times like these, when strident voices make hubbub of the days and the ugliest things are often the loudest, and what men would have us think and do is dinned into our ears with noisy propaganda, there is desperate need of men and women who have learned this deep, essential art of the spiritual life, giving the Highest a hearing. Only so come free souls, free in the only way souls ever can be free, their dominant control not clamor without but a voice within. So Elijah, of the still small voice, was the most titanic moral figure in Israel's history for four centuries.

In the second place, note that however practical we try to make this truth and however for from creed and church we carry its illustration, we are dealing here with the essence of religion. If nothing else were accomplished this morning, I should be glad for the benefit of some to translate the meaning of prayer into the terms of this truth. Few things make more evident our obsession with strenuousness, activity, aggressiveness, than our habitual treatment of praying as though it meant mainly or merely our talking to God. Even when we pray, many of us will not drop our aggressive self-assertiveness. But look at the Hebrew prophet: "After the fire a still small voice. And it was so, when Elijah heard it, that he wrapped his face in his mantle, and went out, and stood." *There* was momentous prayer, with momentous social consequences, but Elijah was not talking; he was listening.

You will understand, then, that our appeal in this matter is no mere modernist endeavor to escape the intellectual difficulties involved in self-assertive praying. Rather, this is part of the great tradition. As the ancient Psalmist said, "I will hear what God the Lord will speak." To be sure, this is not the only kind of prayer. Communion with God is a great sea fitting every bend in the shore of human need. But he who never listens when he prays never prays. Here is a meaning of prayer which makes it an indispensable attitude of the soul. In a very noisy world prayer is giving the Highest a hearing.

Indeed, here is a function of the church which, recovered and exalted, would enable us to meet one of the deep needs of human life. Men and women desperately need help in giving the Highest a hearing. One evening I had finished my serious reading and was casually scanning the advertisements of a magazine when to my surprise my eye fell on this statement about an insurance company: "We are an old, conservative company, operating on old-fashioned principles." "Why!" said I, "here is a strange thing; almost everything advertised today is praised because it is new. Buy this article, the advertisers say; it is the latest thing, in the most modern mode. But here is another note—'We are an old, conservative company, operating on old-fashioned principles.'" There may be things, then, which we profoundly need that are not merely modern. In automobiles we would wish the latest smartness, but not necessarily in insurance companies, on which security depends. So, while I am a modernist in religion to my finger-tips, if it be old-fashioned to conceive the central function of the church as helping men and women in a turbulent time to hear their divine voices within, whose quiet persuasion makes the best personal character and social progress that we know but whose appeal can be so easily drowned out by the world's uproar, then so be it!

None of us can easily learn this fine art of listening to the Highest. It takes technique; it requires practise; it calls for a fellowship of friends in kindred endeavor trying to make divine voices imperiously clear. Even listening to music is an art. But to listen to an inner voice that talks of high motives in a world ridden by low motives, of cleanness in an age blatant with uncleanness, of Christ in a social order that still crucifies him—in such a world, where the lowest so commonly is the loudest, we need a fellowship to help us give the Highest a hearing.

In the third place, not only personal religion but, to a degree that at first one might hardly guess, personal character is involved in our truth. If some one has been saying that it is possible to over-emphasize giving the Highest a hearing, that on that point the New Testament itself issues a warning which the preacher had better heed: "Be ye doers of the word, and not hearers only, deluding your own selves," I agree. Hearing truth without doing anything about it is a peril to character. But, after all, lack of aggressiveness is not our prevalent disease; activism is our chronic state of mind; whatever else we are, in church or out of it, we are doers. Without much fear of betraying this audience into lack of balance, therefore, I plead that, while of course it is a danger to be a hearer and not a doer, for many of us it is even a greater peril to try to be doers—restless, impatient, aggressive doers—when all the time the interior voices of divine guidance have been drowned out in the world's uproar, so that like a ship with its compass out of order we go plunging strenuously on, off our course.

When we trace back great character to its genesis, we commonly come to a listening ear. We think, for example, that we know much more about child psychology than our forefathers did, but many a story in the Bible goes to the quick of a child's life. Once a young boy named Samuel, for whose coming his mother had prayed before he was conceived and who had been dedicated to the service of God while still she carried him beneath her heart, was taken to the temple to serve the altar. So, that little lad, thus prepared, heard God talking to him in the night. It is an old story but how timeless the record sounds—"And the Lord came, and stood, and called as at other times, Samuel, Samuel. Then Samuel said, Speak; for thy servant heareth."

Not only does the genesis of great character commonly go back to such experience, as many of us know well, but the maintenance of great character goes back to its repetition. Indeed, my sermon had come thus far on when I remembered that somewhere in William James' *Psychology* was a famous passage in which the essence of will was interpreted in terms of the capacity to pay attention, so that when we try to understand what free will is—the power of choice— we come at bottom to this mysterious faculty within us by which we pay attention to one thing rather than another. So, turning to his *Principles of Psychology*, I found it: "Effort of attention is thus the essential phenomenon of will." That is to say, what we give habitual hearing to inevitably determines our choices.

Then to my surprised eyes the next sentences presented my sermon from a psychologist's point of view. For William James describes a man in a passion, the turbulence of cupidity or lust or temper noisy within him, in a fit mood to ruin himself withal, and fighting off all listening to the cool, calm voices of reasonable ideas. Concerning this familiar situation James says, "Passion's cue accordingly is always and everywhere to prevent their still small voice from being heard at all," to which he adds, "The strong-willed man . . . is the man who hears the still small voice unflinchingly."

That is pertinent to every one of us. That situation is reduplicated how continually in this company! On how many hearts are memories engraved of tragedy that need never have taken place had we but listened! What tragedies today are on their way, due to arrive tomorrow, that would never happen if some soul now would listen! Strange, penetrating word of the Master, so often quoted, so little understood: "He that hath ears to hear, let him hear."

Finally, I do not see how any man can maintain his courage and morale in a day like this if he hears nothing but the noisy voices. Recovery of morale is not commonly associated with uproar but with quiet places. So the twenty-third Psalm strikes a universal note—

> He leadeth me beside still waters.
> He restoreth my soul.

Elijah himself was a whipped and beaten man when he left for the wilderness, a disillusioned public servant, a tired liberal, a disheartened prophet ready to quit, but he heard something in that still small voice that sent him back to his work again like an army with banners, his soul restored. Far from feeling deserted, he was convinced now that there was a strong minority in Israel that had not bowed the knee to Baal, that the cause he had thought was lost need not be lost at all, that, though he had been defeated in a moral battle, he could still be victor in the moral war. He came back to fight again, confident that the future of the world belonged, not to the noisy forces, but to the still small voices.

Human history can be told in terms of the successive victories of quiet forces over their noisy enemies. Repeatedly in science, as well as morals, in politics as well as religion, some new idea has come so silently that it caught at first but the inner ear of one who listened and then was heard by but a few, like the twelve disciples about our Lord in Galilee, and all around these still small voices raged the antagonistic world. But again and again the ultimate victory has come, not to the shouts upon the street corner, but to the voice heard in the inner chamber, as Jesus said.

Has some one here been saying that the supreme need today is for courageous minds to build a better social order and a new international system? You know how cordially I agree with that. But because we do so desperately need men and women of undiscourageable faith and effort whom this world can neither whip nor tame, we need this deeper thing we have been speaking of.

> Breathe through the heats of our desire
>   Thy coolness and thy balm;
> Let sense be dumb, let flesh retire;
> Speak through the earthquake, wind, and fire,
>   O still small voice of calm!

Decision of Character

JESUS once met a teacher of his people, a high-principled, thoughtful man, who answered the Master's questions, we are told, discreetly. To him Jesus offered a new venture of spiritual experience but the man missed it, almost rose to it but not quite, and went away with little or nothing to show for the most critical opportunity of his career. And Jesus summed up the situation in words which many of us need to hear: "Thou art not far from the kingdom of God." So! Not far, nearly, almost, not quite—and "a miss is as good as a mile."

This familiar experience is not commonly enough recognized. With our rough and ready methods of classification, we divide people into black and white. Good or evil, we say, right or wrong, successful or a failure, well or sick. So we chop life in two and catalogue the opposites. We are in a hurry; there is not much time for finesse in shading; we see folk as one thing or the other. That, however, misrepresents real life. Real life is made up mainly of the not-fars, the almosts, the not-quites—nearly right, nearly successful, nearly well—skirting boundary lines where it seems as though a single step would carry us over.

Indeed, in this realm lie how many of our tragedies! The motorist tries to take a corner at forty miles an hour and almost succeeds. The student depends for his promotion on passing an examination and almost gets through. The airman tries a long non-stop flight and nearly arrives. A friend of ours is very ill and almost pulls through. A business man is trusted with a new responsibility in his corporation and comes not far from making good. A youth stands wavering between his lower and his better self and almost takes the upper path. That is real life.

One of the bitterest memories of the Great War, so far as the Allies are concerned, is Gallipoli. One who has been there since, as I have been, can picture the courage and gallantry of that expedition which, landing under fire at the place where the Dardanelles and the Ægean meet, fought its way almost to Constantinople and then turned back again. Now we learn that the Turks had given up hope, that, reduced to their last rounds of ammunition, they supposed they were beaten, and that the order for the evacuation of Constantinople already had been written. Almost, nearly, not quite!

Week after week in this congregation we are mainly interested in trying to see what *is* right, charting a course on this stormy sea that we may know where we ought to steer. Accordingly we elucidate and clarify, argue and discuss. But all the time another problem lurks in the shadows of our lives. There are rights and duties we do see, truths and values we know well enough to act upon, but we do not act. Not lack of knowledge but feebleness of will is our trouble there—not ignorance but indecision. We skirt boundaries on the other side of which are the duties we do know, the rights we do behold, the values we do acknowledge—not far from chosen, almost, not quite.

Let us see then what we can make of this experience, so familiar but so commonly neglected.

In the first place, some of us skirt the boundary lines of a better life, not far from them, not quite crossing them, because of an instinctive fear of a new experience. The fear of the new, while it is a common human trait recognized by everybody, is not often applied to this realm—we are afraid of our own spiritual possibilities and of venturing on a new life that requires giving up an old one. The psychologists have made this fact vivid, if not lurid, by showing how many children suffer from it as they grow up. A child likes being a child, nestles into the comfort and security of a beautiful home, so that, when the inevitable hour strikes for the emerging responsibilities of youth, the child shrinks back. He does not want to leave his cocoon and trust the spread of his own wings. Only those on the inside know the emotional wreckage caused by the fear of children about growing up. Here is one of the major causes of the emotional collapses, the nervous breakdowns, the suicides even, of adolescent and early college youth. Concerning such a case one often hears it said, He was so fortunately reared, he had so beautiful a home, why—? The fortunate security of the child's home was the precise reason why, when the emerging independence of maturity arrived and especially the dreadful necessity of making good or of failing on his own, he shrank back. He was afraid. He may never have said it to himself—he rationalized; he made up other reasons for it—but he was afraid of the responsibilities of maturity.

Most of us have gotten past that, although everybody here had a nervous time doing it, but we are not past the basic fact which that illustrates—fear of a new experience when its acceptance involves giving up an old one.

Almost every one seems to think that the experience of the Prodigal Son, for example, when he left the companionship of swine for the welcome of his father's home, was beautiful. But any one who knows what is involved in such an experience entertains dour imaginations of it. For the Prodigal Son had accustomed himself to the far country. He had chosen it, committed himself to it, staked his reputation on it, become habituated to it, so that now, although hating it, when the thought rose that he might leave it and try the venture of going home, what derisive voices must have spoken in him! You belong here, they said. You cannot go home. Your father will not welcome you. You have not strength to maintain your life there if you should go. You chose this; you belong here. How often, think you, did that Prodigal almost decide to start, not quite, nearly? And in this so-called respectable congregation, how many of us, think you, in some moral problem know, in some degree, what he went through before he brought himself to acting on his determination, "I will arise and go to my father"?

In many a chemical experiment all the ingredients are in the test tube waiting for the decisive jar of the operator's finger to precipitate the crystals, and in many lives all the ingredients of knowledge are present, waiting for the determinative stroke of the volition to act. But there we fail. "I will arise"—there we shrink back, bogged down and sunk, not far from the kingdom of God! If we could know how many of the worst men in history came close to being the best, and how many of the best men in history came close to being the worst, what fascinating information would be revealed!

Of course, this is as true about man's social life as it is of his individual experience. We know that sometime we will have to leave the war system and trust the peace system for our security, but see how we hold back! When the pithy moment of decision comes we shrink back upon the old, absurd, suicidal methods of militaristic security. As another put it, Disarmament is like a social function where nobody wishes to arrive until he is sure that every one else is already there. So the world continues on the verge of doing something decisive for peace—almost, nearly, not quite.

It is of our individual problems, however, we are thinking today. Throughout this congregation there are people within reaching distance of a moral good which would redeem to a new quality our personal habits, our family relationships, our business practises, our spiritual resources. We could, as it were, take a single step and be there, and we do not. I knew a man once who became a Christian from that very situation. My friend, walking with him in the evening, saw how close he was to a superior spiritual life, and, with his cane drawing a line upon the street, he said, "You are as near as that to being a Christian. Will you?" Well, will *you*? Or shall we remain forever among the nearlies, almosts, not-fars, and not-quites?

In the second place, some of us skirt boundary lines not far from a better life but do not quite cross them, because of the inherent difficulty of making up our minds. The hardest work in the world is to decide. Even when we have light enough upon the subject and clarity as to what ought to be chosen, the hardest work in the world is decision. Doubtless this is one of the reasons, as the psychiatrists say, for the multiplying rate of nervous breakdowns and even mental collapses. For one has only to imagine back a long generation to find a time when individuals did not have to decide for themselves so many details of belief and behavior as they do now. To be sure, Matthew Arnold spoke of the "perplexities and confusion" of his time. Every generation seems to its inhabitants sufficiently disturbing, but some of us remember a day when individuals did not have to decide so many things as now. That is to say, there was a social consensus of opinion, a general body of agreement about belief, about behavior, about right and wrong. The individual was not so much dependent upon himself in making up his mind. He was sustained, directed, sometimes fairly coerced by the community's consensus of moral judgment. But now, in a city like New York, for multitudes of individuals there is no social consensus. Almost any kind of belief or of behavior can find backing somewhere. The individual is thrown back upon himself alone, amid conflicting codes and standards, to make up his mind about almost everything he is to think or do. And the result, alas, is commonly not rugged individualism but feeble individualism; a condition, that is, where individuals, forced to decide amid multitudinous possi-bilities of choice, crack up under the strain. They cannot carry so heavy a load of decision, and so the breakdowns multiply and the asylums fill up.

If some of us have managed to get through this difficult time, the reason is not far to seek. We kept around us, for one thing, the family group, with its great traditions, with its consensus of moral judgment, so that, when the times for decision came too thick and fast, we were supported and directed by a home, to which, above all else, we wished to be loyal. And we have kept around us the church group, with its high heritage, its fellowship of the noble living and the noble dead, by whose strong, stabilizing, confirming tradition we have been steadied when the demand for individual decision would have swamped us. For it is hard to decide. This sermon comes out of poignant sympathy with people who find it so. Deciding is the most difficult task in the world.

When some man whom we admire makes a decision, all we see is the result. We cannot see the conflict in his mind, the pros and cons that clashed there, the narrow shave between the choice he made and another choice altogether that he nearly made. A man like Charles Darwin, for example, seems intellectually predestined for biology. As a matter of fact, Darwin became a biologist by the skin of his teeth. For one thing, like many another boy he could have made a failure of his life, and apparently he almost did, for his father told him when he was a youth, "You care for nothing but shooting, dogs, and rat-catching, and you will be a disgrace to yourself and all your family." When young Darwin did wake up, he intended to be a practising physician like his father, his brother, and his uncle, and we are assured by his biographer, after a series of if-clauses, that if this long and varied series of events had not dovetailed together there is not one chance in ten that Darwin would have been *Darwin*. How tight the squeaks are! How hairbreadth the escapes! Some of us almost missed the thing we got and some of us almost got the thing we missed. We have close elections in politics but they are nothing to the close elections in the commonwealth of one's soul.

Indeed, how many do you suppose are here today in whom a little moral decision now would save no end of misery hereafter? How many are there in whom a fine decision might even bear results that the world would hear about? So Walt Whitman summed up his intellectual adolescence: "I was simmering, simmering, simmering," he said; "Emerson brought me to a boil." You have put me in this pulpit, in a university community, and asked me week by week to try to make the things of the spirit more real to you. By God's grace I will try. But how can I help thinking of the people, young people in particular, who year after year go on simmering and simmering? A greater than Emerson, Christ, calls to them as long ago he called to the young scholar of his people, and still they simmer. They are not far from the boiling point. That is the tragedy—nearly, almost, not quite.

Some of you have been on the Bernina Pass in Switzerland, with the Engadine on one side and on the other the far stretches of Italy. Do you remember those two small lakes there, with but a narrow watershed between them? It is strange to think that, so near at the beginning, they should be so far apart in destiny. For one flows into the Adriatic and the other, at last, into the Black Sea. I suppose that not a week passes without there being some one here on his Bernina Pass. You may resent it if you want to— sometimes I do—that the far sundered destinies of men should so depend on hairbreadth escapes, but an honest minister, who is not responsible for having made this universe, can only tell you the truth. And it is the truth. Some one here may some day flow into his Black Sea and remember this hour when with him it was *almost*.

Finally, many people skirt the boundary of a better life,

not far from it, not crossing it, because they think they can remain undecided, go on all their lives balancing tentatively the pros and cons. They forget one of the most pertinacious facts in life, that while a man may hold his opinions in suspense he cannot hold his living in suspense. Life gets made up one way or another. To be sure, there are wide ranges of theoretical discussion where one may remain undecided till he dies. Which of the various theories concerning the origin of the Aurora Borealis is correct I do not know. One does not have to know. One does not even have to guess. One does not have to make up his mind about that because one does not have to make up his life about that. Thus there are wide ranges of argument where one can be undecided till he dies. But today we are thinking not of that discursive realm of argument, where one can hold his opinion in abeyance forever, but of a realm far deeper, more vital, where, though we may succeed in not making up our minds, we cannot help making up our lives.

I was brought up alongside the Niagara River, where with a deep and powerful current it flows out from Lake Erie toward the Falls, and many an evening, after a fishing trip, I have fought my way back in a rowboat across that obdurate current to my landing place. Ever since, I have been meeting people who remind me of a man in a rowboat going down the Niagara River and debating the relative advantages and disadvantages of stopping at Buffalo. There may be many considerations pro and con that an open and unprejudiced mind might wish to consider. Continue, I should say, your debate as to the advisability or inadvisability of stopping at Buffalo, but in the meantime the inexorable sweep of Niagara has not waited for the conclusion of your debate and, if you cannot settle it by discussion, the Niagara will settle it. You will not have stopped at Buffalo.

How much like life that is! Perhaps some one here cannot quite make up his mind about the principles on which to manage his love experience, whether to be true to the high ideals of monogamy, with continence before marriage and loyalty afterward, or whether to take refuge in temporary liaisons or promiscuity. He knows the opposing arguments that throng the minds of men in a town like this. He cannot quite make up his mind. But, man, you cannot help making up your life. Life gets lived one way or the other.

Or here is one who, however blind he may be, cannot fail to see that an evil habit is thrusting him into thraldom. As Epictetus put it: "See children thrusting their hands into a narrow-necked jar, and striving to pull out the nuts and figs it contains: if they fill the hand, they cannot pull it out again, and then they fall to tears." To such a child one would say sensibly, You must let go; you never will be free until you let go. But still the child might stand, desire for the nuts and figs on one side, desire for freedom on the other, not able to make up his mind. Surely that childish situation is reduplicated here today. Some indulgence on one side, desire for freedom on the other—you cannot make up your mind. But your life is being made up. Indecision is a fantasy. There is no such thing. Life gets made up.

Deeper yet, here we are in this mysterious pilgrimage between two eternities, with its strange birth, its varied fatalities, its hardships and cruelties, its love and joy, and then its death, and all this, some people think, must be lived with no more strength than a man can somehow succeed in engendering within himself. Life may be lived, however, as the great saints have lived it—sinking shafts within the soul which strike the nether springs where power comes in from beyond ourselves, bringing such reserve and resource that, though life be hard and troubles thick, "they that are with us are more than they that are with them." Surely, I know the pros and cons of debate concerning religion and irreligion. Surely, I know the conflict of arguments between Christ and Antichrist. But that does not mean we are not deciding.

We may hold our opinions in suspense. We cannot hold our living in suspense.

Friends, it is because this range of fact is so true and so powerfully operative that we never can quite reduce living to a pure science. Pure science does remarkably well in keeping itself tentative, open-minded, uncommitted. To be sure, even pure science has to decide some things. At Al Azhar, the orthodox Moslem university at Cairo, my friend asked one of the professors what astronomy they taught there— that the sun goes around the earth or that the earth goes around the sun—and with a bland and amiable open-mindedness he answered, "We teach both." Even pure science has to be more decisive than that. Yet pure science does extraordinarily well at being tentative, indeterminative, open-minded, holding back decision for more light. But *life* cannot be like that. Life, like an inexorable Niagara, sweeps on. Life gets made up one way or another.

So, always in great living there is a kind of sporting wager, a man gambling, shall I say? on the best he can see, the noblest he can perceive, the truest he can get his eye upon, staking his life on the high against the low, on Christ against Antichrist.

At Carnegie Hall the other day, after the orchestra had finished a glorious symphony, my friend said, "After all, in spite of life's brutalities and cruelties, its Hitlers and Mussolinis and rumors of war, there must be something noble in man worth living for if he can dream such glories and so play them." There is the essential platform of a great life. Granted life's sordidness and brutality. Granted that you cannot always get the argument finished in a neat Q. E. D. Will you wager your life on the best you can see, the finest you can get your eye upon? "Will you?" said Jesus. Again and again you have that phrase, Will you?

Some time ago Mussolini's agents caught a man whom they had long been looking for. He was an anti-fascist and had fled across the boundaries of Italy into Austria. They knew where he was living just over the border. So they framed a situation that brought him to the frontier, and they caught him on the line. That is where most of us are caught, on the frontier, not far from the kingdom of God—nearly, almost, not quite.

There Is No Death

E VEN here on earth we live in the presence of some things for which there is no death. "Three times three equals nine"—there is no death for that. From everlasting to everlasting, always and everywhere, that will live on. To be sure, the counters on which we figure it and to which we apply it are transient and will pass away. But "three times three equals nine" moves in another realm, invisible, intangible, immutable, eternal.

Here lies the reason why great mathematicians are always reverent and are commonly religious. Mathematicians do not live in a transient and fugitive world where one can sum up life by saying, "Change and decay in all around I see." They live in a world where one naturally might say, "O thou who changest not, abide with me!" Nothing more awe-inspiring is known to the intellect of man than the vista which the higher mathematics opens into the infinite, and even to ordinary folk like us it reveals the possibility of living here and now in an eternal world.

Why, however, should the experience of the eternal be limited to that realm alone? If man is thus capable of living here and now in an imperishable realm, why should one suppose that a capacity so profound and meaningful is restricted to one area only? Such questions mankind, especially from the days of Plato on, has been asking. And the message of Easter morning comes in answer. For some things, it says, there is no death. They do not belong in the realm where death moves. Death can get no hold on them, can do nothing against them, is as irrelevant to them as though a man with a sword should try to slay the truth of a mathematical formula. So, as the Fourth Gospel reports it, Jesus said to Martha when

[261]

her brother lay dead, "Whosoever liveth and believeth on me"—that is, whosoever enters into and shares my quality of life—"shall never die"—that is, death has nothing it can do to that. "Believest thou this?" said Jesus.

Note at once that thus to say, You shall never die, is not the way in which immortality is usually referred to. As the matter commonly stands in man's imagination, death is unescapable. Man is mortal and we all shall die—so runs the tale—and the question is, After death has thus done its ruinous work, can we hope for restoration to life again? Go through this congregation even on Easter morning and note how many of us so put the question, postponing eternal life until after death. That however, is not the New Testament's way of conceiving the matter. Here and now, it says, we are in the presence of the eternal. Here and now we can enter into and experience the world invisible, intangible, imperishable. Here and now we need not be merely fugitive and transitory creatures but can have within ourselves eternal life. For that there is no death; in the story of that, what we call death is only an incident; that never dies. Ah, my soul, deep and difficult though it is for our earth-bound imagination to conceive, if we can make that real to ourselves today, this will be an Easter morning.

Consider, in the first place, that this way of putting it provides the only reasonable starting point for believing in immortality at all. If our world now is altogether transient and fugitive, what possible reason is there for supposing that after death we can suddenly be ushered into a world eternal and imperishable? What magic potency can death possess so to transfer us from a life with nothing eternal in it to a life that is eternal? Such an account of the situation sounds like a fairy tale and it is a fairy tale. No wonder intelligent people do not believe it.

That picture, however, does not represent the facts. Here and now, from mathematics up and down, we deal with invisible, imperishable things, which the tooth of time cannot gnaw nor the scythe of death mow down. What we are believing in on Easter morning is not the restoration to life of something that is transient, but the continuance in life of something that has always been, by its very nature, eternal.

This, of course, is what the New Testament means by eternal life. Always in the New Testament, eternal life is a present possession here and now. Indeed, it is so urgently a present possession that one might almost say that in the New Testament eternal life is a matter of now or never. Whatever hope of the future we have, the New Testament teaches, depends upon whether now we have in our lives an eternal quality. Transient things are transient, here or anywhere. They cannot last. Eternal things are eternal, here and everywhere. They cannot help lasting. So the New Testament calls us to a quality of life that is eternal now: "He who hears my word and puts his faith in Him who sent Me, has eternal life"; "We know that we have crossed over from death to life, because we love"; "He that hath the Son hath the life"; "This is eternal life—to know Thee, the only true God, and Jesus Christ, whom Thou hast sent." So, always in the present tense, eternal life is not a postponed affair but is an immediate, exigent, urgent quality, a kind of living with which death has nothing to do.

This way of putting the matter, as you see, brings the difficult question of immortality within the factual realm. I mean that, as a matter of actual fact, we live now in two worlds—the one visible, tangible, temporal, the other invisible, intangible, with a sense of timelessness in it. "The things which are seen are temporal," says Paul. Granted! But that does not comprise all our life or the realest portion of it. What about that other world we live in even here and now— the things that are not seen?

Every minister at some time has heard a man deriding faith in God on the ground that God is invisible, impalpable, and therefore unreal. The New Testament, a man says, it may be with a touch of scorn, tells the truth on at least one matter—"No man hath seen God at any time." I fail to get the force of that argument. No man has seen a thought at any time although thoughts are immensely creative forces in human life. No man has seen love at any time although love is the builder and maker of the city of God on earth. No man has seen faith and courage or the interior fellowship of soul with Over-Soul. Indeed, no man has even seen himself. His body, this essentially transient thing, yes, but himself—self-conscious personality with powers of intelligence, purposefulness, and goodwill—none ever saw that. In two worlds we live, with one of which visibility, time, and death have everything to do, but in the other of which there is a sense of timelessness, as though truth and love and beauty and character might go on expanding forever.

Friends, we iron our lives down too much, make them too flat and simple. That is why we cannot believe in great things. But our lives are far more mysterious now than commonly we think. A little girl in school, anxious about her acquisition of knowledge in comparison with the whole realm of knowledge to be acquired, asked the teacher, "Do I know now as much as I don't know?" Ah, child, you never will know as much as you do not know. That's the mystery. Always the realm of knowledge, like every other spiritual realm, encompasses us, infinite, unfathomable, inexhaustible, eternal. And this is the greatest mystery of all, that already we live in such realms—the things seen, temporal; the things not seen, eternal.

We are not saying that this proves life after death. No one can prove life after death, for proof involves verification. But this way of putting the matter opens wide the doors to it. If we live now in eternal realms, why should that part of us, the most important part, stop for death? We are not saying that death takes transient lives and makes them imperishable. We are saying that what is eternal is eternal and that for it there is no death. Believest thou this?

In the second place, let us note that, at any rate in a reasonable universe, death ought not to stop eternal life so begun here. That is what John Fiske of Harvard meant when he spoke of belief in immortality as "a supreme act of faith in the reasonableness of God's work." For consider the alternative to what we have been saying. The alternative is that death ends everything, both what seems to us temporal and what seems eternal, and puts a final period after both.

To be sure, some here must have tried to escape the full force of that alternative by saying, But, while we die, while all of us is obliterated so that we are no more, still what we have stood for, our influence, goes on; in that sense not all of us dies; in that sense we are eternal. Well, I should say in answer, if that is all the eternal you can believe in, then that is all the eternal you can believe in, but you surely should understand that you are using the wrong word when you call it eternal. The earth itself is not everlasting. Once uninhabitable, it will be uninhabitable again. There is no such thing as an eternal influence on a transitory planet. Rather, if death ends all of us, then some day we shall all be dead and our children all dead and their children all dead, and, on a burned out cinder of a planet, everybody will be dead. As one scientist put it, "Nothing will remain, not even the ruins" and both what we call temporal and what we call eternal will be ended together as though they had not been at all. Thus to bring into being spiritual values that seem essentially eternal and then snuff them out like guttering candles, make of them a mere flash in the pan against the vast background of cosmic time, would not be the work of a reasonable universe.

Moreover, consider what this attitude does to us as individuals. Certain chemists, we are told, with a flair for statistics, figured out the chemical constitution of an average man and put the result into easily understandable terms, thus: An average man contains enough fat to make seven bars of soap, enough iron to make a medium-sized nail, enough sugar to fill a shaker, enough lime to whitewash a chicken-coop, enough phosphorus to make twenty-two hundred match tips, enough magnesium for a dose of magnesia, enough potassium to explode a toy cannon, together with a little sulphur. And the chemists figured that at market rates then current these chemical elements could be obtained for about ninety-eight cents. That's what we are made of. That's what all our seers and prophets, the great musicians, the great poets, the great leaders of the race, have been made of, about ninety-eight cents worth of chemical materials. And if death ends everything, they were made of nothing else, merely these fugitive, transient elements, and all that seemed eternal in them, our glory and our hope, was but an accidental by-product of ninety-eight cents' worth of chemicals. Man, if you can believe that, you can believe anything.

No, it is the eternal in us that even here is the realest part of us. We hear a violinist playing on his violin and think the music beautiful. But what is it that plays upon the violinist? For he too is an instrument, a physical, chemical instrument made of materials worth some ninety-eight cents, nowhere nearly so valuable as the Stradivarius he plays upon, and something must play upon the violinist before he can play upon the violin. That something is invisible, intangible, spiritual; it partakes of timelessness and eternity. Whatever is of most value in any life comes, to use Jesus' words, as though born from above, as though, out of a world spiritual and eternal, goodness and truth and beauty played upon us. You cannot describe *that* in terms of ninety-eight cents' worth of chemical materials. Surely, to bring into being such a realm of spiritual values, "the visitations of the divinity in man," only to snuff them out, would not be the work of a reasonable universe. So, on Easter morning, I believe Jesus as he speaks to Martha: Whoever thus liveth and through faith enters into the quality of life I have revealed, abides already in a realm where death cannot operate. Believest thou this?

In the third place, consider that only when so approached does immortality become even desirable. Many take it for granted that immortality, whatever else may be said of it, is certainly desirable. Were we, however, to take a vote of all the people on earth who believe in immortality, a majority, I suspect, would be found dreading it. The great mass of the devotees of Indian religion, for example, with their rebirth on rebirth in endless cycles, dread it, so that Buddha, promising relief from the unending necessity of going on and on, was a welcome savior to millions. What makes life desirable is not quantity but quality. As another has put it, "A soul might conceivably live forever and yet never enter into life."

The New Testament, therefore, puts its finger on the nub of the whole matter when it makes eternal life a matter of quality, beginning now. How much alive are you? it seems to say. In mind, in spirit, in fellowship with the eternal, in devotion to aims endlessly worth serving, how much alive are you? No mere extension of existence is eternal life, only quality of life worth going on with. And the time to begin that is here. Listen to Sir Wilfred Grenfell: "I am very much in love with life. I want all I can get of it. I want more of it, after the incident called death, if there is any to be had." So! That is quality of living, and that begins now.

Here is the trouble with what some one has called those "clergymen's heavens, which members of other professions might find something of a strain." I should say so! Even a healthy clergyman would find them a strain, with their perpetual psalmody and never-ending Sabbaths. Though they be baptized with Christian names, they are pagan and they mislead the imagination of multitudes as to what eternal life is all about.

Who wants reward like that for being good? What does a woman in travail desire? Reward? No, successful creativity, that she may bring forth a life that even before birth she has loved. So said Paul: "The whole creation groaneth and travaileth in pain together until now," waiting—for what? —waiting for "the revealing of the sons of God." That is to say, there is something everlastingly worth while going on here in which we can have a share, and one who is really alive has allied himself with this creative purpose and wants to go on with it, not for love of reward but for the love of sharing in something so infinitely worth while. What does an artist want in the struggle and sometimes agony of his composition? Reward? No, successful creativity, that the beauty which is the voice of God may get itself spoken through him at last. So says Jesus. Whosoever thus really liveth shall never die. This Easter morning, grasp this truth about yourselves and about others whom you have loved and lost—not that such souls die and then may live again, but that such souls already have eternal life, which death can never touch.

Finally, let us go on to say that, one way or another, in good logic what we have been saying involves continuance of personal life. To be sure, I am impatient with the little, popular imaginations of what that means, as though our small egos went on living with themselves forever much as they are now. Of all things, that would be most intolerable. In so vast a universe, with its endless possibilities, the continuance of personal life is capable of infinitely expanded meanings beyond our utmost imagining. Nevertheless, one way or another, continuance of personal life is involved in what we have been thinking. We began by saying that "three times three equals nine" is true forever. But "three times three equals nine" is a truth perceived only by mind, realized only in mind, and if all personal minds should vanish, just how real would "three times three equals nine" be? So everything of which

[268]

we have been speaking that is eternal in quality is a personal experience. Somehow or other, it is persons who enter into the eternal and live by it.

To be sure, not all persons do. There's the tragedy. We have said there is no death, but, alas, there is death. "To be carnally minded," said Paul, "is death." So here and now, dead men and women walk our streets continually, with nothing eternal in them, carnally minded—that is to say, living only by temporary, fugitive, perishable things. That is death. And it may be true of such that, being dead already, with nothing imperishable in their experience, what we call death for them will be the end. What is there in them to go on? At any rate, before death can become to any one an irrelevant incident, there is a condition to be fulfilled. Whosoever liveth, Jesus assures us, and by faith enters into his quality of life, shall never die.

Does some one here feel this mystery too great for his imagination? I sympathize with him. This is a mysterious universe, any way one looks at it. But I beg of you, get the mystery in the right place. It is not so much the survival of spiritual life that is a mystery; it is the arrival of such life in the first place. And the arrival of spiritual life has taken place. That is here in souls whom we have known and loved. There is the mystery, the arrival of a quality of living essentially timeless and eternal. Would it not be a mystery if, having arrived, it did not survive?

In India, they tell us, fakirs sit beside pools of water with piles of colored dust beside them and so skilfully drop the dust upon the still surface that they make for you recognizable portraits of distinguished characters. Then the breeze ruffles the pool and the picture disappears. Is that God's business? Does he take colored dust and drop it on life's water and, lo! Plato, or Isaiah, or Christ himself, or nearer souls whom we have known and loved—and then does the breeze disturb the water and they disappear? That would be a strange business for God! If such quality of life is not to survive, how did it ever happen to arrive? Its destruction would be the real mystery.

No! To him that has entered into life there is no death. A Canadian soldier in the Great War saw his best friend blown to pieces by a shell. Standing silent for a moment, he said, "It will take more than that to stop you." So Christendom addresses Christ on Easter morning. The nails that pierced his hands and feet did not pierce his truth. The spear thrust into his side could not reach his faith. The final paroxysm of his body did not shake his soul. There at Calvary his own words came true—"Be not afraid of them that kill the body, and after that have no more that they can do." Aye, no more that they can do! Death deals only with the transient, not with the eternal. Believest thou this?